Accelerating Climate Action

REFOCUSING POLICIES THROUGH A WELL-BEING LENS

OECD
BETTER POLICIES FOR BETTER LIVES

Please cite this publication as:
OECD (2019), *Accelerating Climate Action: Refocusing Policies through a Well-being Lens*, OECD Publishing, Paris, *https://doi.org/10.1787/2f4c8c9a-en*.

ISBN 978-92-64-80127-1 (print)
ISBN 978-92-64-91396-7 (pdf)
ISBN 978-92-64-78984-5 (HTML)

Revised version, December 2020

Photo credits: Cover © Shutterstock / Soloviova Liudmyla

Corrigenda to publications may be found on line at: *www.oecd.org/about/publishing/corrigenda.htm*.

Preface

At the very moment when we need strong, co-ordinated and far-sighted action to safeguard our collective future, the willingness and ability to act for the common good is in very short supply. This deficiency hinders international efforts to tackle climate change and biodiversity loss, on which our current and future well-being depend. While there undoubtedly has been – sometimes impressive – progress in tackling greenhouse gas emissions, it is clearly insufficient. Moreover, powerful interests remain that continue to oppose stronger climate action.

With global warming currently at around 1°Celsius, we are witnessing many damaging extreme weather events. Worldwide, July 2019 was the hottest month ever on record, and 9 out of the 10 hottest Julys have occurred since 2005, according to the National Oceanic and Atmospheric Administration (NOAA). The current projected pathways set out by national governments will take us to a world that will be around 3°Celsius warmer by 2100. This is a dangerous prospect, and people – particularly young people – around the world are increasingly voicing their frustration.

The climate goals agreed upon in 2015 in Paris, while challenging and ambitious, are also achievable and necessary. This report aims to provide both a changed perspective and the underpinning analysis to support an acceleration of climate mitigation action and to halt the increase in the global average temperature to well-below 2°C. In doing so, it takes an explicit political economy approach to the transitions needed across five economic sectors: electricity, heavy industry, the residential sector, surface transport and agriculture. They are responsible for more than 60% of global greenhouse gas emissions. This changed perspective is in line with the recent IPCC Special Report, Climate Change and Land, which shows the interlinkages across climate change mitigation, food security, and land degradation issues.

Limiting climate risks is fundamental to our collective well-being. The synergies between mitigation policy and other well-being goals can be leveraged around jobs, income, health, education and wider environmental quality. In many cases however, concerns about the affordability of energy and the impact of climate policies on jobs may limit policy action, either pre-emptively or through policy roll-back. There is also an increasing need to reverse a trend of growing economic and social inequalities, within and between countries, that influence many dimensions of well-being.

Reframing climate policies through a well-being lens is necessary in order to make these synergies and trade-offs systematically visible, thus enabling decision-makers to increase the former and anticipate, manage and minimise the latter. This requires us to rethink our societal goals in terms of well-being, reframe our measures of progress and refocus policy-making accordingly. Such a fresh perspective is essential if we are to make our climate goals a reality.

Angel Gurría

Secretary-General, OECD

Foreword

Insufficient progress in climate change mitigation is driving the climate system into unchartered territory with severe projected consequences. The report builds on the OECD Well-being Framework and applies a new perspective, the ***well-being lens***. This new perspectives analyses synergies and trade-offs and creates two-way alignment between climate change mitigation and broader well-being goals across five economic sectors (electricity, heavy industry, residential, surface transport, and agriculture) that are responsible for more than 60% of global greenhouse gas emissions.

Three specific actions are identified as central to generating a two-way alignment between climate and other well-being goals. Namely, rethinking societal goals, refocusing measures of progress, and reframing climate policies through a well-being lens. This report is focused on the first two. While work focusing on the third action was originally planned as a second part of this report, the decision has been made to instead release a series of sector-specific policy papers. These will still draw on the work featured in this report and cover the same five sectors (i.e. residential, agriculture, surface transport, electricity and heavy industry).

An opening chapter "Increasing incentives for climate action using a well-being lens" is dedicated to discussing the general climate context and setting out the main rationale of the report. The rest of the report contains five sector-specific chapters that address the change in perspective, through:

- **Rethinking societal goals**: For each sector, the report reassesses current policy priorities, discussing the need for these to effectively guide the sector towards climate and other well-being and sustainability goals.
- **Reframing the measurement system:** A more comprehensive set of indicators can help monitor and set criteria to ensure progress on multiple policy priorities, making synergies and trade-offs between them systematically visible. A number of new and complementary indicators are introduced and discussed in relation to existing indicators, including those included in the SDGs and the OECD Well-being Framework.

As argued in chapter 1, these two actions are necessary and provide the basis for r***efocusing climate policies through a well-being lens:***

Acknowledgements

This report is part of the work programme of the OECD's Environmental Policy Committee and benefitted particularly from feedback and inputs from delegates to its Working Party on Climate, Investment and Development. The work was carried out by the mitigation team of the OECD's Climate, Biodiversity and Water (CBW) Division, comprising Aimée Aguilar Jaber (Team Lead), Brilé Anderson, Hélène Blake, Mariana Mirabile, Daniel Nachtigall, and Fatoumata Ngom. Simon Buckle, Head of the CBW Division provided inputs, support and guidance at different stages. The report was produced under the overall guidance of Rodolfo Lacy, the Director of the Environment Directorate of the OECD and benefited from the input of many colleagues from the OECD and elsewhere as detailed below.

The different chapters were developed by OECD analysts, while also drawing on inputs and collaboration with external experts, as follows:

- Chapter 1 was drafted by Simon Buckle (ENV/OECD), with support from Aimée Aguilar Jaber (ENV/OECD), Brilé Anderson (ENV/OECD), Mariana Mirabile (ENV/OECD), and Fatoumata Ngom (ENV/OECD).
- Chapter 2 was drafted by Daniel Nachtigall (ENV/OECD), with support from Fatoumata Ngom, drawing on inputs from and in collaboration with Karsten Neuhoff and Jörn Richstein (German Institute for Economic Research - DIW) and Pao-Yu Oei (Technical University of Berlin).
- Chapter 3 was drafted by Brilé Anderson, drawing on inputs from and in collaboration with Chris Bataille (Institute of Sustainable Development and International Relations- IDDRI- and Simon Fraser University).
- Chapter 4 was drafted by Aimée Aguilar Jaber, with support from Fatoumata Ngom, drawing on inputs from and in collaboration with Catalina Turcu (The Bartlett School of Planning-UCL).
- Chapter 5 was drafted by Aimée Aguilar Jaber and Tatiana Samsonova (ITF/OECD).
- Chapter 6 was drafted by Hélène Blake (ENV/OECD) and Mariana Mirabile, drawing on inputs from and in collaboration with Emile Frison (International Panel of Experts on Sustainable Food Systems- iPES Food).

Authors are grateful for the valuable comments and inputs of other colleagues from the OECD and other external institutions, namely: Thibaut Abergel (IEA/OECD); Geraldine Ang (ENV/OECD); Jenitha Badul (Department of Environmental Affairs in South Africa); Adam Baylin-Stern (IEA/OECD); Alexander Blackburn (UNECE); Rodney Boyd (British Business Bank); Nils Axel Braathen (ENV/OECD); Peter Borkey (ENV/OECD); Enrico Bota (ENV/OECD); Ruben Bibas (ENV/OECD); Miguel Cárdenas (ENV/OECD); Aris Christodoulou (JRC-European Commission); Lisa Danielson (ENV/OECD); Rob Dellink (ENV/EEI); Koen Deconinck (TAD/OECD); Simon Devisme (ENV/OECD); Dimitris Diakosavvas (TAD/OECD); Alexandros Dimitroupolos (ENV/OECD); Assia Elgouacem (ENV/OECD); Jane Ellis (ENV/OECD); Carrie Exton (SDD/OECD); Benjamin Fairbrother (European Comission); Florian Flachenecker (Joint Research Centre of the European Commission); Florens Flues (CTP/OECD); Andrés Fuentes-Hutfilter (ECO/OECD); Catherine Gamper (ENV/OECD); Santiago Guerrero (TAD/OECD); Guillaume Gruère (TAD/OECD); Enrique Gutiérrez (ENV/OECD); Alejandro César Hernández

(IEA/OECD); Marit Hjort (ENV/EHS); Peter Janoska (IEA/OECD); Emmanuel Kasese (Green Cape in South Africa); Reinhard Klenke (Helmholtz Centre for Environmental Research); Nicolina Lamhauge (ENV/OECD);Elisa Lanzi (ENV/OECD); Hannah Leckie (ENV/OECD); Peter Levi (IEA/OECD); Luca Lore (IEA/OECD); Yuki Matsumoto (TAD/OECD); Gianpiero Mattera (STI/OECD); Yuki Matsumoto (TAD/OECD); Matteo Ordinanovich (European Commission); Sarah O'Carroll (Green Cape in South Africa); Michael Pahle (Potsdam Institute for Climate Impact Research); Joshua Paternina (ITF/OECD); Stephen Perkins (ITF/OECD); Marissa Plouin (ELS/OECD); Andrew Prag (IEA/OECD); Mikaela Rambali (ENV/OECD); Rasmus Raabjerg Nielsen (Trade Union Advisory Committee to the OECD); Uwe Remme (IEA/OECD); Dirk Röttgers (ENV/OECD); Alexandre Santacreu (ITF/OECD); Jehan Sauvage (TAD/OECD); Guido Schmidt-Traub (United Nations Sustainable Development Solutions Network); Abel Schumann (CFE/OECD); Filipe Silva (STI/OECD); Will Symes (ENV/OECD); Cecilia Tam (ENV/OECD); Aayush Tandon (ENV/OECD); Janek Toepper (ENV/OECD); Stephanie Venuti (DAF/OECD); and Shunta Yamaguchi (ENV/OECD).

We are also grateful to Janine Treves (PAC/OECD) for her editorial support in the preparation of the report; as well as to other colleagues from the OECD publications team and our internal staff in the Environment Directorate: Sama Al Taher Cucci (ENV/OECD) and Beth Del Bourgo (ENV/OECD) for their communications support, and Florence Guerinot (PAC/OECD); Audrey Garrigoux (PAC/OECD); Carmen Fernández (PAC/OECD), Sandrine Levain (PAC/OECD); Nassera Belkhiter (ENV/OECD); Jane Kynaston (ENV/OECD); Shellie Phillips (ENV/OECD); Inés Reale (ENV/OECD); Anna Rourke (ENV/OECD). We would also like to thank. Romy de Courtay for her support in editing the report.

Table of contents

FIGURES

INFOGRAPHICS

TABLES

Executive Summary

General approach

Climate change is an urgent and unprecedented challenge with far reaching implications and it is happening now. The world has already warmed by an average of 1°Celsius relative to pre-industrial temperatures and July 2019 was the hottest July ever recorded. Ice sheets are melting and sea level rising. Extreme weather events exacerbated by climate change are already taking their toll across the globe and will only become more frequent and more intense as a result of inaction. To limit global warming to well-below 2°C and towards 1.5°C, a key aim of the Paris Agreement will require a significant scaling up and acceleration of action by governments and other stakeholders.

Delaying such action will lead to the further locking-in of highly emitting infrastructures and systems and increase severity of future climate impacts. In advance of 2020, many countries are looking to increase the ambition of their national actions contributing to the goals of the Paris Agreement. Yet they also face other pressing challenges. Unless carefully designed, climate policy action may therefore unintentionally exacerbate some of these problems thereby slowing down progress in reducing emissions. Conversely, where climate action can also help address other societal challenges, such as air pollution, health, or equity there may be potential to further accelerate climate change mitigation action.

Systematically putting people's well-being at the centre of decision-making is therefore key to creating the social and political support needed for more ambitious climate action. This report investigates the potential advantages of adopting a well-being lens to climate mitigation policies. It focuses on five major sectors of the economy (electricity generation, heavy industry, residential, surface transport[1] and agriculture), to identify key synergies and trade-offs between climate change mitigation and broader well-being outcomes.

The OECD's well-being framework provides a comprehensive approach to the determinants of both current and future well-being, beyond such aggregate measures such as GDP. It encompasses multiple dimensions, such as income, jobs, health, knowledge and skills, safety and the quality of the environment, as well as the economic, natural, human and social capital stocks needed to sustain well-being over time. Adopting a well-being lens means that climate and well-being goals should not be pursued independently. Specifically, it means that: (i) policy goals should be defined in terms of well-being outcomes (including the risks and impacts of climate change) and are systematically reflected in decision-making across the economy; (ii) decisions should be taken consider multiple well-being objectives, rather than focusing on a single (or very narrow) range of objective(s) independently of others; and (iii) the interrelations between the different economic sectors and systems in which a policy intervenes are sufficiently well understood

Applying a well-being lens when designing climate mitigation policies has the potential to deliver wider well-being benefits both in the short and the long term. One example relates to the synergies between simultaneously reducing air pollution and GHG emissions. Reducing the combustion of fossil fuels would

[1] For the purposes of this document, "surface transport" includes road and rail transport, walking, cycling, and public transport (including overground and underground metro systems). Maritime transport is excluded.

cut carbon dioxide (CO_2) emissions, but also the related particulate matter and other chemical compounds yielding climate air quality and health benefits. Opportunities for enlarging the synergies between climate and well-being outcomes can be found in all the sectors considered. Identifying and quantifying these synergies – sometimes through new metrics and indicators – is key to designing policies and investments that could realise these benefits.

A well-being lens can also help to highlight where significant trade-offs may exist between climate and well-being objectives. As such trade are sometimes hard to avoid, it is crucial to anticipate them in order to address them. Pricing policies aiming at reflecting the social costs of different activities, such as burning fossil fuels for heat or transport, may have damaging distributional impacts. Decision makers need to assess whether these trade-offs are material, perhaps even sufficiently important to jeopardise the feasibility of such policy measures. Where this is the case, such concerns can be addressed through targeted compensation (e.g. free emission allowances for emissions intensive firms) or the provision of suitable alternatives (e.g. public transport as a substitute for private vehicle use). By considering potential trade-offs early in the decision-making process, policy makers can design policies in order to reduce unwanted impacts, particularly distributional impacts, and thereby avoid the risk that policies will be rolled back in the future.

A well-being approach calls for a reframing of the measurement system around well-being outcomes. A broader set of indicators to track performance and guide decision-making is presented and discussed for every sector considered. They include SDG indicators and indicators from the OECD well-being framework.

Sectoral application

Electricity is central to people's well-being as it delivers a broad range of basic services, economic infrastructure and activities. However, the combustion of fossil fuels for electricity generation is not only the largest contributor to GHG emissions globally, but is also damaging to human health and environmental quality. Adopting a well-being lens to this sector implies to go beyond the traditional objectives of the energy trilemma (affordability, reliability and decarbonisation), also accounting for objectives such as public health and safety, preservation of ecosystems and provision of high-quality employment. Adopting a well-being lens also means taking a systematic view of the entire power system, including the plant level, the network infrastructure and the demand side. Such a holistic approach enables policy makers to identify and exploit synergies between mitigation and other well-being priorities (e.g. reduced pollution from coal plants and coal mines) while managing the trade-offs (e.g. supporting coal-dependent regions and workers in the transition), increasing the social and political acceptability of climate action. Systematically measuring all areas of electricity-related well-being using the appropriate set of indicators (e.g. on health, jobs, ecosystems) is key for identifying the many synergies and trade-offs while enabling better targeted policies, for example by adopting indicators that better identify households at risk of energy poverty to effectively address potential energy affordability problems.

A shift of focus in heavy industry is also crucial for climate. Heavy industries produce the materials and chemicals that we need for our daily lives: for infrastructure, housing, vehicles, packaging, fertilisers, and so on. However, it is important that decisions are not focused only on maximising production to meet the demands of a growing population; they need to address the harmful effects of current industrial production on the air we breathe, soil and water quality and on natural resources, as well as the need to reduce GHG emissions. This requires that heavy industries over time decarbonise their production, adopting circular and resource-efficient processes and engaging in RD&D to overcome the technological and commercial obstacles to decarbonising some processes. This transition to sustainable production would be facilitated by the development and monitoring of indicators that show whether production is increasing at the expense of air, land, water, soil and materials pollution and climate stability.

Buildings generate 27% of global CO_2 emissions in 2017, with the residential sector accounting for 60% of these. However, targeting the dwelling – in itself - is insufficient to reach ambitious climate reductions in the sector. Recognising that housing is a “bundled good” is essential to reaping greater emission reductions, for example, in order to identify opportunities for integrating the location of housing with existing natural and manmade infrastructure.,. It would also enhance synergies between climate and people’s immediate well-being. For instance, housing developments that are transit-friendly, provide educational, leisure and employment facilities and safer streets while mitigating GHG emissions.

Re-designing mobility systems around accessibility, instead of physical movement, is key to invert the current growth in car ownership and use, and related GHG emissions from transport (now accounting for approximately 23% of global CO_2 emissions). Accessibility is a combination of mobility and proximity, i.e. ensuring that people are able to easily reach jobs, opportunities, goods, services and amenities. Enhancing accessibility by giving priority to sustainable modes and creating proximity between people and places can importantly contribute (along with the improvement of vehicle technologies and fuels) to enlarging mitigation potential, while also improving life quality through delivering better equity, health, economic, road safety, and wider environmental outcomes. Such an approach will lead to a redistribution of budgets and public space that is better aligned with climate and wider well-being goals. Developing and using the right indicators to articulate the shift in focus towards accessibility is an important step, which has already supported some cities for planning transport networks and city development. This would be usefully supplemented by criteria on safety and security, as well as air quality.

Agriculture and the food sector comprise nearly 30% of global GHG emissions. They also impact on the feasibility of stringent global mitigation goals through their impact on land-use (e.g. deforestation to expand production) and by the potential to sequester carbon in plants and soils. Economic criteria (GDP, trade and farmers’ livelihoods) are currently the main drivers for decisions in agriculture and associated food systems. Integrating wider social objectives as priorities is key for current and future well-being, as the way food systems are shaped strongly affects people’s health, the environment (water and air quality) and natural resources (water resources). More particularly, when shaping climate mitigation policies in the agriculture and food sector, a strong focus should be made on providing a healthy diet for a growing global population. This key challenge can only be answered by a full endorsement from all actors of the food system, including consumers. Dietary changes and the reduction of food loss and waste, for instance, have the potential to mitigate GHG emissions from agriculture, improve people’s health, food security and the environment. These benefits can only be reached with the collaboration of stakeholders and consumers.

1 Increasing incentives for climate action using a well-being lens

This chapter argues that approaching climate change mitigation through a well-being lens can help countries identify and implement measures to reverse rising greenhouse gas emissions, avoid lock-in of carbon-intensive technologies and reduce long-lived carbon dioxide emissions to zero on a net basis by the middle of the 21st century, or shortly thereafter. The implications of this approach are likely to differ across jurisdictions, reflecting their levels of development and the particular challenges and opportunities they face. Adopting and adapting a well-being approach will put governments in a better position to reach their climate and broader well-being goals.

The statistical data for Israel are supplied by and under the responsibility of the relevant Israeli authorities. The use of such data by the OECD is without prejudice to the status of the Golan Heights, East Jerusalem and Israeli settlements in the West Bank under the terms of international law.

In Brief

Increasing incentives for climate action using a well-being lens

The world has already warmed by an average of 1°Celsius and July 2019 was the hottest July ever recorded. Extreme weather events are taking their toll across the globe. Without accelerated mitigation action, risks to human health and food and water security will continue to grow, threatening our ability to meet the Sustainable Development Goals (SDGs). We need to reverse and then rapidly reduce global CO_2 emissions to zero on a net basis by 2050 or shortly thereafter.

The low-emissions transition requires an unprecedented scale of transformation in our societies but this is not happening quickly enough to achieve international goals. Investments in renewable technologies such as wind and solar have stalled, despite being cheaper than fossil-fuel alternatives in many places. Coal plants, particularly young plants in Asia, are still responsible for 30% of energy-related CO_2 emissions, which according to the IEA are increasing faster (2.9% in 2018) than the overall growth in such emissions (1.7%).

Systematically placing people's well-being at the centre of decision-making is necessary to increase the political and social support for more ambitious mitigation action and to overcome the barriers to change. The concept of well-being goes beyond economic welfare and incorporates such aspects as political and social rights, health, education, security and environmental quality. This report refers to present and future well-being and is a synonym of sustainable development.

Climate change mitigation has the potential to deliver wider well-being benefits for current generations and to underpin the resources needed for future well-being. Importantly, the potential trade-offs between climate policy and other goals such as affordability, competitiveness and jobs constrain the ambition of climate action. Using a well-being lens helps make these synergies and trade-offs visible, allowing decision-makers to increase "two-way alignment" between climate change mitigation and broader well-being objectives.

Adopting a well-being lens means ensuring that decisions aim to deliver simultaneously on multiple well-being objectives, including climate. It also requires an economy-wide perspective, rather than focusing on a single or very narrow range of output-related objectives, independently of others. For example, tackling damaging air pollution problems by eliminating fossil-fuel combustion takes advantage of one of the major synergies between climate action and health. In terms of trade-offs, addressing in advance the potential impacts on the affordability of transport from increased fuel prices through targeted compensatory measures or investments in public transport infrastructure, makes such price increases more acceptable and effective.

We can improve our collective chances of limiting climate change, while securing important well-being improvements, by applying a well-being lens to key sectors. This report examines five economic sectors (electricity, heavy industry, residential, surface transport, and agriculture), which together represent over 60% of global GHG emissions. It explains how reassessing policy priorities and adapting the set of indicators used to track progress and guide decisions in each sector can support governments in creating "two-way alignment" between climate and a number of other well-being benefits, such as public health and safety, affordability, reliability, natural resource management, and new employment opportunities. It also discusses how climate policies in these sectors can be implemented, designed and evaluated while taking into account potential synergies and trade-offs.

Infographic 1.1. Increasing incentives for climate action using a well-being lens

Strong climate action is the foundation of our **future economic and wider well-being**.

with a **production** lens:

with a **well-being** lens:

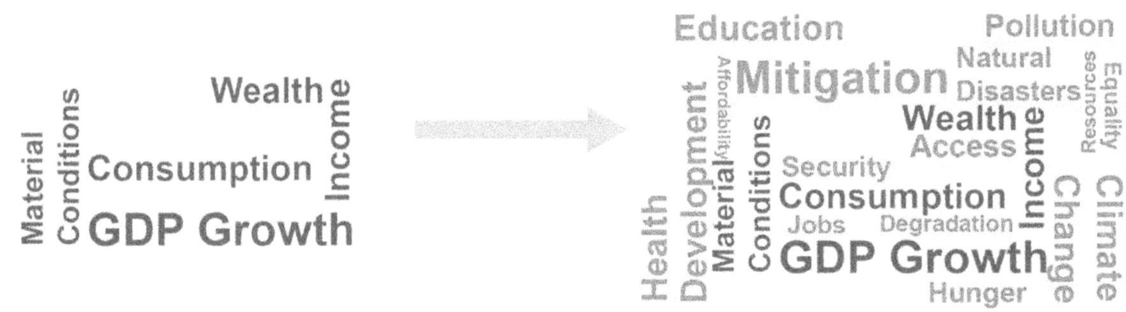

There are synergies between climate policies and **larger societal goals** that can be leveraged around jobs, income, health, education, environmental resources…

Focusing on 5 sectors responsible for 60% of GHG emissions, we can meet ambitious climate goals while also delivering wider societal benefits.

We need an enhanced measurement system that can help improve policy design.

[J]ust as any comprehensive well-being agenda must feature strong climate action as necessary to underpin human quality of life, we need to put people at the centre of climate policy to ensure equitable outcomes across countries, communities, individuals and generations. (Angel Gurría, OECD Secretary-General)

1.1. The climate context

Climate change is happening now. Without accelerated efforts to reduce greenhouse gas (GHG) emissions, it will transform the world in which society has evolved over several millennia. The global average surface temperature has already increased by around one degree Celsius (°C) relative to pre-industrial levels, largely driven by higher atmospheric concentrations of GHGs and the complex effects of atmospheric aerosols resulting from human activities (Berkeley Earth, 2017[1]). The impacts of climate change on human well-being are increasingly being felt (Watts et al., 2015[2]) and the risks of "severe, pervasive and irreversible" impacts will grow as the global temperature increases (IPCC, 2014[3]). The recent Intergovernmental Panel on Climate Change (IPCC) report, Global Warming of 1.5°C (IPCC, 2018[4]), highlights the significant benefits of restricting the global temperature increase stemming from GHG emissions to 1.5 degrees Celsius (°C) instead of 2°C or higher, particularly in terms of preventing impacts on unique and threatened systems (e.g. coral reefs), and reducing the impacts of extreme weather.

To meet individual countries' climate mitigation goals, carbon dioxide (CO_2) emissions into the atmosphere – the major driver of climate change – will need to reach zero on a net basis in the early second half of the 21st century, i.e. in 30 years' time or slightly later, depending on the stringency of the mitigation goal. This will require deep reductions in emissions across the whole economy in all countries, with differences in priorities and phasing depending on country circumstances and capabilities. High-income economies will need to reach zero net emissions earlier, to give low-income countries more time. The extent to which emissions of other non-CO_2 GHGs are reduced will influence the level of cumulative CO_2 emissions consistent with a given global temperature goal. State-of-the-art modelling suggests that recourse to large-scale atmospheric carbon dioxide removal (CDR) technologies would be needed to achieve stringent mitigation goals, effectively relaxing the very tight limits on remaining cumulative CO_2 emissions consistent with such goals.[1] However, in the absence of large-scale demonstration and deployment of key technologies,[2] large uncertainty prevails about the availability of CDR technologies at a sufficient scale, as well as their cost and potential implications for land use and water resources. These uncertainties reinforce the need for much stronger near-term reductions in CO_2 emissions. "Hoping for the best" is not a policy the OECD recommends.

As a way to support greater near-term mitigation action, this report argues for approaching climate change mitigation through a well-being lens in order to increase the political and societal support for ambitious, early action to reduce GHG emissions. Adopting a well-being lens means that societal goals are defined in terms of well-being outcomes (including the risks and impacts of climate change) and are systematically reflected in decision-making across the economy. Moreover, multiple well-being objectives need to be taken into account simultaneously and the interrelations between them sufficiently well understood.

The report reviews efforts to move beyond gross domestic product, a key step for placing climate and wider well-being at the centre of decisions across the economy. Initiatives addressed include the Sustainable Development Goals (SDGs) and the OECD Framework for Measuring Well-being and Progress (henceforth the OECD well-being framework). The report proposes a change in perspective on policy making for five different sectors: electricity, industry, residential, transport and agriculture, and identifies key policy priorities that are central to promoting the wider sustainable and well-being goals captured by the SDGs and the OECD well-being framework. A key issue is the need to develop adequate measurement systems that allow policy makers to capture potential synergies and trade-offs between multiple priorities in each sector and across systems.

Adopting the well-being lens across sectors and using more adequate indicators to track performance as well as criteria in decision-making will greatly influence policy design and prioritisation. Where climate action is concerned, this new approach will result in policy packages that can tackle climate change more effectively and garner more consensus, by yielding several other benefits. These are the focus of Part II of this report, which examines policy practices to achieve this "two-way alignment" for each of the sectors mentioned above.

1.1.1. A decisive moment

The required transitions are of an unprecedented scale (IPCC, 2018[4]). They will require significant new investment in low-emission technologies and infrastructure (OECD, 2017[5]), as well as maintaining and restoring ecosystems that are important in drawing down and sequestering atmospheric CO_2. The OECD, UN Environment and World Bank Group in their report, *Financing Climate Futures: Rethinking Infrastructure*, further explore the transformative agenda governments must take in key areas including planning, innovation, public budgeting, private finance, development finance and cities (OECD/The World Bank/UN Environment, 2018[6]).

At the same time, meeting the 17 SDGs – of which climate is just one, but one on which progress towards many of the others depends – is an urgent challenge. Achieving the goals of no poverty, zero hunger, quality education for all, gender equality, sustainable cities, and biodiversity on land and in the oceans depends on the collective ability to limit climate risks. Clearly, these agendas cannot be pursued separately, either financially or substantively. The SDGs are intimately interconnected, and well-designed action to address them can yield significant synergies across many different goals.[3]

The resource costs of making these simultaneous transitions in many different sectors will undoubtedly be large, but they can easily be overstated. In some areas, they will be outweighed by reduced fuel costs (OECD, 2017[5]) and offset by (non-climate) benefits, even before the main benefits of reduced climate-risk become apparent. A recent World Bank study (World Bank, 2019[7]) finds that achieving full decarbonisation by the end of the century in lower- and middle-income countries need not cost most than more emission-intensive development pathways.

Indeed, as recently highlighted by (Zenghelis, 2019[8]), the costs of a transition in the energy sector are endogenous and depend on the pathway chosen. The radical and rapid reductions in the cost of renewables technologies over the past decade or so were not widely anticipated, but have completely overturned the traditional logic of decarbonisation in the electricity sector. Indeed, many projections for the share of solar energy in the energy mix by 2050 look set to be exceeded.[4] Similar progress is both needed and achievable in other sectors, albeit more easily in some than in others. An effective response to climate change will require a steep change in innovation and the diffusion of a wider range of technologies for sustainability. It will also require changes in financial systems and regulations, lifestyles and the management of ecosystems (to name just a few).[5] At the core of these many changes is the need to rethink the priorities guiding decisions and policies across the economy, ensuring they are consistent with the ultimate goals set for the climate and other transitions needed to ensure human well-being, now and in the future. Encouraging and supporting the revision and rethinking of policy priorities across the economy is a central aim of this report.

The world stands at the junction between different alternative futures. Even if achieved in full, the stated scale of national action to reduce GHG emissions (the so-called nationally determined contributions [NDCs] for post-2020 action) does not yet, in aggregate, match the ambition of limiting warming to well-below 2°C or even 1.5°C (UNEP, 2018[9]). Without additional mitigation efforts, emissions are expected to rise to levels that would result in temperature increases of 3°C above pre-industrial levels by the end of the century – yet G20 countries collectively are not yet on track to meet their NDCs (UNEP, 2018[9]).

It is now known that an increase of such magnitude in global mean surface temperatures will have major systemic impacts. The recent IPCC special report, *Global Warming of 1.5°C* (IPCC, 2018[4]), notes that "Climate-related risks to health, livelihoods, food security, water supply, human security, and economic growth are projected to increase with global warming of 1.5°C and increase further with 2°C." Disadvantaged and vulnerable populations, and those dependent on agricultural or coastal livelihoods, are most exposed to these risks (IPCC, 2018[4]). How can the broader range of SDGs be achieved against such a headwind?

To achieve either a 1.5°C or below 2°C goal, the IPCC assesses that global CO_2 emissions will need to fall by 20-45% by 2030 relative to 2010.[6] Yet energy-related CO_2 emissions rose by an estimated 1.7% in 2018, driven by rapid increases in energy demand.[7] Data compiled by the Global Carbon Project (Figure 1.1) show no sign that global CO_2 emissions are approaching a peak, a prerequisite for achieving zero net emissions early in the second half of the century. According to the International Energy Agency (IEA), the bulk of emission increases in 2018 came from coal power plants, with the majority located in Asia. These plants are only 12 years old on average, thus constituting a major lock-in of CO_2-intensive generation assets. Worryingly, recent OECD analysis suggested some 200 GW of coal capacity (equivalent to 10% of current installed coal-generation capacity) will be constructed over the next five years. In the absence of massive deployment of carbon capture and storage (CCS) technologies, this is not compatible with a goal of well below 2°C, which would require coal capacity to fall rapidly in coming decades (Mirabile and Calder, 2018[10]). Adding to these concerns is a flattening of investment in new renewables capacity and energy efficiency in 2018, despite continuing cost reductions in renewables (IEA, 2019[11]). The evidence shows that the continued prevalence of fossil-fuel subsidies (OECD, 2018[12]) significantly reduces investment in renewable generation capacity (Röttgers and Anderson, 2018[13]).

In his 2015 speech, the Governor of the Bank of England, Mark Carney, famously highlighted a key challenge facing climate action, the "tragedy of the horizon", in which, "the catastrophic impacts of climate change will be felt beyond the traditional horizons of most actors – imposing a cost on future generations that the current generation has no direct incentive to fix," (Carney, 2015[14]). Building on this seminal contribution, the OECD Secretary-General, Angel Gurría, in his 2017 climate lecture, highlighted a further challenge, namely, overcoming a purely national horizon in addressing what is actually a global challenge (OECD, 2017[15]). Underlining the importance of subnational and other non-state actors for climate action, Mr Gurría also stressed that action on issues (such as local air pollution) with important shorter-term benefits can help align short-term national incentives with longer-term goals for climate action, and that adopting an inclusive approach is essential to this agenda.

Figure 1.1. Global fossil CO_2 emissions: 36.2 ± 2 $GtCO_2$ in 2017, 63% over 1990

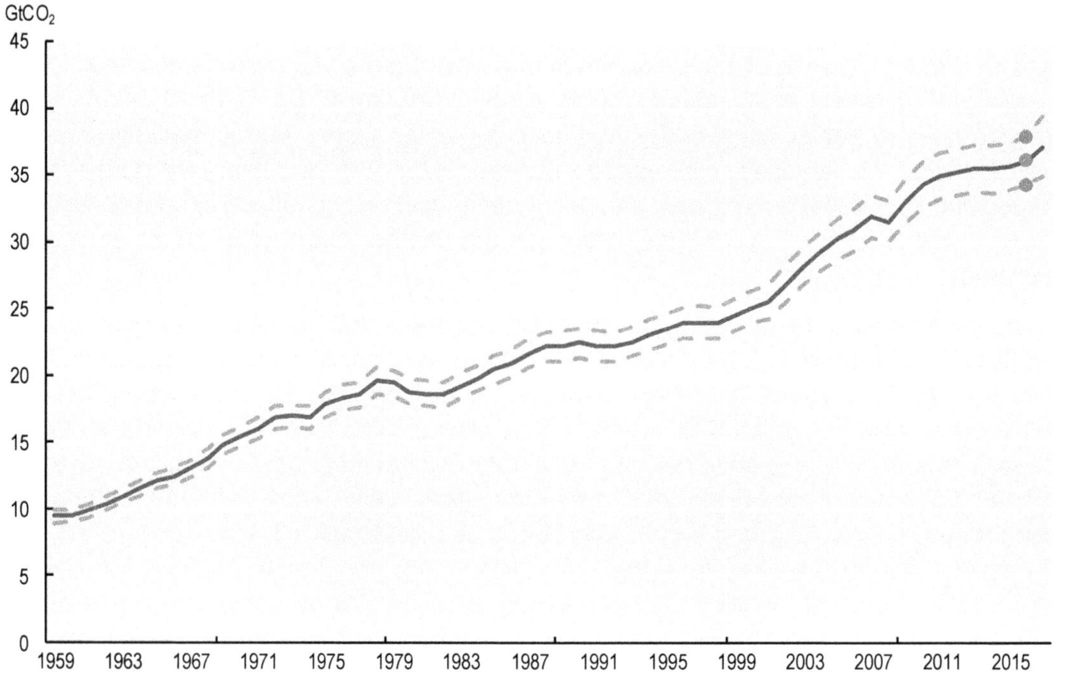

Note: The level of total emissions estimated by the Global Carbon Project differs from that used by the IEA, but provides a consistent picture of the trend. Red dot represents a projection for 2018: 37.1 ± 2 GtCO2, 2.7% up on 2017 (range 1.8% to 3.7%).
Source: (Le Quéré et al., 2018[16]).

StatLink https://doi.org/10.1787/888933992952

> There is a strong argument that, even from a purely national perspective, current NDCs are insufficiently ambitious... Incentives to reduce emissions should also be enhanced by the co-benefits of mitigation action, such as improved health from reduced air pollution and reduced traffic congestion from greater use of public transport. (Angel Gurría, OECD Secretary-General).

A conceptual model can help illustrate how these different effects play out at different timescales, abstracting from the challenges of co-ordination and co-operation across different countries (Figure 1.2). The model consists of two periods in which the current generation lives and a long term in which a new generation will make its own decisions. The model captures the fact that the world is only one investment cycle away from locking in severe climate damages.[8] Box 1.1 discusses the model further, highlighting some critical issues in determining the scale and timing of climate action. These include that initial income and the emissions intensity of the production technology is important in shaping the mitigation response, while the weight placed on long-term outcomes and the nature of climate damages will also influence the extent of mitigation action.

Figure 1.2. Conceptual model of climate action

Today's choices impact tomorrow's livelihoods and the well-being of future generations

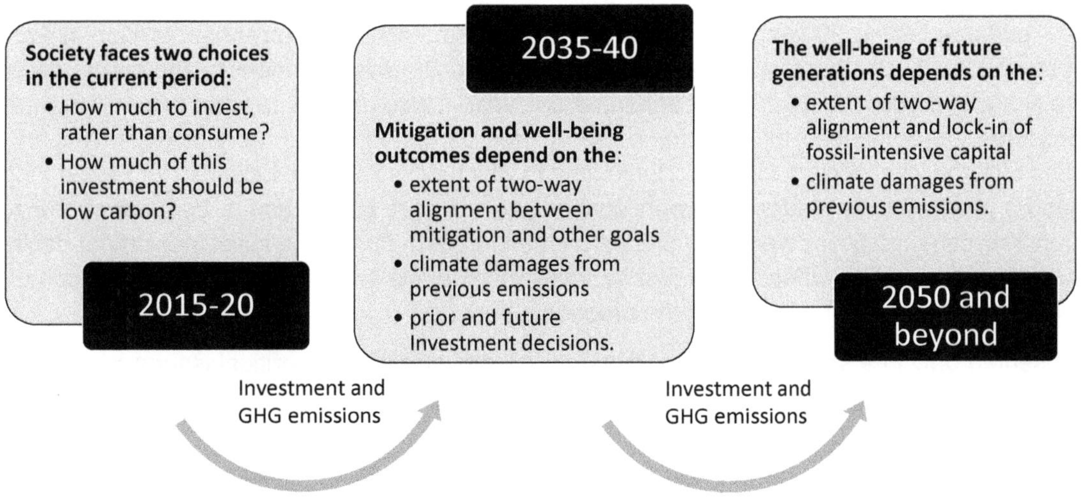

Source: Based on the model developed in (Buckle et al., 2014[17]).

This stylised model does not capture the political economy issues surrounding the impact of the transition on incumbent firms and workers – and yet these are also critical in determining the ambition of mitigation action. One of the key advantages of applying a well-being lens (see below) to climate change mitigation is that it helps identify synergies and trade-offs between mitigation and other well-being goals. It also helps build a broader political constituency for mitigation action and addresses the concerns of individuals who might otherwise face adverse consequences, e.g. workers in industries that may disappear during a transition to a low-emission economy - an issue addressed by the 2015 ILO guidelines for a just transition (ILO, 2015[18]). Other complementary approaches – e.g. adopting the recommendations of the Financial Stability Board's Task Force on Climate-related Financial Disclosures – will also be important to drive changes in financial and corporate strategies, governance, risk management and metrics.[9] Over time, as more companies focus on the benefits and opportunities of strong climate action, these will change the dynamics of the political economy.

In light of the troubling emission and investment trends mentioned above, and the implications of the aggregate level of ambition in the first round of NDCs under the United Nations Framework Convention on Climate Change (UNFCCC) process, what can be done to improve society's collective chances of limiting climate change to well-below 2°C? Much analysis and commentary has focused on the extent to which decision-making should and does factor in the long term. In itself, moral exhortation to care more about future generations will only have limited impact. In many, particularly low-income countries, it will be met with the understandable reaction that the poor of the current generation need to be prioritised. Institutional mechanisms to enshrine a duty to future generations could change the nature and dynamics of decision-making. Arguably, the United Kingdom's Climate Change Committee fulfils this role, Wales has a Future Generations Commissioner, and New Zealand has a Parliamentary Commissioner for the Environment.[10] The recent youth protests about climate inaction also have the potential to change the political calculus. Like efforts to enhance firms' climate disclosure, these mechanisms could address the tragedy of the horizon, increasing the priority placed on future generations in current decisions.

Box 1.1. Critical issues in determining the scale and timing of climate action

Each of the periods in the stylised model illustrated in Figure 1.2 can be thought of as relatively long lifetimes – perhaps lasting 20 years – of infrastructure investments. The current generation in Period 1 (starting around 2015-20) inherits a capital stock with a given CO_2 emission intensity and makes decisions about the share of production it will either consume or invest. It also decides to what extent investment in future production is composed of low-carbon rather than carbon-intensive technologies. This, in turn, determines both the level of production and the extent to which emissions are locked in for Period 2 (2035-40). Period 2 production is shared between consumption in that period and a bequest to the future generation, reflecting the policy weighting placed on the long term during the initial investment decisions. The value of any bequest is affected not just by investment levels but also, critically, by the cumulative CO_2 emissions from production in both of the preceding periods.[1]

While presented only in a stylised way, the model highlights some of the critical issues and incentives facing decision makers with regard to climate action, including:

- **Starting points matter.** The initial income and emission intensity of the production technology is important in shaping the mitigation response: the higher the level of locked-in emissions from current production relative to desired cumulative CO_2 emissions, the higher the incentive to mitigate from a social welfare perspective. Locked-in emissions, in turn, depend on both the level of production (GDP) and emission intensity of the economy. Other things being equal, in a very low-income world – or one with very clean technology – the incentives for mitigation would therefore be lower than in an economy with a higher GDP and a dirtier technology. The initial level of atmospheric CO_2 also matters, the incentives are lower with lower atmospheric CO_2 concentrations, than with higher concentrations, as climate damages would be lower. Current atmospheric CO_2 concentrations are far higher than at any time in the last 800 000 years, and CO_2 emissions continue to rise rapidly.
- **Current income determines levels of investment and mitigation**. According to the well-known inter-temporal effect, future consumption from an investment today is discounted relative to current consumption, owing to a component related to time preferences and another reflecting aversion to risk or income inequality. It follows that the marginal cost of investment in terms of, foregone Period 1 consumption, influences its extent. All things being equal, a lower initial income would tend to make investment in any technology more costly in terms of foregone consumption. To the extent that cleaner technologies are more (or less) expensive than carbon-intensive alternatives, this effect would be augmented (or reduced). However, if there exist other social costs from production (e.g. the impacts of air pollution on health), these would increase the incentive to invest in clean versus dirty technologies. Significant social and economic adjustment costs are also likely to exist in real-life; these might reduce investments in clean technologies relative to established technologies.
- **The value placed on the long-term is an important determinant of the stringency of mitigation action.** This is essentially the tragedy of the horizon: conventional economic decision-making frameworks, and political and economic actors, may underweight the long term. Cost-benefit analysis can address concerns about undervaluing the long term by using discount rates that decline over time. (Stern, 2006[19]) argued for strong climate action based on a low discount rate, but a case for stringent mitigation action can be made even with higher discount rates (Sterner and Persson, 2008[20]).
- **The nature and severity of climate damages.** The level and degree to which climate damages increase with rising CO_2 concentrations also significantly influence a country's incentive to mitigate. There exist strong arguments suggesting countries have not adequately factored into

their decision-making the full range of climate damages or the "likelihood of severe, pervasive, and irreversible impacts," (IPCC, 2014[21]). Countries are intimately linked through intricate trade and global value chains. Hence, damages elsewhere in the world can have impacts that countries may not fully understand or value if they evaluate investments based on purely national climate damages and do not consider the risks transmitted through such value chains.

Source: Authors, based on (Buckle et al., 2014[17]).

1. In reality, of course, generations overlap. But the sharpness of this distinction helps make clear the different inter-generational incentives at play. In this model, everything is determined by the initial investment decisions, assuming that subsequent social welfare is maximised in the light of preferences.

1.2. Two-way alignment and the well-being lens

Mitigation policies are likely to be easier to implement politically, economically and socially – and more cost-effective – when there is ***two-way alignment*** between climate action and the broader goals of human well-being and sustainable development. The first imperative is that action in non-climate policy areas should support rather than undermine the pursuit of climate change mitigation goals. This was a major theme of the OECD publication *Aligning Policies for the Low-carbon Economy* (OECD/IEA/NEA/ITF, 2015[22]). Examples of misalignments needing to be resolved include lower tax rates for company cars or a faster depreciation rate for tax purposes for fossil-fuel infrastructure compared to renewables, which incentivises perpetuating emission-intensive activities. The *Investing in Climate, Investing in Growth* report (OECD, 2017[5]) examined transition pathways that are inclusive, progressive and good for business.

The second imperative is that to be more attractive, climate change mitigation should also meet other important societal goals, or at least not have negative impacts on key dimensions of well-being. Any well-being effects will often be realised on a shorter timescale than those of climate change mitigation policies, which accrue over the longer term. In the case of well-being benefits, their greater immediacy will help counter the short-termism pervasive in decision-making at all levels, from individuals to governments, that inhibits climate mitigation action. Where there are negative well-being impacts, e.g. on jobs in certain sectors or affordability of key services such as energy or transport, these are likely to inhibit further or even roll back action on climate change mitigation.

Two-way alignment is a condition that is currently insufficiently achieved, constituting a major obstacle for governments and society to accelerate mitigation action. This report argues for the systematic inclusion in decision-making of the wider well-being impacts of climate change mitigation as a central step to making potential synergies and trade-offs visible and manageable, and thus, contributing to generating the two-way alignment and putting mitigation action back on track. It refers to this change in perspective to policy making as ***adopting a well-being lens,*** which in this report means that: [11]

- Policy goals are defined in terms of well-being outcomes (including the risks and impacts of climate change) and are systematically reflected in decision-making across the economy.
- The decisions taken consider multiple well-being objectives, rather than focusing on a single (or very narrow range of) objective(s) independently of others.
- The interrelations between the different economic sectors and systems in which a policy intervenes are sufficiently well understood.

Viewed through a well-being lens, climate change mitigation has the potential to deliver wider well-being benefits for current generations and underpin the resources needed for future well-being.[12] The most obvious is perhaps that of improved health from reduced air pollution (see Box 1.2 in this chapter) from reduced emissions from electricity generation (Chapter 2), transport (Chapter 4) and agriculture (Chapter

6). Reducing fossil-fuel combustion will cut CO_2 emissions but will also reduce levels of air pollution due to fine particulate matter and chemical compounds, some of which are precursors of highly damaging tropospheric ozone. As documented in (Perera, 2017[23]), children and the developing foetus are more vulnerable to many of the effects of toxic air pollutants than adults. Thus, fossil-fuel combustion doubly impacts on future generations, not only through future climate damages, but also through current health and developmental potential. That both of these impacts disproportionately affect the poor only amplifies the injustice. But there are many other benefits that can be realised throughout the economy that would justify a far greater level of mitigation action than is currently undertaken at an aggregate level. For instance, earlier and stronger mitigation action targeting long-lived GHGs (such as CO_2) will also limit the inevitable increases in sea level that could threaten major concentrations of economic and social capital in both coastal cities and rural communities forced to retreat in the face of rising seas (OECD, 2019[24]).

Equally important, a well-being approach also brings into sharp focus the need to consider potential trade-offs between climate change mitigation and wider well-being goals. Trade-offs between policy goals cannot always be avoided, but adopting a *well-being lens* is key to identifying and assessing them, thus improving policy design and prioritisation of mitigation actions across the economy. For instance, to the extent that mitigation action raises household costs for key energy and transport services, distributional issues affecting the political feasibility and sustainability of such actions may arise in the absence of compensating measures or alternatives (e.g. public transport). In each such case, a detailed analysis of the issues is required. Overall, such trade-offs may be related to socio-economic inequalities, but non-income aspects are also important. The discussion in OECD (2019[25]) about the recent "Gilets Jaunes" protests in France emphasises that re-distributional policies may not always be the answer to problems more deeply rooted in societal exclusion – an important dimension of a well-being approach.

The character of the resulting two-way alignment is likely to differ across jurisdictions, reflecting their development levels as well as the particular challenges and opportunities they face. By adopting this approach, governments will be in a better position to secure both their climate and broader well-being goals in a way that is appropriate to their situation. Looking at climate action through a well-being lens is therefore necessary to assess and better manage political economy factors. With respect to employment, there are clear similarities between this approach and the discussion of opportunities, challenges and guiding principles for the Just Transition (ILO, 2015[18]).

An international consensus is emerging on some key ingredients of a well-being approach. The concept of well-being goes beyond economic welfare: it incorporates such aspects as political and social rights, health, education, security and environmental quality (OECD, 2014[26]). In broad terms, reaching well-being "requires meeting various human needs, some of which are essential (e.g. being in good health), as well as the ability to pursue one's goals, to thrive and feel satisfied with [one's] life" (OECD, 2011[27]). Throughout this report, the term "well-being" refers to present and future well-being. As such, it is a synonym of sustainable development (Brundtland, 1987[28]).

The OECD well-being framework comprises both current well-being outcomes and the resources that help sustain it over time. It acknowledges that maximising current well-being could come at the cost of depleting future resources and recognises the need to monitor both dimensions in parallel. Ultimately, policy must be able to balance the sometimes differing interests of current and future generations, addressing both the tragedy of the horizon and issues of two-way alignment. The well-being framework is also part recent progress in improving measurement systems "beyond GDP", including through the SDGs and a number of country initiatives (Exton and Shinwell, 2018[29]). The next section describes efforts to underpin this change in perspective with changes in measurement systems at an economy-wide level and provides more detail on the OECD well-being framework. The following chapters illustrate how adopting a well-being lens could be done in the five economic sectors selected for this report, including discussions on how measurement systems at sector specific level would also need to be adapted.

1.2.1. Measuring progress: Moving beyond GDP

GDP is a measure of the production of goods and services in a given country and period,[13] but is widely used as a proxy for well-being. Although criticisms on the relevance of GDP as a measure of well-being are as old as the measure itself, GDP has maintained its position as the main metric to gauge societal progress or "success", which can be problematic (Durand et al., 2018[30]; Boarini and Mira D'ercole, 2013[31]). The correlation between GDP and certain well-being dimensions can also be negative depending on the chosen well-being dimension, e.g. air pollution (see Box 1.2). Hence, focusing on GDP outcomes alone can lead to suboptimal outcomes, particularly where major externalities exist.

Van den Bergh (2009[32]) argues that while positive correlations exist between certain well-being dimensions, they change over time and depend on country characteristics. Additionally, approaches that are limited to GDP completely obscure income, spatial and social differences. That said, better measures of well-being will come with an extra level of complexity, which will be need to be justified if they are to gain acceptance. The contention here is that climate change mitigation is one of those areas where the benefits should far outweigh the costs of adopting a more sophisticated approach. The need for urgent and effective action to address a number of major intra- and intergenerational externalities simultaneously and in an integrated manner demands a step change in the sophistication of the policy tools used.

Macroeconomic policymaking is always going to depend on economic indicators such as the components of GDP, if not the aggregate measure itself. The real issue is when GDP is misused and the growth maximisation doctrine spills over into all aspects of policy, regardless of the quality of GDP growth and distributional issues. Some of the key problems in this regard are (Van Den Bergh, 2008[33]):

- GDP is a flow and not a stock measure. It does not directly capture the change over time of the different types of capital or "wealth" (environmental, economic and social), although measures of physical capital can be constructed from its investment component. Therefore, GDP does not directly provide information about the sustainability of the economic activity or the possibility of achieving well-being over time (Boarini and Mira D'ercole, 2013[31]; Fleurbaey, 2009[34]).
- GDP does not provide information on factors beyond the material conditions that affect well-being, such as security, social rights, health or leisure time (OECD, 2011[27]).
- GDP has nothing to say on the distribution of "income" across society, which is an important feature for individual and societal well-being, particularly at a time of intentional structural change.
- GDP includes activities that can negatively affect well-being or that remediate the social or environmental costs generated by the production of goods and services ("regrettables"), rather than increasing well-being. Examples include higher transportation costs due to congestion, the costs of remediating environmental destruction (e.g. the cleaning of coastal areas after an oil spill) and increased consumption stemming from reduced ecosystem services (e.g. bottled water or masks due to undrinkable water and unbreathable air) (OECD, 2011[27]; Fleurbaey, 2009[34]).
- GDP generally values the supply of goods and services at market prices, which may reflect marginal costs but not the welfare derived from it, as in the case of cheap food staples.
- GDP excludes non-market activities potentially contributing to well-being, such as services produced by households (e.g. childcare) (OECD, 2011[27]; Giannetti et al., 2015[35]).

These considerations have important policy implications, particularly for addressing climate change through public policy approaches that avoid stark trade-offs between climate and economic policy. Among others, OECD (2017[5]) has demonstrated that such trade-offs are avoidable. In specific cases where a pro-growth policy could be harmful to well-being, policy makers should look for ways to improve policy design so that negative well-being impacts are neutralised or even turned into positive impacts. The same is true for mitigation activities that reduce GHG emissions, but have significant negative impacts on wider well-being goals. Conversely, some mitigation policies may improve well-being, while reducing or changing the composition of GDP, which may be wrongly valued precisely because of deficiencies in GDP as a well-being indicator. For example, policies promoting a modal shift from motor vehicles to bicycles may be undervalued if analysed solely in terms of economic output, as their positive impacts on health, air quality, equity and reduced emissions may be only partially captured and may also reduce GDP. Furthermore, GDP does not provide the information needed for efficient management of natural resources and waste (i.e. in a circular economy).

Growth and well-being are inextricably linked through factors such as income, earnings, jobs and economic capital. Clearly, a well-being lens would provide a much stronger rationale for a policy with compelling well-being gains and neutral growth impacts than a strategy with a simple growth objective. This is a very important concrete advantage of adopting a well-being approach. It focuses on the quality of economic growth and its well-being outcomes, rather than just the magnitude of that growth. Additionally, a well-being approach explicitly forces attention on those things (e.g. social connections and a clean environment) that money alone cannot buy, and GDP does not value. Perpetuating the current model of economic activity (i.e. with insufficient regard for environmental, distributional and social impacts) would ultimately put everyone's long-term well-being at risk.

Box 1.2. Air pollution and climate change mitigation

CO_2 and other GHG emissions are strongly linked to air pollution. Reducing energy use and emissions could increase well-being through improved air quality, environmental quality and health. Exposure to outdoor air pollution from combustion engines (i.e. PM2.5, PM10 and ozone) is associated with premature mortality, cardiorespiratory disease, lung cancer and asthma (WHO, 2015[36]).

The burden of disease from ambient outdoor PM2.5 contributed to 3.7 million premature deaths globally in 2012, 88% of which occurred in low- and middle-income countries (WHO, 2015[36]). Without additional action, the market and non-market costs of outdoor air pollution reported in (OECD, 2016[37]) will grow rapidly, reaching an estimated 1% of GDP by 2060 (market) and USD 18-25 trillion in 2060 (non-market), compared to USD 3 trillion in 2015. Indoor air pollution from the use of polluting fuels for basic cooking, heating and lighting is estimated to have caused 4.3 million premature deaths, mostly of women and children (WHO, 2015[36]). The deployment of modern forms of energy could reduce emissions and improve the health of the world's 3 billion poorest people (Shindell et al., 2017[38]).

Children suffer the most from the health impacts of air pollution, which impairs their development (WHO, 2018[39]) and can diminish their educational outcomes substantially and lastingly (Heissel, Persico and Simon, 2019[40]). Air pollution is also linked to the incidence of dementia (Bishop et al., 2018[41]). Finally, it reduces worker productivity, lowering agricultural yields (OECD, 2016[37]).

These health benefits of reducing carbon emissions have led many to argue for prioritising action on short-lived climate pollutants (SLCPs), which include methane, black carbon and hydrofluorocarbons. Although the major health benefits are unambiguous, the climate benefits of SLCP reductions are context-dependent (Pierrehumbert, 2014[42]). SLCP mitigation will be most effective when CO_2 emissions are already decreasing rapidly; it will be largely irrelevant to reduce the scale of climate change if CO_2 emissions continue to increase and are not close to reaching zero on a net basis. It is therefore important not to substitute mitigation action to reduce SLCPs for action on CO_2, which would only provide limited short-term benefits in terms of temperature reduction early on for far higher temperatures later. Many CO_2 mitigation measures will also reduce emissions of SLCPs, and some action on SLCPs may also reduce CO_2 emissions (Shindell et al., 2017[38]).

Rethinking societal goals and the definition of progress is increasingly recognised as crucial to putting well-being and sustainability at the centre of policy decisions (e.g. when considering the criteria for implementing policies) (EUROSTAT, 2010[43]). In recent years, significant efforts have been made to improve measurement systems to go "beyond GDP" (see Box 1.3). In January 2019, the Prime Minister of New Zealand, Jacinda Ardern argued at the World Economic Forum that well-being should be the metric used to gauge societal progress, instead of GDP. On 30 May 2019, New Zealand launched its Well-being Budget, explicilty contrasting this new approach with traditional measures of successon such as GDP. The budget required new governmental spending to be directed towards five social goals: taking mental health seriously; improving child well-being; supporting the aspirations of indigenous people; building a productive nation; and transforming the economy (including climate change mitigation). All new spending will be assessed against 61 indicators to measure well-being. The approach aims to foster cross-government co-operation to achieve these goals, while addressing fiscal sustainability, infrastructure investment and support for the economy.[14]

Box 1.3. Global initiatives for well-being

Initiatives focusing on the development of alternative measures of progress or well-being have increased and accelerated over the last decade in the wake of the (so-called) Stiglitz-Sen-Fitoussi report (Stiglitz, Sen and Fitoussi, 2009[44]) and the EU communication entitled "GDP and Beyond: Measuring progress in a changing world" (European Commission, 2009[45]).

The Stiglitz-Sen-Fitoussi (2009[44]) report highlighted the need for a "shift of emphasis from a production-oriented measurement system to one focused on the well-being of current and future generations, towards broader measures of social progress." It described the limitations of GDP as an indicator of progress, and provided 30 recommendations for data collection to move beyond GDP and improve measures of well-being and progress (Stiglitz, Sen and Fitoussi, 2009[44]).

The European Commission outlined a set of actions – captured in a roadmap – to improve progress indicators to better respond to citizens' concerns, as well as capture the complexity of a globalised world with environmental constraints and a population of over 7 billion (European Commission, 2009[45]). Motivated by numerous academic publications calling on Europe to end "growth dependency", ten Members of the European Parliament organised a Post Growth Conference in 2018 (EEB, 2018[46]).

In 2009, the Conference of European Statisticians, jointly with the United Nations Economic Commission for Europe, the OECD and Eurostat, established the Task Force for Measuring Sustainable Development (TFSD), with the goal to develop a broad conceptual framework (Europe, 2014[47]).

In 2011, the OECD launched the OECD Better Life Initiative, following many of the recommendations issued by the Stiglitz-Sen-Fitoussi report, the TFSD, and national and international initiatives (Durand et al., 2018[30]). The resulting OECD well-being framework provides an analytical tool to study the multidimensional concept of both current and future well-being.

In 2013, as a response to the United Nations Conference on Sustainable Development outcome document "The Future We Want" (United Nations, 2012[48]), an Open Working Group was established and developed the SDGs, which country leaders officially adopted in 2015.

In parallel, various countries have developed national well-being frameworks involving diverse agencies and institutions (e.g. environmental agencies, and finance and health ministries). In 2011, for example, New Zealand presented the Living Standards Framework, aiming to achieve higher living standards and sustainable well-being for New Zealanders. The framework follows a capital approach: natural, human, social, and financial/physical capital, described as interdependent, are the basis for the country's achievement of well-being outcomes. Many other countries, including Italy (Measures of Equitable and Sustainable Well-being), Germany (Well-being in Germany) and Sweden (New Measures for Prosperity) have developed well-being metrics, as described in Table 1.1 of the New Zealand Economic Survey 2019 (OECD, 2019[49]).

Globally, the SDGs adopted in 2015 are a list of internationally agreed policy commitments aiming to address global challenges and acknowledging they are all interconnected. The SDGs include poverty and inequality reduction, climate change mitigation, environmental conservation and justice. The OECD well-being framework is an analytical tool aiming to assess societal progress through the lens of well-being. It is structured around both current well-being and the resources needed for future well-being (see Figure 1.3).[15] All these approaches recognise that societal progress is about improving people's present and future well-being, moving away from a sole focus on GDP to include multiple well-being dimensions. As argued above, such approaches are important to increase the ambition of climate change mitigation policies.

1.2.2. The OECD well-being framework

The OECD recognises that promoting better policies for better lives requires rethinking societal goals and shifting from the current focus on economic growth to a focus on improving people's well-being (OECD, 2018[50]). The OECD well-being framework provides an analytical tool to examine the multidimensional concept of well-being beyond its purely economic aspects. Focusing on individuals and households – rather than aggregating them at the level of the economy – it allows analysis of the distribution of well-being across the population. The framework also looks into both current and future well-being, a particularly relevant distinction for climate change mitigation policies (Boarini and Mira D'ercole, 2013[31]).

Figure 1.3. The OECD well-being framework

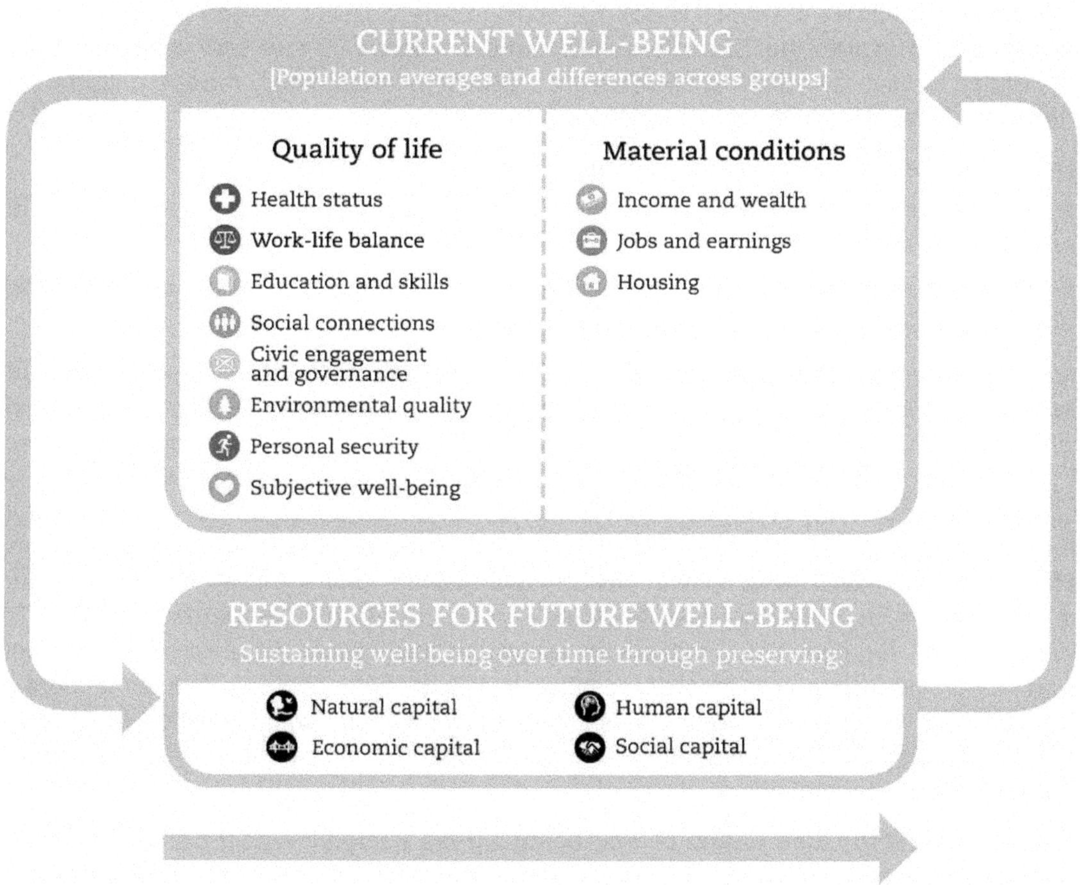

Source: (OECD, 2013[51]).

Figure 1.3 presents the conceptual framework proposed by the OECD. In line with a large body of research[16], **current well-being** is defined as falling into two domains, material conditions and quality of life, broken down into 11 dimensions. **Future well-being** is assessed in terms of the availability of the natural, economic, human and social capital stocks necessary to maintain well-being for current and future generations. Figure 1.4 illustrates the capital stocks (middle column) needed to sustain the different dimensions of well-being over time (right column), as well as the drivers that may influence these stocks. The drivers – represented in the left column – include investments (e.g. to increase the stock), depreciation or depletion (e.g. loss of soil quality for farming, or deforestation), and emissions and waste (OECD, 2013[51]). Current well-being is related to the long-term sustainability of well-being, because current consumption and production decisions have an impact on investment and hence the productive base of future well-being.

The OECD well-being framework – as well as other "beyond GDP" alternative measures, such as the SDGs or the country initiatives described in Box 1.3 – can provide the evidence and language for politicians and policy makers to explain the rationale behind more ambitious climate change mitigation policies. Analysing policies through a well-being lens has the potential to inform policy makers on three important aspects that are not reflected in the measure of GDP, as follows:

- How do policies affect the different dimensions of well-being today?
- How do policies affect the distribution of well-being across society (e.g. are they key for ensuring an inclusive transition to a low-carbon economy)?
- How do policies incentivise a sustainable utilisation of resources (to ensure future generations can achieve well-being)?

How do policies affect the different dimensions of well-being today? Analysing policy actions through a well-being lens allows examination of trade-offs and synergies between the different well-being dimensions. Using this perspective, policies can be assessed according to their potential impact on the different dimensions of well-being, rather than simply their economic impact. For example, the negative impacts of fossil-fuel subsidies on present well-being, due to increased air pollution, and on future well-being, due to the depletion of non-renewable resources and increased likelihood of climate change, would be more visible through a well-being lens. In this light, policies that increase quality of life or resources for future well-being would be valued more positively than policies focusing more narrowly on GDP. The well-being framework still requires policy makers to weigh the implications for income, wealth, jobs and earnings. It will provide them with greater incentive to design better policies that offer more win-win outcomes, or at least win-neutral outcomes. While the well-being approach can reveal, clarify - and ideally quantify - the synergies and trade-offs, it does not of itself deliver the synergies or resolve the trade-offs; that remains the job of governments.

How do policies affect the distribution of well-being across society? A poor distribution of well-being has present and future impacts across the whole of society, through reduced economic development; risks of political instability stemming from people's low trust in institutions or perceptions of injustice, intolerance and discrimination; and limited connections to others owing to "social barriers". Analyses of GDP do not capture the increasing levels of inequality, including in OECD countries over the last 30 years as found in OECD (2015[52]) and OECD (2016[53]). Inequalities are often analysed in terms of income distribution, through indicators such as the Gini coefficient. Although a balanced income distribution is a key element for societal well-being, it is not the only "type" of inequality that matters in terms of achieving a good life. Looking at inequality through a well-being lens allows expanding the measurement to outcomes such as life expectancy, exposure to air pollution, education and skills, and health status.

Figure 1.4. Capital stocks and their drivers in relation to well-being outcomes

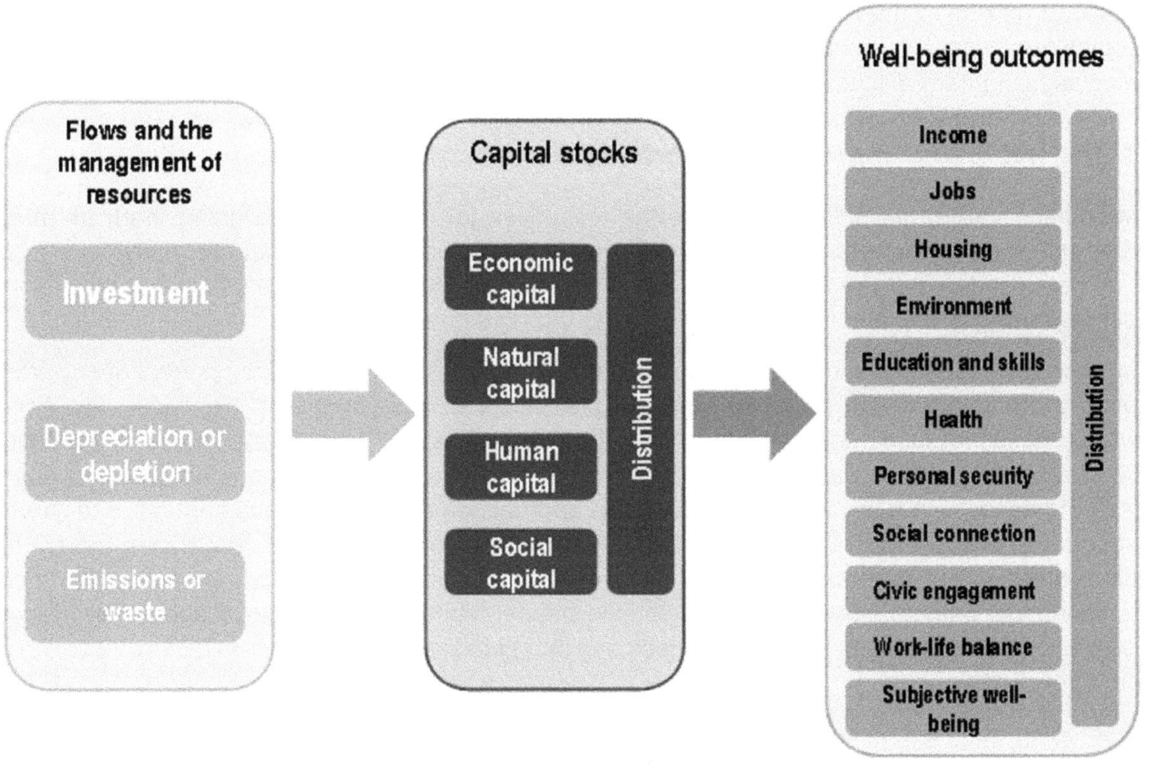

Source: Extracted from (OECD, 2013[51]).

Information on the distribution of the different dimensions of well-being can help policy makers understand the interaction of the impacts of specific policy decisions on different parts of society. This information is particularly relevant to ensuring that climate change mitigation policies result in an equitable transition to a low-emission economy, rather than increasing existing inequalities.

Designing policies to ensure the costs and benefits of the transition are fairly shared across society also reduces the likelihood of political resistance to climate change mitigation policies. For example, identifying the impact of mitigation action on different regions or job categories can help governments design policies that take into account the adverse impacts of these policies on specific regions and job types. There are clear similarities here with the approach advocated in (ILO, 2015[18]). Similarly, carbon-pricing instruments that typically put a higher burden on lower-income households can be designed in a non-regressive manner. This type of approach could avoid exacerbating pre-existing economic inequalities; with proper design, it could even benefit lower-income households, eventually prompting them to support transition (Van Dender and Marten, 2019[54]).

How do policies incentivise a sustainable utilisation of resources? The notion of capital is helpful to assessing sustainability. One generation's choices regarding the accumulation or depletion of capital stocks influence the next generation's opportunities to achieve well-being (OECD, 2013[51]). For example, failure to mitigate the current unsustainable levels of GHG emissions will affect the livelihoods and subsistence of future generations, which will bear the impact of climate change on their economic, natural, social and human capital.

Thus, informing policy by viewing it through a well-being lens can help governments develop more comprehensive policy packages that exploit synergies between the different well-being dimensions, duly considering the potential trade-offs and barriers to policy implementation. As such, the OECD well-being framework, as well as the other frameworks introduced in Box 1.3 and the sector-specific analysis offered in this report (linking to the SDG and OECD well-being frameworks throughout), can be useful tools for developing long-term low-emission development strategies (LT-LEDS), briefly described in Box 1.4. The following section briefly discusses the relationship between carbon pricing and the well-being approach.

1.2.3. The well-being approach and carbon pricing

The well-being framework aims to increase the incentives for mitigation by aligning them as much as possible with other well-being goals that may weigh more heavily in cost-benefit analyses and other decision frameworks. It also acknowledges and helps identify potential trade-offs between mitigation and broader well-being goals, and highlights the need to manage these trade-offs.

Focusing on carbon pricing and fossil fuel subsidy reform remains an essential component of any effective approach to climate change mitigation, including applying a well-being lens. However, low-emission pathways require profound transformations rather than changes at the margin, entailing a political economy perspective to navigate the transition(s). In some sectors, carbon pricing alone is not going to drive the necessary changes, e.g. in terms of coherent approaches to urban development and transport infrastructures. Effective carbon rates are highest in the transport sector, but elasticities are such that carbon pricing may not change behaviour and technologies that much. Moreover, while the right pricing is vital to encourage both investment and innovation in cleaner technologies, concerns about the implications for well-being (e.g. affordability, competitiveness and jobs) are likely to be important factors inhibiting more stringent policy settings.

The well-being approach is used to assess "two-way alignment" between climate and other well-being goals in order to better identify and manage the synergies and trade-offs. In this context, it calls for full cost accounting – including through carbon pricing – or at least factoring in the (sometimes uncertain) costs of externalities. It embraces and stresses the importance of pricing externalities, but looks at this critical policy component from the broader perspective of supporting the transition to a low-emission development pathway while achieving broader well-being goals and avoiding some of the negative trade-offs that may arise from a sole focus on carbon pricing and other climate policy instruments.

1.3. Moving from theory to practice

This report aims to encourage and support governments in meeting their national and international climate change mitigation goals. It explains how adopting a well-being lens could lead to different policy approaches and change the overall perspective on policy making in specific economic sectors, namely, electricity, heavy industry, residential, surface transport and agriculture, which together represent over 60% of global GHG emissions (IPCC, 2014[3]). It highlights that setting priorities across sectors to deliver multiple well-being and sustainability outcomes both enhances the potential benefits, and helps identify the opportunities and needs for co-operation and co-ordination in order to meet stringent mitigation goals.

For policy makers to be able to adopt a well-being lens for policy making, the measurement system used to track progress, set criteria for decision-making frameworks and evaluate policy outcomes needs to capture multiple well-being objectives. Decisions are often based on a single objective or a very limited number of objectives; the associated measurement and monitoring systems often have limited ability to capture broader well-being impacts, often conflating outputs with well-being outcomes. In transport, for example, measurement focuses on the number of passengers and tonne-kilometres, instead of the access to opportunities and services provided by transport. A measurement system that better monitors diverse well-being outcomes can also be a crucial step for setting shared goals and targets across governments, where co-operation and co-ordination are key to delivering climate and other well-being goals.

> Without political commitment to act on them, the development of indicators is a symbolic exercise.

Box 1.4. An opportunity for sustainable development and more ambitious climate change mitigation policies: Long-term low-emission development strategies (LT-LEDS)

LT-LEDS are a powerful planning instrument that allows countries to deliver on climate change mitigation while improving the well-being of current and future generations. Article 4.19 of the Paris Agreement calls on signatory countries to formulate "long-term low greenhouse gas emission development strategies, mindful of Article 2 taking into account their common but differentiated responsibilities and respective capabilities, in the light of different national circumstances," (UNFCCC, 2015[55]). While the Paris Agreement provides no methodological insights about how LT-LEDS should be developed, a rapidly developing literature identifies several key characteristics and requirements for such strategies to generate the structural change needed to reach the well-below 2°C goal.

The Institute for Sustainable Development and International Relations (IDDRI) defines LT-LEDS as "structured strategy exercises [should be] embedded in the national policy process and represent a useful way of structuring national policy debates in a transparent, productive and ambitious way. The point of departure should be national socio-economic objectives, alongside the well below 2°C objective," (IDDRI, 2016[56]).

IDDRI defines a set of principles for developing a multi-stakeholder framework. In line with the two-way alignment, it aims to: i) review climate and non-climate policies that deliver on climate-change mitigation and other dimensions of well-being; and ii) explore cross-sector linkages, as well as the need for meeting mitigation, adaptation and other SDGs. This report discuss these linkages in more detail for each sector (Electricity; Heavy Industry; Residential; Surface Transport; and Agriculture).

Developing LT-LEDS is not a straightforward process. Adequate mechanisms for interactions between all parts of the government (e.g. between ministries and different levels of government), as well as between government and other stakeholders, will be necessary. Governments may also need to expand their technical capacity (e.g. by developing adequate modelling tools or improving interactions between the different models used) and address numerous political economy factors, such as government revenues' dependence on fossil fuel and vested interests. The rest of the report examines a range of political economy factors in each of the five sectors, notably those related to affordability and acceptability, which are central to guaranteeing an equitable transition.

LT-LEDS are likely to be one of many planning instruments in national frameworks (e.g. sectoral plans, local plans and strategies focusing on the delivery of other policy goals, such as improved health through reducing air pollution). If efforts to develop LT-LEDS are in line with the set of principles introduced above, this process could become an opportunity to rethink economy-wide policy priorities, and align other planning instruments at the national and subnational levels with these. Designing effective and coherent policies for meeting multiple goals related to well-being outcomes and the SDGs is the major purpose of the OECD Framework for Policy Coherence for Sustainable Development (OECD, 2018[57]).

While some of the indicators proposed in this report are relatively new, many are not. The novelty lies in the recognition that they need to be widely available (since only a few countries or databases may have them), and considered simultaneously and with the same level of priority, rather than viewed in isolation and with a hierarchical order (e.g. focus on GHG emissions, regardless of the impacts on agricultural soils). In addition, a change in the measurement system can be a significant step towards more ambitious climate change mitigation policies only if the new approach is effectively used to inform policy decisions, as "without political commitment to act on them, the development of indicators is a symbolic exercise" (Winston and Eastaway, 2008[58]). The evidence base that enables this to happen still needs to be built, including by embedding well-being indicators in policy evaluations. Discussions across sectors focus on this point and provide examples of good practice where available.

The report discusses how the well-being lens could be applied in different sectors and the type of measurement system that could support the shift in perspective needed to decarbonise that particular sector while achieving two-way alignment. While chapters have a sectoral focus, they also make linkages across sectors, where this is important (e.g. for electricity, and for the residential and transport sectors in particular). Rethinking policy goals and reframing the measurement system is central to designing, evaluating and implementing climate policies while taking into account potential synergies and trade-offs, thereby to better aligning incentives towards both climate change mitigation and wider well-being benefits.

References

Berkeley Earth (2017), *Global Temperature Report for 2017*, http://berkeleyearth.org/global-temperatures-2017/. [1]

Bishop, K. et al. (2018), *Hazed and confused: the effect of air pollution on dementia*, http://www.nber.org/papers/w24970 (accessed on 3 July 2019). [41]

Boarini, R. and M. Mira D'ercole (2013), *Going beyond GDP: An OECD Perspective*, http://www.bls.gov/iif (accessed on 25 August 2018). [31]

Brundtland, G. (1987), *Our Common Future (The Brundtland Report)*, http://dx.doi.org/10.1080/07488008808408783. [28]

Buckle, S. et al. (2014), "Prospects for Paris 2015: do major emitters want the same climate ?", *CORE Discussion Papers*, https://ideas.repec.org/p/cor/louvco/2014008.html (accessed on 3 July 2019). [17]

Carney, M. (2015), *Speech: Breaking the tragedy of the horizon – climate change and financial stability*, https://www.bis.org/review/r151009a.pdf (accessed on 12 December 2017). [14]

Durand, M. et al. (2018), "Countries' Experiences with Well-being and Happiness Metrics", https://s3.amazonaws.com/ghc-2018/GHC_Ch8.pdf (accessed on 5 June 2018). [30]

Durand, M. and C. Exton (2019), *Adopting a Well-Being Approach in Central Government: Policy Mechanisms and Practical Tools*, https://s3.amazonaws.com/ghwbpr-2019/UAE/GH19_Ch8.pdf (accessed on 3 July 2019). [61]

EEB (2018), "Beyond-gdp-growth-debate-at-postgrowth-conference.". [46]

European Commission (2009), *GDP and beyond : measuring progress in a changing world*, https://eur-lex.europa.eu/legal-content/EN/TXT/?uri=CELEX:52009DC0433 (accessed on 3 October 2018). [45]

Europe, U. (2014), *Conference of european statisticians recommendations on measuring sustainable development*, https://www.unece.org/fileadmin/DAM/stats/publications/2013/CES_SD_web.pdf (accessed on 3 July 2019). [47]

EUROSTAT (2010), "Sigma the bulletin of european statistics: gdp and beyond", http://www.pixelio.de. (accessed on 19 September 2018). [43]

Exton, C. and M. Shinwell (2018), "Policy use of well-being metrics: Describing countries' experiences", *SDD working paper.*, No. 94, OECD, Paris, http://www.oecd.org/sdd/publicationsdocuments/workingpapers (accessed on 6 November 2018). [29]

Fleurbaey, M. (2009), "Beyond GDP: The Quest for a Measure of Social Welfare", http://dx.doi.org/10.1257/jel.47.4.1029. [34]

Giannetti, B. et al. (2015), "A review of limitations of GDP and alternative indices to monitor human wellbeing and to manage eco-system functionality", *Journal of Cleaner Production*, Vol. 87, pp. 11-25, http://dx.doi.org/10.1016/j.jclepro.2014.10.051. [35]

Heissel, J., C. Persico and D. Simon (2019), *Does Pollution Drive Achievement? The Effect of Traffic Pollution on Academic Performance*, https://www.nber.org/papers/w25489.pdf (accessed on 3 July 2019). [40]

IDDRI (2016), *Long-term low emissions development strategies and the Paris Agreement – Why, what and how?*, https://www.iddri.org/en/publications-and-events/policy-brief/long-term-low-emissions-development-strategies-and-paris (accessed on 6 September 2018). [56]

IEA (2019), *World Energy Investment 2019*, https://webstore.iea.org/download/direct/2738?fileName=WEI2019.pdf (accessed on 3 July 2019). [11]

ILO (2015), *Guidelines for a just transition towards environmentally sustainable economies and societies for all*, http://www.ilo.org/publns (accessed on 8 August 2019). [18]

IPCC (2018), *Global Warming of 1.5 C*, https://ipcc.ch/report/sr15/ (accessed on 17 October 2018). [4]

IPCC (2014), *Climate Change 2014 - Summary for Policymakers*, https://www.ipcc.ch/pdf/assessment-report/ar5/syr/AR5_SYR_FINAL_SPM.pdf (accessed on 20 August 2018). [21]

IPCC (2014), *Climate Change 2014 - Synthesis Report*, Gian-Kasper Plattner, http://www.ipcc.ch. (accessed on 3 July 2019). [3]

Le Quéré, C. et al. (2018), "Global Carbon Budget 2018", *Earth System Science Data*, Vol. 10/4, pp. 2141-2194, http://dx.doi.org/10.5194/essd-10-2141-2018. [16]

Liebreich, M. (2018), *Scenarios for a solar singularity*, https://www.linkedin.com/pulse/scenarios-solar-singularity-michael-liebreich/. [59]

Loorbach, D., N. Frantzeskaki and F. Avelino (2017), "Sustainability Transitions Research: Transforming Science and Practice for Societal Change", *Annual Review of Environment and Resources*, Vol. 42/1, pp. 599-626, http://dx.doi.org/10.1146/annurev-environ-102014-021340. [60]

Mirabile, M. and J. Calder (2018), "Clean power for a cool planet", *OECD Environment Working Papers*, Vol. 140, https://dx.doi.org/10.1787/2dc84376-en. [10]

OECD (2019), *OECD Economic Surveys: New Zealand 2019*, OECD Publishing, Paris, https://dx.doi.org/10.1787/b0b94dbd-en. [49]

OECD (2019), *OECD Regional Outlook 2019: Leveraging Megatrends for Cities and Rural Areas*, OECD Publishing, Paris, https://dx.doi.org/10.1787/9789264312838-en. [25]

OECD (2019), *Responding to Rising Seas: OECD Country Approaches to Tackling Coastal Risks*, OECD Publishing, Paris, https://dx.doi.org/10.1787/9789264312487-en. [24]

OECD (2018), *Meeting of the Council at Ministerial Level. Strategic orientations of the secretary-general*, http://www.oecd.org/officialdocuments/publicdisplaydocumentpdf/?cote=C/MIN(2018)1&docLanguage=En (accessed on 29 August 2018). [50]

OECD (2018), *OECD Companion to the Inventory of Support Measures for Fossil Fuels 2018*, OECD Publishing, Paris, https://dx.doi.org/10.1787/9789264286061-en. [12]

OECD (2018), *Policy Coherence for Sustainable Development 2018: Towards Sustainable and Resilient Societies*, OECD Publishing, Paris, https://dx.doi.org/10.1787/9789264301061-en. [57]

OECD (2017), *Climate Action -Time for implementation*, http://www.oecd.org/canada/munk-school-climate-action-time-for-implementation-canada-2017.htm (accessed on 1 October 2018). [15]

OECD (2017), *Investing in Climate, Investing in Growth*, OECD Publishing, Paris, https://dx.doi.org/10.1787/9789264273528-en. [5]

OECD (2016), *Income inequality remains high in the face of weak recovery*, http://www.oecd.org/social/OECD2016-Income-Inequality-Update.pdf (accessed on 3 July 2019). [53]

OECD (2016), *The Economic Consequences of Outdoor Air Pollution*, OECD Publishing, Paris, https://dx.doi.org/10.1787/9789264257474-en. [37]

OECD (2015), *In It Together: Why Less Inequality Benefits All*, OECD Publishing, Paris, https://dx.doi.org/10.1787/9789264235120-en. [52]

OECD (2014), *Understanding National Accounts*, https://www.oecd-ilibrary.org/docserver/9789264214637-16-en.pdf?expires=1533575592&id=id&accname=ocid84004878&checksum=811571AB6B21D2670BA3ED9BE8F33A46 (accessed on 6 August 2018). [26]

OECD (2013), *How's life? 2013: measuring well-being*, OECD Publishing. [51]

OECD (2011), *How's Life?: Measuring Well-being*, OECD Publishing, Paris, https://dx.doi.org/10.1787/9789264121164-en. [27]

OECD/IEA/NEA/ITF (2015), *Aligning Policies for a Low-carbon Economy*, http://www.oecd-ilibrary.org/docserver/download/0315021e.pdf?expires=1510835480&id=id&accname=ocid84004878&checksum=CAF8D360F2C9DCED4002CAE73DD7F463 (accessed on 16 November 2017). [22]

OECD/The World Bank/UN Environment (2018), *Financing Climate Futures: Rethinking Infrastructure*, OECD Publishing, Paris, https://dx.doi.org/10.1787/9789264308114-en. [6]

Perera, F. (2017), "Multiple Threats to Child Health from Fossil Fuel Combustion: Impacts of Air Pollution and Climate Change.", *Environmental health perspectives*, Vol. 125/2, pp. 141-148, http://dx.doi.org/10.1289/EHP299. [23]

Pierrehumbert, R. (2014), "Short-Lived Climate Pollution", *Annual Review of Earth and Planetary Sciences*, Vol. 42/1, pp. 341-379, http://dx.doi.org/10.1146/annurev-earth-060313-054843. [42]

Röttgers, D. and B. Anderson (2018), "Power struggle: Decarbonising the electricity sector", https://dx.doi.org/10.1787/900f4c72-en (accessed on 2 July 2019). [13]

Shindell, D. et al. (2017), "A climate policy pathway for near- and long-term benefits", *Science*, Vol. 356/6337, pp. 492-493, http://dx.doi.org/10.1126/science.aaj2350. [38]

Sterner, T. and U. Persson (2008), "An Even Sterner Review: Introducing Relative Prices into the Discounting Debate", http://dx.doi.org/10.1093/reep/rem024. [20]

Stern, N. (2006), *The economics of climate change: The Stern Review*, Cambridge University Press, http://dx.doi.org/10.1017/CBO9780511817434. [19]

Stiglitz, J., A. Sen and J. Fitoussi (2009), "Measurement of Economic Performance and Social Progress", http://ec.europa.eu/eurostat/documents/118025/118123/Fitoussi+Commission+report (accessed on 2 May 2018). [44]

UNEP (2018), *Emissions Gap Report 2018*, http://www.un.org/Depts/Cartographic/english/htmain.htm (accessed on 2 July 2019). [9]

UNFCCC (2015), *Adoption of the paris agreement - Paris Agreement text English*. [55]

United Nations (2012), *The future we want*, https://sustainabledevelopment.un.org/content/documents/733FutureWeWant.pdf (accessed on 3 July 2019). [48]

Van Den Bergh, J. (2008), "The GDP paradox", http://dx.doi.org/10.1016/j.joep.2008.12.001. [33]

van den Bergh, J. (2009), "The GDP paradox", *Journal of Economic Psychology*, Vol. 30/2, pp. 117-135, http://dx.doi.org/10.1016/j.joep.2008.12.001. [32]

Van Dender, K. and X. Marten (2019), "The Use of Revenues from Carbon Pricing", *OECD Tax and Environment Working Paper Series*, OECD. [54]

Watts, N. et al. (2015), "Health and climate change: policy responses to protect public health", *The Lancet*, Vol. 386/10006, pp. 1861-1914, http://dx.doi.org/10.1016/s0140-6736(15)60854-6. [2]

WHO (2018), "Air pollution and child health: prescribing clean air", *WHO*, https://www.who.int/ceh/publications/air-pollution-child-health/en/ (accessed on 3 July 2019). [39]

WHO (2015), *Reducing global health risks Through mitigation of short-lived climate pollutants Scoping report for policymakers*, https://apps.who.int/iris/bitstream/handle/10665/189524/9789241565080?sequence=1 (accessed on 3 July 2019). [36]

Winston, N. and M. Eastaway (2008), *Sustainable Housing in the Urban Context: International Sustainable Development Indicator Sets and Housing*, Springer, http://dx.doi.org/10.2307/27734657. [58]

World Bank (2019), *Beyond the Gap – How Countries Can Afford the Infrastructure They Need while Protecting the Planet*, https://www.worldbank.org/en/topic/publicprivatepartnerships/publication/beyond-the-gap---how-countries-can-afford-the-infrastructure-they-need-while-protecting-the-planet (accessed on 3 July 2019). [7]

Zenghelis, D. (2019), "Endogenous Growth, Convexity of Damage and Climate Risk: How Nordhaus' Framework Supports Deep Cuts in Carbon Emissions", Vol. 125/583, pp. 574-620, http://dx.doi.org/10.1111/ecoj.12188. [8]

Notes

[1] See the discussion in (IPCC, 2018[4]), "Summary for Policymakers".

[2] Such as carbon capture and sequestration, which could be combined with biomass combustion to deliver so-called negative emissions.

[3] See for example, https://sdgindex.org/news/behind-the-numbers:-joint-research-centre-audit-of-the-sdg-index-and-dashboards/.

[4] See the discussion in (Liebreich, 2018[59]).

[5] Loorbach (2017[60]) notes that "The energy transition is thus much more than merely a technological shift; it is a power struggle and a socio-cultural change having a deep effect on incumbent institutions, routines, and beliefs."

[6] The 45% reduction for a 1.5°C goal assumes little overshoot of CO_2 emissions and therefore limited requirement for atmospheric CO_2 removal. The 20% figure corresponds to a 66% chance of keeping the temperature change below 2°C.

[7] See: https://www.iea.org/geco/emissions/.

[8] It should be noted, however, that this simple framework does not capture the dynamic nature of innovation in the context of climate modelling.

[9] For more information, see: https://www.fsb-tcfd.org/.

[10] Hungary had a Parliamentary Commissioner for Future Generations during 2008-12.

[11] See also the discussion in (Durand and Exton, 2019[61]), outlining that "Putting people's well-being at the heart of policy requires better data, but this alone is not enough. It also requires building well-being into the machinery of government, and the tools used to take decisions."

[12] A point highlighted in the OECD Secretary-General's 2017 speech and related to the way in which current income determines levels of investment and mitigation in the description of the conceptual model.

[13] Or equivalently, a measure of income and expenditure.

[14] See https://treasury.govt.nz/sites/default/files/2019-05/b19-wellbeing-budget.pdf.

[15] There exists a significant overlap in how well-being is defined in the SDGs and the OECD well-being framework (as well as in many individual country initiatives). A key difference between the two frameworks is that the OECD framework is an analytical tool, while the SDGs are a set of goals and targets agreed internationally, with the aim of achieving sustainable development. As such, the SDGs are a concrete example of a move towards improving well-being in practice.

[16] See (Stiglitz, Sen and Fitoussi, 2009[44]) for a literature review.

2 Catalysing change through a sustainable electricity sector

This chapter analyses the electricity sector through a well-being lens. The first part discusses a number of policy priorities beyond the traditional concerns of reliability, affordability and decarbonisation – the so-called "energy trilemma". It highlights the importance of considering different scales (plant, network and demand level) and how these scales can help governments better ensure synergies between climate and other priorities, strengthening two-way alignment. For instance, it shows how activating the role played by the demand side can enhance both affordability and system flexibility, allowing a higher share of variable renewable energy resources to be integrated in the generation mix. The second part of the chapter proposes a set of indicators enabling policy makers to track progress towards multiple priorities, assessing the synergies and trade-offs between climate action and other well-being priorities.

The statistical data for Israel are supplied by and under the responsibility of the relevant Israeli authorities. The use of such data by the OECD is without prejudice to the status of the Golan Heights, East Jerusalem and Israeli settlements in the West Bank under the terms of international law.

In Brief

Catalysing change through a sustainable electricity sector

Electricity is at the heart of human well-being since the energy it delivers supports a broad range of basic services, economic infrastructure and activities, and facilitates education and gender equality among other things. Despite improvements in energy efficiency, global electricity demand grew by 115% between 1990 and 2016, much faster than the increase in population over the same period (41%). This trend will likely continue due to economic growth and increasing access and electrification of end-uses.

Current electricity generation, notably through the combustion of fossil fuels, is the single largest contributor to global GHG emissions, pollutes the air, damaging public health and ecosystems, all of which harms current and future well-being. While decarbonisation of the electricity sector has become a policy priority, the sector is still off-track to meet global mitigation goals. Worryingly, electricity-related GHG emissions rose by 2.5% in 2018, due to large increases in gas and coal generation, a problematic trend for decarbonising industry, transport and housing that increasingly rely on a supply of low-carbon electricity. Coal-fired electricity accounted for 30% of global energy-related CO_2 emissions in 2018, mostly due to relatively young plants in Asia that could lock-in high-levels of emissions for the next 30 years.

Exploiting synergies and addressing trade-offs between climate and other priorities is an opportunity to accelerate decarbonisation while bringing other well-being benefits. For example, phasing out coal reduces GHG emissions and air pollution, creating immediate health benefits that can increase the social and political acceptability of more stringent climate action. Coal phase out, however, impacts employment opportunities and people's livelihoods, creating difficulties for some communities. These difficulties can be addressed by appropriate policy design to mitigate negative impacts on particular population groups.

Adopting a well-being lens entails incorporating objectives beyond the energy trilemma (affordability, reliability, decarbonisation), and looking at the entire power system. Setting priorities like ensuring public health and safety, sustainably managing natural resources, preserving ecosystems and providing high-quality employment opportunities is central for shifting to a sustainable energy sector. Delivering these multiple priorities requires looking beyond the plant level, examining the network infrastructure and the demand side (e.g. households, industry). For example, activating and transforming the demand side through energy efficiency improvements (e.g. using efficient household appliances and electric motors in industry) and active demand management can reduce energy bills for households and industrial consumers while enhancing system flexibility and improving the integration of variable renewable energy sources such as wind and solar photovoltaic into the grid.

Systematically monitoring all areas of electricity-related well-being is essential to supporting this shift. For example, indicators allowing to better identify households at risk of energy poverty will enable policy makers to better target income transfers and allocate infrastructure costs. These and other indicators that monitor other priorities (e.g. health, safety, ecosystems) are needed for identifying synergies and trade-offs. In addition, complementing current measurement of production-based carbon intensity with consumption-based metrics, and monitoring the extent to which governments are unlocking the potential of demand management, provides better information for setting priorities. Policy packages will need to include carbon pricing, renewable energy support and unabated coal phase-out (plant level), network planning and electricity market design (network level), and the creation of adequate regulatory conditions to activate the demand-side.

Infographic 2.1. Catalysing change through a sustainable electricity sector

Electricity supports a broad range of services and economic infrastructure across sectors. It is the highest emitting sector but it is not on track to meet global mitigation goals.

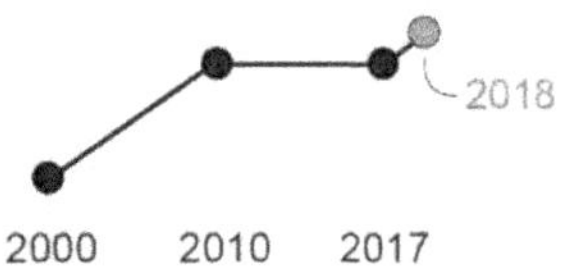

Electricity-related CO_2 emissions are on the rise again

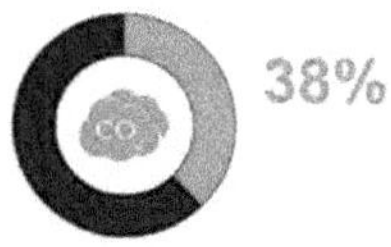

In 2018, the electricity sector contributed to 38% of global energy-related CO_2 emissions

With major impacts on health, biodiversity and natural resources

Looking beyond affordability and reliability, we can accelerate decarbonisation by exploiting wider synergies across all levels of the power system.

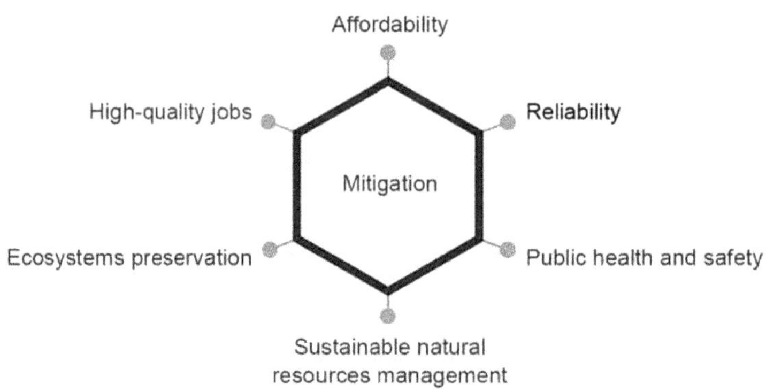

To accelerate climate action, we urgently need to:

Reframe measurement

- Identify households at risk of energy poverty
- Monitor impacts on health, ecosystems and jobs
- Apply consumption-based carbon intensity

Refocus policies

- Integrate well-being objectives into renewable energy support
- Price carbon and phase out coal
- Democratise electricity generation to include households and industry

2.1. Introduction

This report argues that a **change in perspective** – i.e. applying a ***well-being lens*** to policy making – is central to assessing the synergies and trade-offs of climate policies, and thus to achieving a ***two-way alignment***[1] between climate and broader well-being objectives. Adopting a well-being lens implies that:

- Societal goals are defined in terms of well-being outcomes (including limiting climate change through mitigation) and are systematically reflected in decision-making across the economy.
- The decisions taken consider multiple well-being objectives, rather than focusing on solving a single objective or a very narrow range of objectives.
- The relations between the different sectors and elements of the system in which a policy intervenes are well understood.

The present chapter applies a well-being lens to the electricity sector. It derives a number of policy priorities characterising a sustainable electricity sector and proposes a set of indicators that can be used to track progress and guide policies, in line with the policy goals proposed. As such, it provides a general framework centred on well-being, used to guide policies.

Electricity, a hugely versatile form of energy, affects human well-being and the Sustainable Development Goals (SDGs) in various ways. On the one hand, electricity allows lighting and heating buildings, which increases the comfort, health and safety of residents (SDG 3); facilitates education (SDG 4) and gender equality (SDG 5); and supports a broad range of basic services, as well as economic infrastructure and activities (e.g. SDGs 6, 7, 8, 9 and 11). On the other hand, electricity generation through the combustion of fossil fuels is a major contributor to global greenhouse gas (GHG) emissions and climate change, with negative impacts on current and future well-being, public health (SDG 3), marine and terrestrial biodiversity (SDGs 14 and 15) and more generally, sustainable development (IPCC, 2014[1]).

Electricity has helped spur economic development in modern societies and is becoming the fuel of choice for many end uses. As a result, the main objective of the electricity sector has been to provide affordable and reliable electricity for all (SDG 7). With the advent of climate change on the political agenda, climate change mitigation is increasingly featured on the list of policy priorities, culminating in the so-called energy trilemma, i.e. the pursuit of reliable, affordable and low-carbon energy.

While the dimensions of the energy trilemma remain key, electricity generation affects human well-being in many other ways, adding complexity to managing the low-carbon transition. For instance, fossil-fuel power plants are a major contributor to air, water, and soil pollution, causing serious impacts on public health, ecosystems and biodiversity. Some low-carbon technologies – notably large hydro dams – often require displacing communities. They cause deforestation and landscape degradation, negatively affecting biodiversity and ecosystems, and compromising current and future human well-being (McCully, 2001[2]). The impacts associated with low-emission technologies such as nuclear energy and large-scale deployment of carbon capture and storage (CCS), include issues related to safety, long-term storage and leakage risks for CCS (IPCC, 2014[3]), which remain a concern and affect public acceptability in some countries. Variable renewable energy (VRE) sources (such as wind power plants) also have some adverse impacts, e.g. on migratory birds and bats (Tabassum-Abbasi et al., 2014[4]).

Many countries are already shifting from fossil-based power generation to renewable energy, but the pace of change in decarbonising the sector is too slow to be consistent with global climate change mitigation goals (IEA, 2019[5]). In fact, stringent mitigation goals require not only rapid decarbonisation of electricity, but also increasing electrification of end-use sectors (IPCC, 2014[1]), (IPCC, 2018[6]). Creating two-way alignment between climate change and other well-being goals by exploiting the synergies and effectively addressing the trade-offs can accelerate the pace of decarbonisation while delivering multiple well-being objectives and enabling the shift towards a sustainable electricity sector that accounts for the impacts mentioned above.

Looking at the entire power system through a well-being lens reveals an even larger number of impacts on current and future well-being (including climate change), increasing the levers of action and offering wider opportunities to deliver multiple well-being goals. Demand reduction through improvements in energy efficiency can lower the energy bill of households and industrial customers while decreasing the investment needs in generation and network capacity, with positive impacts on ecosystems and finite natural resources (land, materials) (IEA, 2018[7]). Equally important, exploiting the potential of distributed energy resources (e.g. demand response, "behind-the-meter generation") and increased sector coupling (e.g. heat pumps, electric vehicles) can enhance flexibility, facilitating the integration of high shares of VRE resources (IEA, 2017[8]).

Section 2.2 discusses how applying a well-being lens to the electricity sector reveals the multiple impacts of electricity on well-being and is fundamental to accelerating the shift towards a sustainable electricity sector. It argues that systematic consideration of multiple well-being objectives is necessary to create two-way alignment between climate change mitigation and other well-being goals, exploiting the many synergies while effectively anticipating and addressing the existing and potential trade-offs between climate change mitigation and other priorities. Such synergies enhance the political and social acceptability of climate action.

Section 2.3 contends that the shift in perspective needs to be supported by a set of indicators that systematically reveal the electricity sector's various impacts on human well-being, and facilitate the design of policies supporting two-way alignment. It proposes a number of indicators for monitoring, evaluating and refining these policies as necessary. The indicators presented are not exhaustive, but provide best-practice examples for tracking progress towards a sustainable electricity sector.

2.2. Shifting perspective: Beyond the energy trilemma and the plant level

Electricity is fast becoming the energy form of choice. Electricity powers digital technologies, communication infrastructure and industrial operations, laying the foundation for economic prosperity (SDG 8), modern infrastructure and industry (SDG 9), and sustainable cities (SDG 11). In developing and emerging countries, ensuring access to electricity (SDG 7) correlates positively with reduced levels of poverty (SDG 1), improved public health (SDG 3), better educational attainment (SDG 4) and more gender equality (SDG 5).

Lack of access to electricity or supply disruptions have very negative impacts on human well-being. Despite significant progress in recent years, the world is not on track to provide universal access by 2030 (IEA et al., 2019[9]): 840 million people (mostly located in Sub-Saharan Africa) still lacked access to electricity in 2017. Even if households have physical access, some may be excluded from electricity consumption owing to fuel poverty, which may force households to reduce space heating or cooling to levels that reduce comfort and therefore well-being. Finally, electricity outages – though rarely observed in developed countries – are associated with large losses in production, damage to equipment and negative impacts on well-being, including risks to health and safety, and loss of leisure time (Linares and Rey, 2013[10]). For example, the July-August 2011 blackout in Cyprus produced a welfare loss of up to EUR 1 billion, equivalent to roughly 4% of the country's gross domestic product (GDP) (Zachariadis and Poullikkas, 2012[11]); this was the largest welfare loss in Europe over the last ten years (European Commission, 2018[12]). Most governments have long acknowledged the importance of electricity consumption in promoting human well-being and economic development. Hence, providing **access to affordable and reliable electricity** has always ranked among governments' top policy priorities.

Nevertheless, electricity generation is associated with significant negative impacts on a number of well-being dimensions: fossil-fuel power plants – especially unabated coal plants – are major contributors to GHG emissions and **climate change**. Electricity generation is the single largest contributor to carbon dioxide (CO_2) emissions, accounting for 38% of global energy-related CO_2 emissions in 2018 (IEA,

2019[13]). From 1990 to 2018, global CO_2 emissions from electricity nearly doubled, from 6.7 $GtCO_2eq$ to 13 $GtCO_2eq$ (IEA, 2019[13]). Coal-fired power plants still account for 60% of global installed generation; 200 GW of coal capacity are currently under construction, which run the risk of becoming stranded assets (Mirabile and Calder, 2018[14]).

Although many governments increasingly consider the mitigation of electricity-related GHG emissions as a policy priority, current policies and recent trends are not sufficient to reach global mitigation goals (IEA, 2019[5]). Acknowledging climate change mitigation as a policy priority alongside electricity affordability and reliability resulted in the so-called **energy trilemma.** However, electricity generation is associated with a number of other detrimental impacts on human well-being, briefly summarised as follows:

- Fossil power plants remain a major contributor to air pollution – e.g. sulphur oxide (SO_x), nitrogen oxide (NO_x) and particulate matter – with serious **impacts on public health** (OECD/IEA, 2016[15]). Despite important progress in reducing air pollution from the power sector in recent years,[2] air pollution remains a serious problem: in 2013, about 22 900 premature deaths in the European Union (EU) could be attributed to currently operational coal plants (CAN et al., 2016[16]), almost equivalent to the number of fatalities in road-traffic accidents (26 000). Coal power plants are also a major source of mercury emissions (EPA, 2016[17]). When airborne mercury enters the water cycle, it interacts with bacteria that convert it into its highly toxic form, methylmercury, which negatively affects aquatic ecosystems and animals, endangering fish-eating birds and mammals, as well as their predators. (EPA, 1997[18]). Finally, thermal power plants are also a major source of toxic waste, which can negatively affect the local environment if not properly stored (National Research Council, 2010[19]).
- Some generation technologies **consume large amounts of finite natural resources (land, materials, water) and impact ecosystems**. Coal mining drastically alters the landscape: it has negative impacts on ecosystems through deforestation and habitat destruction, and can pollute the groundwater through leaks from coal waste sites or acid mine drainage – the flow of acidic water into nearby rivers and streams (Epstein et al., 2011[20]). Thermal power plants' energy-conversion efficiency has not improved significantly in the last decades (Ayres, Turton and Casten, 2007[21]), as they continue to reject large amounts of waste heat using water as a coolant; the subsequent release of hotter water has negative impacts on ecosystems and biodiversity (Goel, 2006[22]).
- Low-carbon technologies can also have negative impacts on public health, ecosystems and biodiversity, while consuming natural resources. Nuclear accidents such as Chernobyl, for which the cumulative death toll related to cancer is estimated at between 4 000 (IAEA, WHO and UN, 2005[23]) and 16 000 (Cardis et al., 2006[24]), and Fukushima-Daichi, have had a range of serious physiological, developmental, morphological and behavioural impacts for terrestrial and marine plants and animals, owing to their exposure to radioactivity (Steinhauser, Brandl and Johnson, 2014[25]). CCS continues to impact on ecosystems through upstream mining activities and water use of thermal power plants (IPCC, 2014[3]). Although large hydro dams interfere with the surrounding ecosystems, many large hydro projects are currently constructed or planned in the world's most biodiverse river basins (Amazon, Congo, Mekong) (Winemiller et al., 2016[26]).[3] Large-scale bioenergy, as foreseen by scenarios compatible with limiting climate change to 1.5 degrees Celsius (°C), can put significant pressure not only on ecosystems and biodiversity, but also on available land and food production (IPCC, 2018[6]). Other renewables (i.e. solar photovoltaic [PV], wind, tidal) can have negative impacts on ecosystems and biodiversity through loss or fragmentation of habitats. These impacts can be addressed to varying degrees by appropriate policy design, so that low-carbon generation does not necessarily come at the expense of other well-being goals (Gasparatos et al., 2017[27]). Solar PV and modern wind turbines require a range of precious and rare earth metals (e.g. silver and indium), whose scarcity may represent bottlenecks in the future (Grandell et al., 2016[28]).

- The electricity sector also plays a large role as an employer. The transition towards an electricity sector with high shares of renewables has important implications for employment opportunities, local communities, and people's livelihoods and well-being. While the transition is likely to have a positive impact on gross employment, it may create difficulties for some regions and communities, notably those that rely on coal extraction (OECD, 2017[29]). These local employment effects put major pressure on the regional development and well-being of the affected communities, and need to be managed carefully. The transition also involves changes in the quality of jobs, e.g. as the number of mine workers decreases and employment in renewables increases.

While managing the dimensions of the energy trilemma is already complex, viewing the electricity sector through a well-being lens shows that it includes dimensions beyond those contained in the energy trilemma. A sustainable electricity sector provides affordable and reliable electricity for all, while: i) limiting climate change; ii) ensuring public health and safety; iii) sustainably managing natural resources; and iv) providing high-quality employment opportunities.

A sustainable electricity sector provides affordable and reliable electricity for all, while: i) limiting climate change; ii) ensuring public health and safety; iii) sustainably managing natural resources; and iv) providing high-quality employment opportunities.

Assessing the generation technologies in terms of well-being requires adopting a **full-cost accounting** approach, which incorporates all relevant external costs, risks and benefits to determine each country's low-carbon generation portfolio compatible with sustainable development. This assessment clearly needs to go beyond the plant level, examining the network infrastructure and the demand side to get a comprehensive picture of the social costs of electricity.

In addition, while the levelised costs of electricity of VREs are already on par with fossil-fuel power plants in many locations, large-scale deployment of VREs in addition to distributed generation requires higher levels of system flexibility (Jairaj et al., 2018[30]). Integrating increasing shares of intermittent VREs cost-effectively while maintaining high levels of reliability requires implementing a set of measures, including operational improvements to the existing fleet, advanced VRE plant design and investments in additional infrastructure (transmission lines, back-up and storage capacity) (IEA, 2017[8]) (2018[31]). But a key measure to provide flexibility also consists in activating the demand side, discussed in the next section.

2.2.1. Broadening the perspective: Activating the demand side

A key element of the well-being lens is to study the entire power system, including the generation fleet, the network infrastructure and the demand side (Figure 2.1). Looking at these scales provides a comprehensive picture of the electricity sector and increases the levers of action to meet multiple well-being goals. For instance, demand reduction (through improvements in energy efficiency) and demand response (by shifting load over the course of a day) contribute to well-being and sustainable development in multiple ways. They improve affordability by reducing not only operational costs (e.g. avoided fuel costs), but also the need for capital expenditures in new generation and network capacity. This, in turn, reduces the energy bill of private and industrial consumers, while lowering the pressure on ecosystems and natural resources. Importantly, demand response also enhances the flexibility of the electricity system, allowing for better integration of VREs.

Figure 2.1. Well-being dimensions and levels of the electricity sector

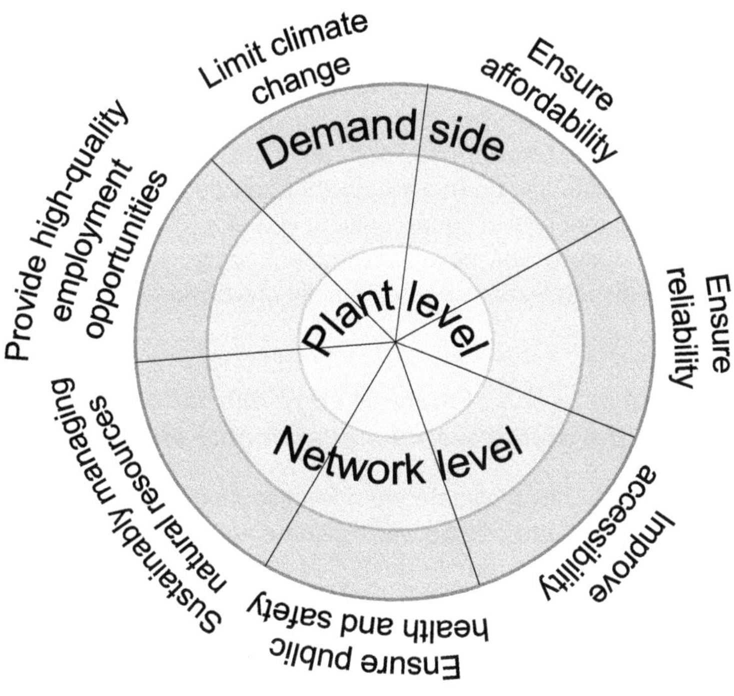

Demand reduction in end-use sectors is critical to curb electricity demand and GHG emissions while delivering other well-being benefits (IEA, 2018[32]). Despite improvements in energy efficiency, global electricity demand grew by 115% between 1990 and 2016 – more than double the rate of growth (52%) in total final consumption of all energy over the same period (IEA, 2019[33]). This trend is likely to continue in the next decades owing to economic growth and the increasing electrification of end-use sectors (IEA, 2017[34]). While energy efficiency will remain key, there exists a paradigm shift – triggered by the penetration of distributed energy resources, combined with digital technologies and increased sector coupling – towards activating the demand side.

While energy efficiency will remain key, there exists a paradigm shift – triggered by the penetration of distributed energy resources, combined with digital technologies and increased sector coupling – towards activating the demand side.

Distributed energy resources encompass a large variety of local energy sources, including small generation units (small hydro, rooftop solar), energy storage, demand response and electric vehicles. Generation "behind the meter" is blurring the traditional boundary between electricity generation and consumption: self-producing customers can now play an active role in the power system, transforming the traditional power system from a unidirectional centralised system towards a bidirectional decentralised system. Similarly, demand response has been limited to large industrial producers, but emerging digital technologies offer great potential for demand response in other end-use sectors, through smart meters and smart appliances (IEA, 2017[35]). In addition, smart-charging and vehicle-to-grid technology, and their aggregated deployment for system services, allows using electric vehicles (EVs) as electric storage (ITF, 2019[36]). Demand and storage aggregators, as well as virtual power plants that aggregate the production of many small-scale producers, can actively participate in electricity markets, enhancing system flexibility cost-effectively.

Sector coupling – i.e. integrating end-use sectors in the electricity system, either by electrifying end uses or producing feedstock from electricity (power-to-gas, power-to-heat) – further increases the levers of system flexibility. While electrifying end uses is key to ensuring a low-carbon pathway for the whole economy, some end uses (e.g. heat pumps for space heating and electric vehicles) can also contribute to system flexibility (IEA, 2018[7]). Using low-carbon electricity to produce synthetic fuels (e.g. hydrogen and ammonia) can also play an important role in decarbonising industry (chemicals) or transport (e.g. fuel-cell electric vehicles) (IEA, 2019[37]). Moreover, power-to-gas technology can enhance the system flexibility, potentially balancing seasonal disparities between electricity production and consumption (ENTSO-E and ENTSOG, 2018[38]).

2.2.2. A two-way alignment between climate change mitigation and other policy priorities is necessary to accelerate the shift towards a sustainable electricity sector

Adopting a holistic approach and tackling climate change mitigation in parallel with other policy priorities can increase synergies and reduce trade-offs between climate action and broader well-being goals. Such an approach can produce important short-term benefits that can enhance social and political acceptability, thereby accelerating the decarbonisation of the electricity sector while ensuring it does not come at the expense of other well-being priorities. Table 2.1 illustrates the benefits of analysing climate change mitigation through a well-being lens by systematically incorporating the policy priorities comprising a sustainable electricity sector.

Table 2.1. Potential two-way alignment benefits from applying the well-being lens to the electricity sector

Other policy priority	Contributing to limiting climate change	
	Generating synergies	Avoiding/reducing trade-offs
Improving or maintaining affordability	Affordable electricity prices for end-use sectors can incentivise electrifying equipment. This is a key strategy to reduce GHG emissions in end-use sectors. Cost-reflective pricing for industrial customers (e.g. lower rates due to more steady demand) subject to international competition can prevent offshoring of electricity-intensive production processes (Chapter 3).	Addressing affordability problems through artificially low electricity prices incentivises wasteful consumption. Instead, targeted lump-sum or income-based transfers maintain the economic incentive to reduce electricity consumption, while also reducing GHG emissions and other negative impacts on the environment. Monitoring households' energy expenditure helps governments identify households at risk of energy poverty, allowing more targeted complementary or compensation policies (e.g. energy cheques).
Ensuring reliability	Fossil fuel-poor states are increasingly deploying renewables, including VREs. This reduces the import dependence on fossil fuels, while mitigating GHG emissions.	In contrast to thermal power plants, the supply profile of most VREs depends on the weather and is therefore volatile. However, enhancing system flexibility through more interconnections and storage capacity and, importantly, activating the demand side enhances the integration of high shares of VREs while avoiding load curtailment.
Improving accessibility	In many cases, providing access to electricity in rural and remote areas (where lack of electricity access is the most prevalent) thanks to decentralised systems based on renewables is already the least-cost solution and avoids costly investments in transmission grid infrastructure. At the same time, electrification can reduce GHG emissions, e.g. by lowering the combustion of local biomass.	Satisfying the additional demand originating from the provision of electricity access with fossil power plants can have lower private costs than renewables. However, removing regulatory barriers for decentralised renewable solutions can improve the cost-competitiveness of renewables versus fossil fuels.
Maintaining a safe and healthy environment	Lowering air, soil and water pollution from fossil power plants through regulation can decrease combustion from fossil fuels, reducing GHG emissions and producing important health and biodiversity benefits.	In some cases, pollution-control technologies for fossil power plants require additional energy input and thus result in higher GHG emissions. However, more efficient control technologies (e.g. Limestone Forced Oxidation's energy input is higher than Lime Spray Dryer) can reduce negative impacts. Wind power plants create noise pollution that can have negative effects on health. However, appropriate zoning requiring minimum distances to residential areas and sensitive ecosystems can mitigate the negative effects.
Sustainably managing natural resources (land, water, natural resources)	Stricter water regulations for thermal power plants increase the operating costs and can lead to less generation from coal or gas-fired power plants, and lower GHG emissions. Lower generation from power plants also reduce the impacts on and increase the benefits to biodiversity (e.g. fewer warm-water effluents and mining activities).	Many renewables have a larger demand for land than conventional power plants. In addition to renewables' direct impact on biodiversity, this can put pressure on biodiversity. However, the design of planning and policy instruments can minimise the adverse impacts. Monitoring both the deployment of renewable energy and its impact on sensitive areas supports governments in undertaking more effective zoning, e.g. by dedicating areas for renewable deployment outside of sensitive ecosystems and habitats.
Providing high-quality employment opportunities	Renewable energy is labour-intensive and an important driver of local employment. Accounting for local employment effects from the installation, manufacturing and operation of renewables can render the deployment of renewables more attractive than conventional power plants. Employment opportunities in renewables are also spread out more evenly across regions, benefiting a larger number of local communities.	Monitoring adverse effects on local employment (e.g. job losses in mining communities) when phasing out electricity generation from fossil fuels helps identify affected regions and workers. This can enable more tailored structural measures (e.g. re-training, structural policies) to mitigate the adverse effects on workers, ensuring a transition that leaves no one behind.

2.3. Indicators for monitoring electricity's contribution to Well-being

As noted in Chapter 1, a change in the measurement system is key to implementing a change in perspective for policy making. This section proposes a set of indicators that policy makers can use to track progress towards a sustainable electricity sector, guide policy decisions and assess two-way alignment. Several initiatives that have developed indicators to track progress towards a sustainable electricity sector already exist ((IAEA, 2005[39]), (ESMAP, 2018[40]), (World Economic Council, 2019[41])), but tend to focus on specific issues related to sustainability (e.g. electricity access, the energy trilemma). The SDGs and the OECD Framework for Measuring Well-being and Progress (henceforth the OECD well-being framework) establish a number of well-being priorities and related indicators at the level of the whole economy. Still, there exists substantial overlap between the policy priorities identified in the previous section and the goals established in the OECD well-being framework and the SDGs (Table 2.2). This section is ordered along the policy priorities identified in Section 2.2. Summary tables at the end of each policy priority offer a recap of the indicators proposed, showing the link to the indicators used for specific SDG targets and the well-being domains of the OECD well-being framework.

Table 2.2. Policy priorities for the electricity sector and their link to the SDGs and the OECD well-being framework

Policy priority	SDG goal and target	OECD Well-being domain	OECD Well-being dimension
Limit climate change	13. Take urgent action to combat climate change and its impacts. 7.2. By 2030, increase substantially the share of renewable energy in the global energy mix. 7.3. By 2030, double the global rate of improvement in energy efficiency. 7.3. By 2030, double the global rate of improvement in energy efficiency	Future well-being: resources.	Natural capital.
Ensure affordability	7.1. By 2030, ensure universal access to affordable, reliable and modern energy services. 7.3. By 2030, double the global rate of improvement in energy efficiency.	Current well-being: material conditions.	Housing. Income and wealth.
Ensure reliability	7.1. By 2030, ensure universal access to affordable, reliable and modern energy services. 7.3. By 2030, double the global rate of improvement in energy efficiency.	Not applicable.	Not applicable.
Improve access	7.1. By 2030, ensure universal access to affordable, reliable and modern energy services. 7.3. By 2030, double the global rate of improvement in energy efficiency.	Not applicable.	Not applicable.
Ensure public health and safety	3.9. By 2030, substantially reduce the number of deaths and illnesses from hazardous chemicals and air, water and soil pollution and contamination. 11.6. By 2030, reduce the adverse per capita environmental impact of cities, including by paying special attention to air quality and municipal and other waste management.	Current well-being: quality of life. Resources for future well-being.	Environmental quality. Natural capital.
Sustainably manage natural resources and preserve ecosystems	14.3. Minimise and address the impacts of ocean acidification, including through enhanced scientific co-operation at all levels 15.5. Take urgent and significant action to reduce the degradation of natural habitats, halt the loss of biodiversity and, by 2020, protect and prevent the extinction of threatened species.	Resources for future well-being.	Natural Capital.
Provide high-quality employment opportunities	8.5. By 2030, achieve full and productive employment and decent work for all women and men. 8.8. Protect labour rights and promote safe and secure working environments for all workers, including migrant workers, in particular women migrants, and those in precarious employment.	Current well-being: material conditions.	Jobs and earnings.

The list of indicators presented here is not exhaustive. Rather, it aims to provide best-practice examples that support governments in tracking progress towards a sustainable electricity sector. It also intends to stimulate informed discussion, as well as reveal data limitations and potential data enhancements.

Systematically using these indicators as criteria guiding decisions enables governments to drive the change towards a sustainable electricity sector. Importantly, policy makers should look at these indicators jointly, instead of adopting a "silo" approach that examines isolated dimensions.

2.3.1. Limiting climate change

The indicators used to track climate change mitigation in the electricity sector are relatively straightforward. They include GHG emissions of electricity production in absolute terms, carbon intensity, and the share of electricity from low-carbon or renewables in total generation. The indicators for SDG 13 focus on policies and the indicator for SDG 7.2 reflects the share of renewables in total final energy consumption, whereas the OECD well-being framework uses GHG emissions from domestic production and CO_2 emissions from domestic consumption (Table 2.3). All of these indicators are aggregated over all the sectors and hence do not provide specific information on the electricity sector. This section briefly reviews widely applied high-level indicators and proposes two new indicators: i) consumption-based carbon intensity, which informs customers on the carbon footprint of electricity consumption and can complement production-based carbon intensity; and ii) marginal carbon intensity (see below), which informs on the impact of demand response on emissions when shifting load from one hour of the day to another. It also provides some analysis on "intermediary" indicators that could be useful for measuring and tracking the extent to which governments are activating demand, i.e. unlocking the potential of demand reduction and response. As discussed in section 2.2, activating the demand is an important lever that governments can use to improve the flexibility of the electricity system, allowing for better integration of VREs, while also contributing to other objectives discussed in later sections, such as affordability and the conservation of ecosystems and natural resources.

Aggregated GHG emissions is the most suitable indicator, as it determines the extent of climate change (Chapter 1). The vast majority of electricity-related GHG emissions stem from CO_2 emissions caused by the combustion of fossil fuels, but other sources of GHG emissions exist, including methane and NO_x emissions from combustion, as well as fugitive emissions from gas leaks (EPA, 2019[42]), or methane emissions from the artificial reservoirs of dams (Deemer et al., 2016[43]). This section focuses on CO_2 emissions from combustion.

The (production-based) carbon intensity of electricity supply condenses the carbon footprint of the current electricity generation mix into one number. Complementing the carbon intensity with other indicators helps identify the various channels affecting intensity. This includes the generation share used by technology to track deployment of low-carbon technologies and identify fuel switches (e.g. from coal to natural gas), as well as the carbon intensity of each technology used to monitor efficiency improvements in the current fleet of power plants. In addition, carbon intensity only includes emissions in power plants' operating phase; it neglects life-cycle emissions, e.g. from the construction (including extraction and process of materials) and decommissioning of power plants (for more details on life-cycle assessments [LCAs], see Section 0).

Complementing the carbon intensity of production with the **carbon intensity of consumption** provides a more comprehensive picture of a country or region's electricity system, and its interconnectedness with neighbouring systems. Production-based carbon intensity measures intensity based on electricity generation by the domestic power-plant fleet, as suggested by the United Nations Framework Convention on Climate Change (UNFCCC) guidelines (IPCC, 2006[44]). Consumption-based carbon intensity measures the true carbon footprint of electricity consumption, i.e. the indirect so-called "Scope 2" emissions, which refer to "the point-of-generation emissions from purchased electricity" (WRI, 2015[45]). Neither measure includes transmission and distribution losses, which in 2016 accounted for around 8% on a global average – exceeding, however, 50% in some countries (IEA, 2018[46]).[4]

Information on consumption-based carbon intensity becomes increasingly important as many national and subnational governments, as well as companies, launch initiatives to reduce their consumption-based GHG emissions. For example, New York City envisages a 30% reduction by 2030 relative to 2006,

Copenhagen aims to become carbon-neutral by 2025, and the British retailer Tesco announced its intent to achieve a 60% reduction in emissions by 2025 relative to 2015 (IEA, 2017[47]). These pledges typically include indirect emissions from electricity consumption (C40 Cities, 2018[48]). Local governments can use this information when introducing local taxes on the carbon content of consumer electricity. Governments can also use this metric to calculate the indirect emissions from their administrations or public projects' carbon footprint.

Calculating consumption-based carbon intensity, i.e. the intensity of production adjusted to the carbon intensity of imports and exports, requires data on: i) the electricity flows across borders, and ii) the carbon content of the electricity traded. While these data are not always publicly available, many transmission system operators provide them, sometimes even in real time, making it possible to calculate instantaneous consumption-based carbon intensity (Tranberg et al., 2018[49]). The numbers reported below follow this approach and are taken from Electricity Map (Electricity Map, 2019[50]).

Most countries have similar ranges of production and consumption carbon intensities, but some imbalances exist, particularly for smaller countries (Figure 2.2). For example, Lithuania has a production-based carbon intensity of 170 g/kWh, but this figure more than doubles to 340 g/kWh when looking at the consumption side. The reason for this discrepancy is that Lithuania imports more than half of its domestically consumed electricity from Belarus and Russia, both of which have relatively high carbon intensities. The reverse pattern holds true in Denmark, which has a relatively high share of coal and gas in the electricity generation mix, but imports large volumes of hydro and nuclear power from Norway and Sweden while exporting rather carbon-intense electricity to Germany.

Figure 2.2. Annual average of hourly production and consumption-based carbon intensity in 2018

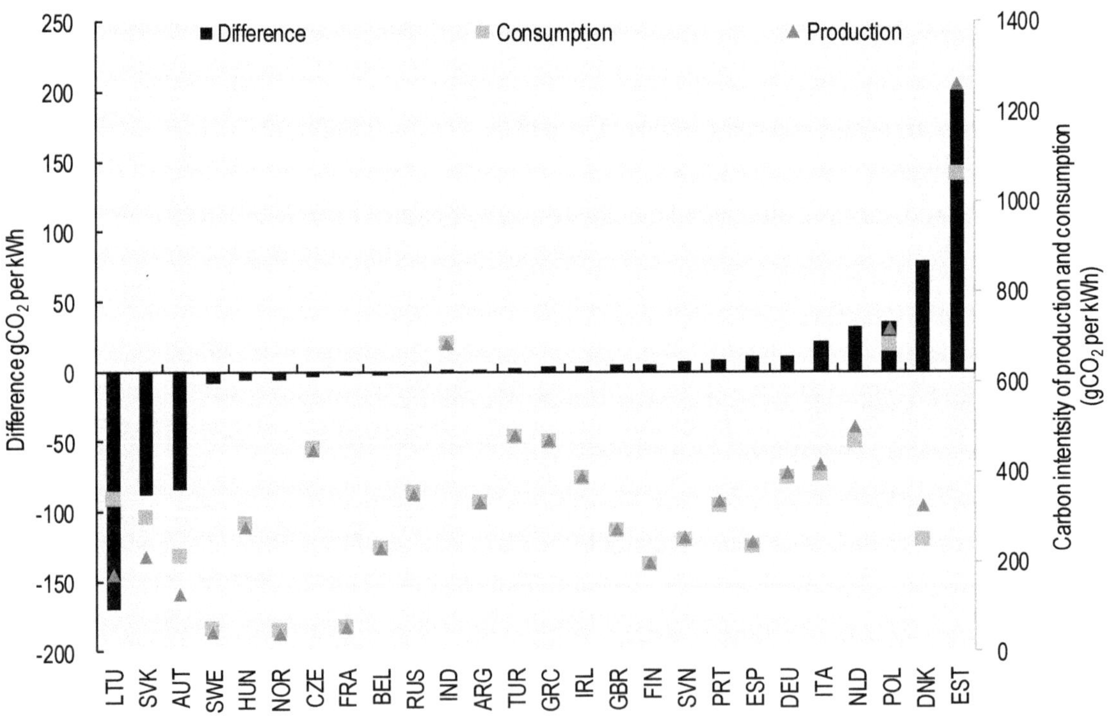

Source: Authors, based on Electricity Map (https://www.electricitymap.org/?lang=en).

StatLink https://doi.org/10.1787/888933992971

Information on carbon intensity patterns *throughout the day* can be used to assess the carbon impact of smoothing demand.[5] Carbon intensity varies across the hours of the day, depending on the current electricity mix at any given point in time. If at a certain hour of the day, the weather conditions for renewables are favourable and renewable generation is high, the carbon intensity will be relatively low, and vice versa. Capturing the impact of shifting demand on CO_2 emissions requires using the *marginal carbon intensity* instead of the average consumption-based carbon intensity. The reason is that to generate one additional unit of electricity supply, the system operator dispatches the marginal power plant, i.e. the plant that provides the additional unit to satisfy the additional demand. This plant's carbon intensity is equal to the marginal carbon intensity.

Smoothing demand (e.g. by dynamic pricing) can have positive impacts on climate change mitigation. Figure 2.3 shows marginal carbon intensity and the net load (i.e. electricity demand less generation from VREs) throughout an average day, exemplified for Austria (a country whose load profile is representative of many other countries) in 2018. Smoothing demand would imply shifting units from the peak demand at 8h00 to the bottom at 2h00. As this illustrative graph shows, this shift would reduce emissions, as the marginal carbon intensity at peak demand is higher than the marginal carbon intensity at 02h00, resulting in 180 - 110 = 70 g savings of CO_2 per kWh. An evaluation of Chicago's Energy-Smart Pricing Plan, a dynamic pricing pilot, show positive impacts of dynamic pricing on GHG emissions (Allcott, 2011[51]). However, these result may not easily transfer to electricity systems with different power-plant fleets (Holland and Mansur, 2008[52]).

Figure 2.3. Carbon intensity and net load exemplified for an average day in Austria (2018)

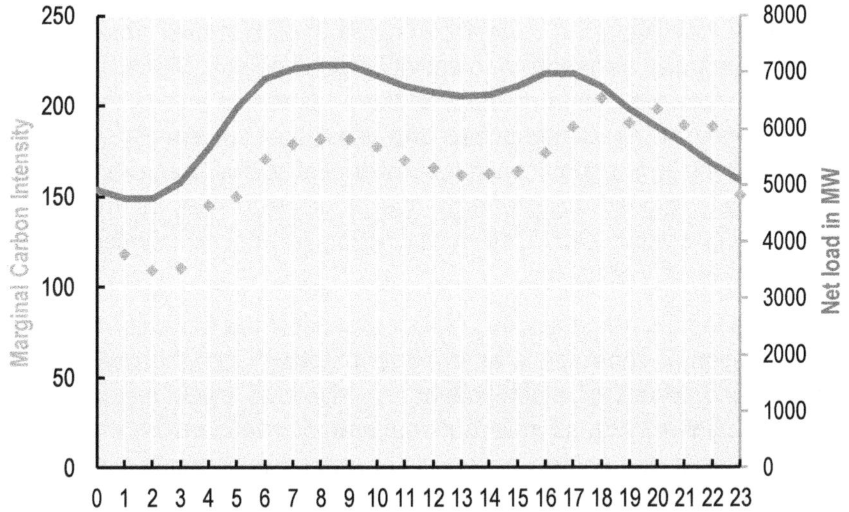

Source: Authors, based on Electricity Map.

StatLink https://doi.org/10.1787/888933992990

Table 2.3. Summary table: Indicators for monitoring progress in limiting climate change and links to SDGs and OECD well-being framework

Policy priority	Proposed indicators	SDG goal and target	SDG indicator	OECD Well-being domain/ dimension	OECD Well-being indicators
Limiting climate change	• Electricity CO_2 emissions (absolute, per capita, by technology). • Share of low-carbon and renewable electricity in total generation. • Carbon intensity (production-based). • Carbon intensity (consumption-based). • Marginal carbon intensity of electricity generation.	13. Take urgent action to combat climate change and its impacts.	Proposed indicators focus on policy progress rather than emissions.	Resources for future well-being: natural capital.	• GHG emissions from domestic production. • CO_2 emissions from domestic consumption.
		7.2. By 2030, increase substantially the share of renewable energy in the global energy mix.	Renewable energy share in total final energy consumption.		

Activating the demand side

SDG 7.3 measures energy intensity as the primary energy per unit of GDP (Table 2.4). While this indicator is straightforward as regards calculating and providing information on the energy intensity of the whole economy, it does not allow identifying the drivers behind its evolution over time. Disaggregating energy use by sector (industry, residential, transport) and activity (space heating, lightning, electric appliances for residential electricity consumption) sheds more light on the progress on energy intensity. For example, the International Energy Agency (IEA) decomposes the evolution of energy consumption into three components: aggregate activity (e.g. population in the residential sector), sectoral structure (e.g. floor-area over population) and intensity (e.g. lightning energy over floor area) (IEA, 2018[53]). This decomposition allows identifying the drivers behind electricity consumption in specific subsectors while isolating the impacts of improvements in energy efficiency.

As discussed before, activating the demand side is key to providing the flexibility needed to integrate rising shares of VREs. Electrification of end-uses is an important strategy to decarbonise end-use sectors and therefore information on the extent of electrification is critical to track the progress. Gathering this information is relatively straightforward, as most national and international databases provide information on electricity consumption as a percentage of total final energy consumption by sector (IEA, 2018[54]). Information on the share of taxes in the electricity price versus the share of taxes in other fuels can reveal barriers to electrification, e.g. when comparing the fuel costs of electric heat pumps with those of gas or oil boilers.

Measuring the flexibility of the power system to assess its capacity to integrate VREs is not straightforward. Many sources can contribute to improving flexibility: flexible power plants (e.g. gas power plants and virtual power plants), interconnections, storage and demand response. One way to assess the power system's capacity to integrate VREs is through output-based indicators. For example, the share of curtailed renewable energy, defined as the ratio between (involuntary) curtailment of renewables and total generation of renewables, provides information on the extent to which the power system fails to integrate renewables. Applying this indicator at a geographically disaggregated level can effectively identify bottlenecks in the integration of renewables, but does not provide information on the cause of the curtailment (e.g. congestion, lack of transmission capacity, excessive supply during low load periods) (Bird, Cochran and Wang, 2014[55]).

Indicators exist to assess the demand for and supply of flexibility. Penetration indicators for renewables, such as the ratio of wind or solar PV generation over demand or the number of hours where this indicator exceeds 100%, can be used to assess the flexibility needed to ensure continuous security of supply (AEMO, 2017[56]). Indicators on the supply side assess the capacity of flexible power plants by type of technology, the storage capacity by technology, and the capacity of flexible demand (IEA, 2019[57]). These supply-side indicators provide information about the extent to which the current power system is capable of integrating excess generation of VREs.

Most currently used indicators focus on the demand response *potential* (BEIS, 2017[58]), because information on the real extent of demand response is more difficult to gather and sometimes not publicly available. The potential for demand response is estimated by aggregating the electricity demand of end uses that can be shifted for every hour of the year, e.g. heat pumps and air conditioners in the residential sector, electric vehicles in the transport sector and aluminium smelters in the industry sector (IEA, 2017[47]). Information on electricity market data can reveal the extent of actual participation in demand response of large industrial customers and aggregators, i.e. intermediaries specialising in aggregating demand response from individual consumers (OFGEM, 2016[59]). Some countries (e.g. Germany) track the deployment of smart metering technologies – an enabling condition for residential consumers to participate in demand response (BMWi, 2016[60]). This indicator can be complemented by indicators on other enabling technologies, including smart appliances or load control software, which allow matching demand to the needs of the overall system in real time (IEA, 2017[35]).

Information on the regulatory framework, i.e. the instruments and regulations for demand response participation in markets, including energy markets and capacity markets, can assess countries' readiness for demand response. In the European Union, SmartEN – a business association for digital and decentralised energy solutions – reviews the regulatory framework for demand response and ranks Member States according to their market readiness along dimensions such as market access, prequalification, payments and penalties (SEDC, 2017[61]).

Table 2.4. Summary table of indicators to measure flexibility and demand side integration

Proposed indicators	SDG goal and target	SDG indicators	OECD Well-being domain/dimension	OECD Well-being indicators
• Electrification rate of end uses. • Share of curtailed renewable energy on renewable energy generation. • (Instantaneous) penetration of VRE sources. • Demand response (actual and potential). • Deployment of smart-meter and other enabling technologies. • Regulatory framework to enable integration.	7.3. By 2030, double the global rate of improvement in energy efficiency.	7.3.1. Energy intensity measured in terms of primary energy and GDP.	Resources for future well-being: natural capital.	No indicators in the framework.

2.3.2. *Improving or maintaining affordability*

Several indicators measure the affordability of electricity or, more broadly, energy poverty. Chapter 3 discusses competitiveness indicators related to energy-intensive, trade-exposed industries. While SDG 7 does not have a dedicated indicator to measure affordability of electricity or energy, the OECD well-being framework reports household income and housing affordability, which subsumes many items, including expenditures on rents, maintenance, gas and electricity (Table 2.5).

Looking at the electricity price alone is not sufficient to assess affordability properly. Retail electricity prices over the long term tend to be uncorrelated with some indicators of energy affordability (Flues and van Dender, 2017[62]). However, short-term changes in electricity prices can impose challenges, notably for low-income households, as adjustment processes still need to materialise. At minimum, assessing affordability requires information on the following elements: household income (or even household wealth – see Chapter 4), the quantity of electricity consumed and finally the retail price, comprising energy costs (wholesale price and supply costs), network costs, and taxes and levies.

Affordability of electricity and energy poverty are multidimensional concepts that are more accurately measured by a set of indicators rather than a single indicator, in order to better understand and monitor the drivers of energy poverty (Rademaekers et al., 2016[63]). Some indicators of energy poverty also include expenditures for space heating – which is reasonable, given that space heating is mostly provided either by electricity or fuels (Chapter 4). Focusing on electricity expenditure only would result in a biased picture, in which households with electrical heating appliances appear to have higher electricity bills, although they may actually have lower energy bills.

The European Union Energy Poverty Observatory has selected several primary and secondary indicators to track energy poverty (European Commission, 2019[64]). The first two primary indicators listed below use self-reported responses to the European Statistics on Income and Living Conditions annual survey (Eurostat, 2019[65]). The two other indicators use values on expenditure from the Household Budget Surveys (Eurostat, 2019[66]). Each of these indicators is available at the country-level and disaggregated by income deciles, urbanisation density and dwelling type (e.g. apartment, detached).

- **Arrears on utility bills:** share of (sub-) population with arrears on utility bills, based on the question, "In the last twelve months, has the household been in arrears, i.e. has been unable to pay on time due to financial difficulties for utility bills (heating, electricity, gas, water, etc.) for the main dwelling?
- **Inability to keep home adequately warm**: share of (sub-) population not able to keep their home adequately warm, based on the question, "Can your household afford to keep its home adequately warm?"
- **Hidden energy poverty:** share of population whose absolute energy expenditure is below half the national median
- **High share of energy expenditure in income:** proportion of population whose share of energy expenditure in income is more than twice the national median share.

Policy makers can use these and other indicators to monitor energy poverty, and evaluate the impact of specific climate policies and energy-tax reforms on affordability ex ante. For example, Flues and van Dender (2017[62]) assess the impact of a hypothetical harmonisation of taxes on heating fuels and electricity across 20 OECD countries, using a carbon component of EUR 45/t CO_2eq. While this reform increases energy-related taxes in most countries, the authors found that if one-third of the additional revenue generated by the reform was recycled through an income-tested cash transfer, the reform would enhance energy affordability in most countries, based on three selected indicators of energy poverty:

- "Ten percent rule" (TPR): the household's energy expenditure share exceeds 10%, and the household is in the bottom-three income deciles.
- Relative poverty line (RPL): the household's disposable income after energy expenditure is below the relative poverty line.
- Low-income, high-cost-share (LIHCS): this indicator combines TPR and RPL.

Table 2.5. Summary table: Indicators for monitoring progress in improving or maintaining affordability and links to SDGs and OECD well-being framework

Policy priority	Proposed indicators	SDG goal and target	SDG indicators	OECD Well-being domain/dimension	OECD Well-being indicators
Improving or maintaining affordability	• Retail price of electricity by component (wholesale price and supply costs, network costs, taxes and levies). • Arrears on utility bills. • Inability to keep home adequately warm. • Hidden energy poverty • Share of energy expenditure in income above 10% (TPR). • Household's disposable income after energy expenditure, below the relative poverty line (RPL). • Low-income, high-cost-share (LIHCS).	7.1. By 2030, ensure universal access to affordable, reliable and modern energy services.	No dedicated indicators for affordability.	Current well-being: material conditions. Housing.	Housing affordability (includes electricity expenditures).
				Current well-being: material conditions. Income and wealth.	Household income.

The chosen indicators have advantages and disadvantages. All three are positively correlated with the subjective indicator on the ability to keep the home warm (Flues and van Dender, 2017[62]). TPR is a good proxy for how many households face relatively high costs for domestic energy. According to RPL, households face affordability risks if they are below the relative poverty line (60% of median income) after energy expenditures, emphasising the income and distribution dimensions of energy affordability. LIHCS is the most selective indicator on affordability risks: by combining TPR and RPL, it identifies households in the low-income group that spend a high share of their income on energy. However, the data requirements for this indicator are relatively great.

2.3.3. Ensuring reliability

Indicators on electricity reliability and security inform policy makers and regulators about the electricity system's current performance (disruptions of electricity supply, supply shortage to satisfy demand). While neither the SDGs nor the OECD well-being framework feature reliability indicators, many regulators provide extensive assessment reports on electricity supply, indicating past trends and highlighting future risks (Reliability Panel AEMC, 2018[67]), (Department of Energy, 2017[68]). These reports typically encompass a large set of indicators that measure the multiple dimensions of reliability, revealing the performance of the electric system and the causes of interruptions in electricity supply. This section gives a very brief overview of frequently used indicators.

Focusing on the distribution and transmission network, high-level indicators include the System Average Interruption Duration Index (SAIDI) and the System Average Interruption Frequency Index (SAIFI), which measure the duration and frequency of interruptions for an average customer during a given period (Reliability Panel AEMC, 2018[67]). Both indicators help policy makers assess the state of the network, comparing reliability both across jurisdictions and across time. In most countries, system operators are required to report whether an outage was planned or unplanned, and to communicate the cause of the interruption (e.g. operating failure, overload or external reasons, such as weather conditions).

Other indicators attempt to measure the ex-ante risk of interruptions in electricity supply. These may include specific information about relevant components of the electricity system (e.g. grid extension, interconnections, reserve capacity, storage capacity), as well as indicators measuring **resource adequacy**, to evaluate the risk of supply shortfalls (Bundesnetzagentur and Bundeskartellamt, 2018[69]). Commonly used indicators include:

- capacity margin: excess of installed generation over peak demand
- de-rated capacity margin: expected excess of *available* generation capacity over peak demand, whereby the available generation capacity refers to the installed capacity that can be expected to be accessible within reasonable timeframes
- loss of load expectation (LOLE): the (statistically expected) number of hours per year in which supply will not meet demand over the long term, based on a probabilistic approach
- expected energy unserved (EEU): expected amount of electricity not supplied to the consumer.

Peak demand affects both types of capacity margins. Policies and regulations encouraging demand response to flatten peak demand will directly translate into the indicators signalling lower risk of load curtailment. Compared to the capacity margin, the de-rated capacity margin explicitly accounts for expected intermittency of the generation fleet that provides capacity only under certain weather conditions (Ofgem, 2011[70]). Many European countries and US markets use LOLE and EEU instead of the de-rated capacity margin as a reliability indicator: although more demanding in terms of methodology and data, their probabilistic approach better captures the impact of increasing penetration of VREs on the security of electricity supply (DECC, 2013[71]).

Policy makers and network operators need to know the customers' valuation of avoided electricity supply disruptions. This valuation is used to assess the damages caused by supply disruptions or in cost-benefit analyses aiming to assess the economic benefits of improvements in electricity infrastructure (de Nooij, Koopmans and Bijvoet, 2007[72]). One commonly used indicator is the **value of lost load (VoLL),** which measures the maximum electricity price customers are willing to pay to avoid load curtailment (ACER, 2018[73]). Using a stated preferences approach directly links electricity reliability to the well-being of customers, who are asked to judge their perceived discomfort in monetary values. EU regulation on the internal electricity market requires EU Member States to state the VoLL for their country and update that estimate at least every five years. For EU Member States, VoLLs range between EUR 1 500/MWh for Bulgaria and EUR 22 940/MWh in the Netherlands, an order of magnitude higher than the average European wholesale price of EUR 40/MWh and EUR 60/MWh (ACER, 2018[73]). VoLL also depends on the type of customer, with commercial and industrial customers typically expressing a higher valuation for a reliable electricity supply than residential users (London Economics, 2013[74]).

Climate change is increasingly challenging the reliability of electricity supply. This calls for a resilient infrastructure: extreme weather events such as storms, forest fires and floods cause supply disruptions; reduced water availability constrains hydro power and the operation of thermal power plants; and rising sea levels affect coastal and offshore energy infrastructure (IEA, 2015[75]). Thus, national and regional risk assessments need to incorporate climate-change risks to assess the impacts on supply security. Indicators on climate risks and infrastructure resilience are currently being developed (OECD, 2019[76]).

2.3.4. Improving accessibility

Indicators measuring (physical) access to electricity typically focus on the number of grid connections in a given area. When reporting access to electricity for measuring SDG 7 (Table 2.6), the IEA focuses on the physical connection to a grid (national grid, mini grid, off-grids), relying on databases sourced by national governments, multilateral development banks and publicly available statistics (IEA, 2017[77]). Depending on data availability, electricity access is mostly inferred either from the existence of a utility pole in a town or village, or from household surveys that explicitly ask about a households' grid connection (SE4A and ESMAP, 2015[78]).

This approach to measuring access has several limitations. First, the existence of a utility pole in a village or town does not necessarily imply that all households are connected to the grid. Second, condensing the measurement of electricity access into a binary variable neglects the multiple dimensions of the quality of access to electricity, including the availability of electricity supply (in terms of hours per day), the voltage of electricity (e.g. low or irregular voltage), and the legality and safety of the connection. Hazardous connections in homes, notably in rural areas and slums, can cause major health issues, injuries and deaths (SE4A and ESMAP, 2015[78]).

A comprehensive assessment requires a more detailed measurement of the multiple dimensions of electricity access, but gives a more accurate picture of the status quo and allows tracking progress more precisely. While the data requirements for this assessment are greater, measurement models are currently being developed and tested, including in developing and emerging economies. The World Bank's Multi-Tier-Framework (MTF) measures the various dimensions of access (as described in the previous paragraph) and evaluates access to electricity through a range of tiers, from 0 (no access) to 5 (full access). The MTF is adaptable and scalable to each country or locality's specificities.

Applying the MTF to a case study in India reveals large differences. For example, a Tier 1 classification implies that capacity ranges from 1 to 50 volts (sufficient for lighting and powering basic entertainment appliances), the electricity supply lasts between 4 and 8 hours, and the connection is illegal. According to the measure founded on the existence of an utility pole in a village, the overall access rate is 96%. However, the MTF surveys show that only 69% of households actually have access to the grid; among them, only 37% enjoy access with at least Tier 1 standards (Jain and Urpelainen, 2016[79]).

The data requirements for the MTF are very demanding, which can hinder its implementation. Even the less demanding simplified framework of the MTF still relies on household surveys (SE4A and ESMAP, 2015[78]). An alternative approach to measuring electricity access is to use night-light data from satellite pictures (Dugoua, Kennedy and Urpelainen, 2018[80]). Using satellite data helps track progress towards universal access without the need to conduct costly and burdensome surveys. On the downside, this low-cost method does not allow assessing the quality dimensions mentioned above. Satellite data can also be used to infer information on the existing electricity infrastructure, e.g. medium-voltage distribution lines (Facebook, 2019[81]).

Table 2.6. Summary table: Indicators for monitoring progress in improving accessibility and links to SDGs and OECD well-being framework

Policy priority	Indicators proposed	SDG goal and target	SDG indicators	OECD Well-being domain /dimension	OECD Well-being indicators
Improving accessibility	• MTF (quality and duration of supply over the course of the day; safety and legality of connection). • Satellite data.	7.1. By 2030, ensure universal access to affordable, reliable and modern energy services.	Proportion of population with access to electricity.	Material conditions: income and wealth and jobs and earnings Quality of life: Education and skills	No indicators on electricity access.

2.3.5. Ensuring public health and safety

Monitoring the electricity-related sources of air, soil and water pollutants helps track progress in cleaning up electricity generation and informs policy makers on the impact of environmental policies. Data on pollution from stationary sources is well established in most OECD countries (OECD, 2000[82]). Beginning in the 1990s, most OECD countries introduced pollutant release and transfer registers (PRTRs) to monitor pollution from stationary sources, including fossil power plants. The OECD has assisted countries in implementing PRTRs and works continuously to improve the methodology (OECD, 1996[83]). The information in PRTRs is publicly available, contributing to transparency and public participation in environmental decision-making.

PRTRs can be used to monitor pollutants originating from the electricity sector. Most PRTRs encompass multiple pollutants, including GHG emissions (e.g. CO_2, methane, hydrofluorocarbon), air pollutants (e.g. SO_x, NO_x, carbon monoxide), heavy metals (e.g. arsenic, mercury, lead), pesticides and inorganic substances (EEA, 2019[84]). For example, the Canadian PRTR, the National Pollutant Release Inventory, currently reports 324 different pollutants (Government of Canada, 2018[85]), supporting the evaluation of policies aiming to reduce the impact of power plants on pollution. Information on the various pollutants, including GHG emissions, can help identify trade-offs and synergies between climate change mitigation and other forms of pollution, enhancing two-way alignment.

LCAs are key to providing information on the aggregate environmental impact of electricity generation technologies. While PRTRs only capture emissions from the operating phase and large combustion installations, LCAs typically cover all phases of the life cycle, from cradle to grave: construction; operation; fuel provision (in the case of biomass, fossil or nuclear plants); and decommissioning (ISO, 2006[86]). While many renewables technologies do not emit pollutants during the operation phase, the construction and dismantling of the power plants causes pollution to air, soil, and water. The bulk of renewables' environmental impact can be attributed to the extraction and procession of materials used in plant construction, e.g. energy-intensive materials such as cement and steel (Chapter 3). However, renewables still perform substantially better than state-of-the-art fossil power plants in terms of life-cycle emissions (IPCC, 2014[1]).

It is still challenging to link the sources of pollution to the respective levels of pollution because of the many non-linearities, requiring atmospheric models to understand the dispersion of air pollutants. SDG 11.6 uses annual mean levels of particulate matter as an indicator to measure pollution levels, but this conceals fluctuation throughout the year (Table 2.7). Instead, the European Environment Agency provides real-time concentrations of various air pollutants (SO_x, NO_x, PM) at different observation sites in Europe (EEA, 2019[87]).[6] Combined with real-time data from point sources (such as PRTR) and air quality models, these data can help governments identify the origin of exceeded air quality limit values, highlight each sector's impact on air quality and provide information on the impact of pollution-control technologies (EPA, 2011[88]).

Table 2.7. Summary table: Indicators for monitoring progress in ensuring public health and safety and links to SDGs and OECD well-being framework

Policy priority	Proposed indicators	SDG goal and target	SDG indicator	OECD Well-being domain/dimension	OECD Well-being indicators
Ensuring public health and safety	• Pollution levels of air, water and soil from stationary sources, derived from pollution-release and transfer registries. • Measuring pollution through life-cycle assessments (LCAs). • Concentration of local pollutants in the atmosphere on average and at peak (by locality).	3.9. By 2030, substantially reduce the number of deaths and illnesses from hazardous chemicals and air, water and soil pollution and contamination.	3.9.1- 3.9.3. Mortality rate attributed to (1) household and ambient air pollution; (2) unsafe water; and (3) unintentional poisoning.	Current well-being: quality of life. Environmental quality.	Air and water quality.
		11.6. By 2030, reduce the adverse per capita environmental impact of cities, including by paying special attention to air quality and municipal and other waste management.	11.6.2: Annual mean levels of fine particulate matter.	Resources for future well-being: natural capital.	Exposure to 2.5PM.

2.3.6. *Sustainably managing natural resources and preserving ecosystems*

Indicators on the land use and water consumption of electricity generation technologies highlight the energy system's impact on these limited natural resources and supports policy makers in identifying environmental pressures. Information on land use is particularly important for countries with limited availability of land, while indicators on water consumption are particularly relevant for countries suffering from water scarcity. Assessing land use and water consumption requires using a life-cycle approach (see previous section). Figure 2.4 provides estimates for both indicators.

In many cases, changes in land use come with considerable losses of biodiversity and may undermine the provision of important ecosystem services, including those needed to maintain freshwater and forest resources (Foley, 2005[89]). Indicators on biodiversity in the SDGs and the OECD well-being framework focus on threatened species (e.g. the Red List Index), but do not assess the risk of extinction attributable to the electricity sector (Table 2.8). It is particularly important to measure the impact on ecosystems of deploying renewables, which will comprise the bulk of most countries' power systems in the future (Section 2.2). Countries having started monitoring systematically the impacts of increasing deployment of renewables in order to identify and address potential trade-offs between renewables and ecosystems. Germany started monitoring the environmental impact of the energy transition, providing indicators that help track the impacts of renewable deployment on the environment and provide a quantifiable basis for policy instruments to address the adverse impacts (Bundesamt für Naturschutz, 2018[90]). As a first step, the German report monitors the geospatial deployment of renewable energy plants over time and compares it with existing data on protected ecologically sensitive areas (Eichhorn et al., 2019[91]). Moreover, the report identifies and quantifies a number of conflicts between renewables and biodiversity, including collision of bats and birds with wind power plants, and the loss and fragmentation of wildlife habitats due to utility-scale solar PV deployment.

Figure 2.4. Water consumption and land use of selected generation technologies

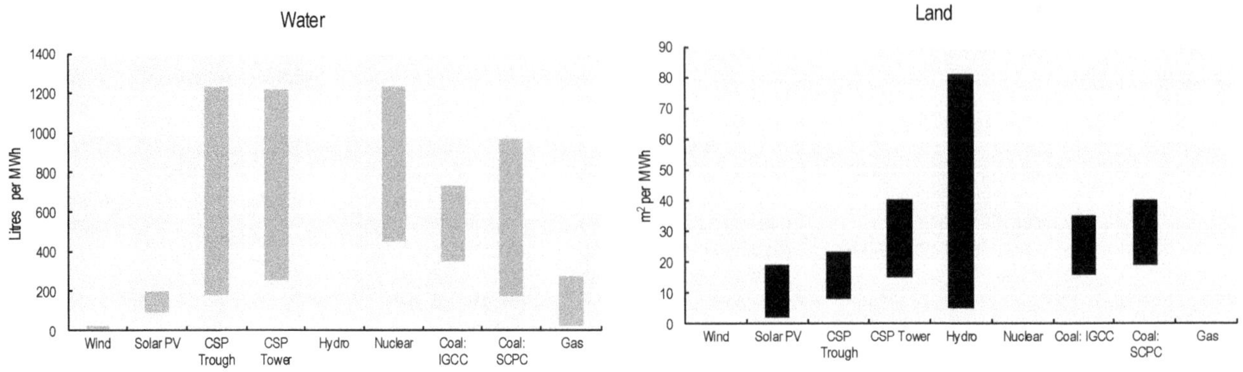

Note: The data show minimum and maximum consumption, depending on the specific technologies used. CSP = Concentrated solar power; IGCC: Integrated gasification combined cycle; SCPC: supercritical pulverised coal.
Source: Authors, based on (Hertwich et al., 2014[92]), (Meldrum et al., 2013[93]) and (Bakken, Killingtveit and Alfredsen, 2017[94]).

StatLink https://doi.org/10.1787/888933993009

Table 2.8. Summary table: Indicators for monitoring progress in sustainably managing natural resources and preserving ecosystems and links to SDGs and OECD well-being framework

Policy priority	Proposed indicators	SDG goal and target	SDG indicator	OECD Well-being domain/dimension	OECD Well-being indicators
Sustainably managing natural resources and preserving ecosystems	• Land use and land-use change by technology. • Water consumption by technology. • Requirement for natural resources. • Siting of power plants and sensitive ecosystems (e.g. migratory routes). • Mapping ecologically sensitive areas.	14.3. Minimise and address the impacts of ocean acidification, including through enhanced scientific co-operation at all levels.	14.3.1. Average marine acidity (pH) measured at agreed suite of representative sampling stations.	Resources for future well-being: natural capital.	• Threatened species. • Freshwater abstractions.
		15.5. Take urgent and significant action to reduce the degradation of natural habitats, halt the loss of biodiversity and, by 2020, protect and prevent the extinction of threatened species.	15.5.1. Red List Index.		

Generating technologies also require a wide range of finite materials, including aluminium, copper, iron and several rare earth metals (Kleijn et al., 2011[95]). Material requirements on a per-unit base for renewables tend to be higher than for conventional power plants (Hertwich et al., 2014[92]). For example, solar PV requires 11-40 times more copper. Monitoring the availability of materials is key to identifying supply bottlenecks. While the availability of most materials is not problematic, the supply of silver, indium, tellurium or ruthenium represent potential bottlenecks for solar PV deployment in the future (Grandell et al., 2016[28]). Similarly, neodymium, praseodymium, dysprosium and terbium are critical elements used in the permanent magnets of wind turbines (Pavel et al., 2017[96]). These potential supply risks highlight the importance of both high recycling rates and a shift towards a circular economy (Chapter 3).

2.3.7. Providing high-quality employment opportunities

The aggregate number of jobs in renewables and fossil generation is an indication of the challenges and benefits associated with the transition towards a sustainable electricity sector. Jobs can be differentiated as direct and indirect positions. Indirect jobs refer to work for suppliers who provide services and intermediate goods for the energy sector. Indirect and direct employment effects are difficult to define and therefore quantify, as not all jobs can be attributed clearly (SRU, 2017[97]). For example, monitoring indirect job numbers in renewables is challenging, as renewable energy suppliers consist of a relatively large variety of firms, most of which also offer other services besides renewables. Distinguishing between direct jobs (working for the mining or power company) and indirect jobs (suppliers) for fossil-fuel companies is, however, easier.

Gross employment growth can be an important driver of continued public support for the transition towards a sustainable electricity sector. The German monitoring report, a comprehensive monitoring system of the energy transition (Box 2.1), explicitly reports employment figures. Figure 2.5 shows the development of employment in fossil fuel and renewables in Germany from 2000 to 2016. The employment figures include both direct jobs and indirect jobs for both sources. Aggregate employment in the electricity sector increased from 554 000 in 2000 to 690 000 in 2016, but has been falling in recent years. The jobs lost in the conventional sector have been outweighed by job creation in the renewables sector, which accounted for almost 50% in 2016. Remaining employment in the fossil-based sector is mostly within the lignite sector, owing to the more labour-intensive mining industry.

Figure 2.5. Development of coal and RES employment in Germany, 2000-2016

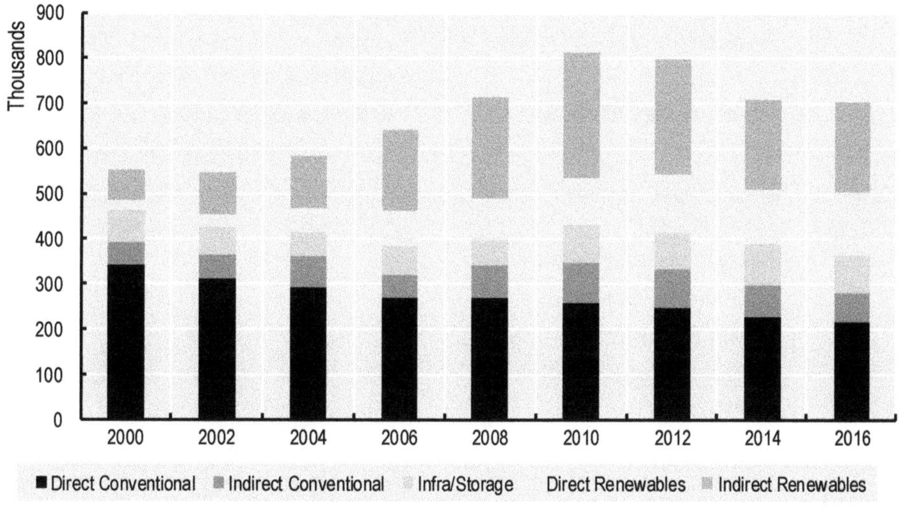

Source: Authors, based on (GWS, DLR and DIW, 2018[98]).

StatLink https://doi.org/10.1787/888933993028

Box 2.1. Tracking progress of the energy transition in Germany

The German monitoring report provides a best-practice example of establishing a measurement system that helps policy makers track multiple policy objectives related to the German *Energiewende* (energy transition). In its energy concept of 2010, the German government set out a number of climate and energy-related targets for the medium term (e.g. a 40% reduction of energy-related GHG emissions by 2020 and 10% improvement in energy efficiency by 10% by 2020).

The monitoring report analyses and condenses available data into appropriate indicators on energy-related, environmental and socio-economic dimensions. While the first part of the report describes the targets established in the energy concept, the second part monitors environmental and socio-economic dimensions beyond the quantitative targets of the energy transition, establishing a multidimensional measurement system (Table 2.9).

Table 2.9. Socio-economic and environmental dimensions of the monitoring process

Dimension	Sub-categories	Indicators
Power plants and security of supply	Power plants.	• Installed capacity by power-plant type and state.
	Supply security.	• SAIDI Index by voltage.
	Nuclear energy phase-out.	• Schedule for phasing out nuclear plants with capacity.
Affordable energy	Final consumer expenditure on energy.	• Aggregate final consumer expenditures for electricity by component (energy costs, network costs, taxes and levies). • Share of nominal GDP comprising final consumer expenditures for electricity.
	Affordability for private households.	• Average annual energy spending of private households. • Retail electricity price by component.
	Affordable energy for industry.	• Aggregate energy costs of industry by energy source. • Electricity prices for industrial companies not covered by special compensation arrangements by component.
Environmental compatibility	Soil, air and water.	• A suitable set of indicators is currently being developed.
	Natural resources and land use.	
	Nature and the landscape.	
	Impacts on human health.	
Integrated development of the energy system	Coupling the electricity, heating and transport sectors.	• Quantity and electricity consumption of electric heat pumps. • Quantity and electricity consumption of electric vehicles. • Degree of electrification of industry.
	Digitisation of the energy transition.	• Share of remote-controllable renewable capacity on total renewables capacity. • Share of metering technologies in the domestic customer sector by type of technology.
Investment, growth and jobs	Investment.	• Investment in renewable energy by type in million euros.
	Growth.	• Imports and exports of green capital goods.
	Jobs.	• Direct employment in the energy industry by type of infrastructure. • Jobs created in renewables, by type.

Source: Authors, based on (BMWi, 2016[60]).

Looking at the aggregate employment figures shows limited reallocation of employment as a result of a transition towards a sustainable electricity sector relative to historic norms (OECD, 2017[29]). However, aggregate numbers conceal the impact of the transition to a sustainable electricity sector at the local level. Regionally disaggregated employment figures exist. For example, the US Energy and Employment Report provides regionally disaggregated data of employment numbers by technology and occupation group on a county level (NASEO and EFI, 2019[99]). This helps identify those counties (and individuals) that are negatively affected by the transition and support governments in better targeting the losers in the transition, so that no one is left behind. In addition, regionally disaggregated data also allows pinpointing the counties that benefited the most, possibly encouraging more stringent climate action at the level of the subnational government.

Assessing the quality of employment needs to account for multiple dimensions. The indicators for SDG 8.5 and SDG 8.8 include average hourly earnings and the frequency of injuries as proxies for a safe working environment (Table 2.10). The OECD Job Quality Framework proposes three dimensions of job quality: earnings quality, quality of the working environment (health and safety conditions), and labour-market security (Cazes, Hijzen and Saint-Martin, 2015[100]). The performance of fossil and renewable jobs in the electricity sector along these criteria differs among countries (notably between OECD and developing/emerging countries), reflecting national circumstances (including trade unions, resource endowment, maturity of the renewable energy sector and workforce education). Information on these criteria informs governments about the synergies and trade-offs associated with the transition towards a sustainable electricity sector, notably employee safety and health.

Table 2.10. Summary table: Indicators for monitoring progress in providing high-quality employment opportunities and links to SDGs and OECD well-being framework

Policy priority	Proposed indicators	SDG goal and target	SDG indicators	OECD Well-being domain/dimension	OECD Well-being indicators
Providing high-quality employment opportunities	• Direct and indirect employment by technology. • Earnings quality. • Quality of the working environment. • Labour-market security.	8.5. By 2030, achieve full and productive employment and decent work for all women and men.	8.5.1. Average hourly earnings. 8.5.2. Unemployment rate.	Current well-being: material conditions. Jobs and earnings.	• Employment rate. • Earnings. • Labour-market insecurity. • Long-term unemployment.
		8.8. Protect labour rights and promote safe and secure working environments for all workers, including migrant workers, in particular women migrants, and those in precarious employment.	8.8.1. Frequency rates of fatal and non-fatal occupational injuries, by sex and migrant status.		

2.4. Conclusion

This chapter argued that applying a well-being lens to the electricity sector reveals a number of well-being priorities beyond the traditional energy trilemma (reliability, affordability and decarbonisation), all of which make up a sustainable electricity sector. It also emphasised the importance of considering different scales (plant, network and demand) that increase the levers of action to create a two-way alignment by exploiting the synergies between climate action and other well-being priorities. The second part of the chapter proposed a set of indicators that enable policy makers to track progress towards a sustainable electricity sector, guide policy decisions, and assess the synergies and trade-offs between climate action and other well-being priorities.

References

ACER (2018), *Study on the estimation of the value of lost load of electricity supply in europe, agency for the cooperation of energy regulators*, Agency for the cooperation of energy regulators (ACER), https://www.acer.europa.eu/en/Electricity/Infrastructure_and_network%20development/Infrastructure/Documents/CEPA%20study%20on%20the%20Value%20of%20Lost%20Load%20in%20the%20electricity%20supply.pdf (accessed on 26 February 2019). [73]

AEMO (2017), *South Australian Renewable Energy Report*, Australian Energy Market Operator, http://www.aemo.com.au (accessed on 7 June 2019). [56]

Allcott, H. (2011), "Rethinking real-time electricity pricing", *Resource and Energy Economics*, Vol. 33/4, pp. 820-842, http://dx.doi.org/10.1016/J.RESENEECO.2011.06.003. [51]

Ayres, R., H. Turton and T. Casten (2007), "Energy efficiency, sustainability and economic growth", *Energy*, Vol. 32/5, pp. 634-648, http://dx.doi.org/10.1016/j.energy.2006.06.005. [21]

Bakken, T., Å. Killingtveit and K. Alfredsen (2017), "The Water Footprint of Hydropower Production-State of the Art and Methodological Challenges", *Global Challenges*, Vol. 1/5, p. 1600018, http://dx.doi.org/10.1002/gch2.201600018. [94]

BEIS (2017), *Realising the Potential of Demand-side Response to 2025: A focus on Small Energy Users*, Department for Business, Energy and Industrial Strategy. [58]

Bird, L., J. Cochran and X. Wang (2014), *Wind and Solar Energy Curtailment: Experience and Practices in the United States*, NREL. [55]

BMWi (2016), *Sechster Monitoring-Bericht zur Energiewende*, http://www.bmwi.de (accessed on 30 January 2019). [60]

Bundesamt für Naturschutz (2018), *Erneuerbare im naturschutzfachlichen Monitoring | Naturschutz und Energiewende*, https://www.natur-und-erneuerbare.de/projektdatenbank/projekte/erneuerbare-im-naturschutzfachlichen-monitoring/ (accessed on 31 January 2019). [90]

Bundesnetzagentur and Bundeskartellamt (2018), *Monitoringbericht 2018*, https://www.bundesnetzagentur.de/SharedDocs/Downloads/DE/Allgemeines/Bundesnetzagentur/Publikationen/Berichte/2018/Monitoringbericht_Energie2018.pdf?__blob=publicationFile&v=3 (accessed on 5 February 2019). [69]

C40 Cities (2018), *Consumption-based GHG emissions of C40 cities*, http://www.c40.org/gpc (accessed on 27 February 2019). [48]

CAN et al. (2016), *Europe's dark cloud*, https://env-health.org/IMG/pdf/dark_cloud-full_report_final.pdf (accessed on 28 February 2019). [16]

Cardis, E. et al. (2006), "Estimates of the cancer burden in Europe from radioactive fallout from the Chernobyl accident", *International Journal of Cancer*, Vol. 119/6, pp. 1224-1235, http://dx.doi.org/10.1002/ijc.22037. [24]

Cazes, S., A. Hijzen and A. Saint-Martin (2015), "Measuring and Assessing Job Quality: The OECD Job Quality Framework", *OECD Social, Employment and Migration Working Papers*, No. 174, OECD Publishing, Paris, https://dx.doi.org/10.1787/5jrp02kjw1mr-en. [100]

de Nooij, M., C. Koopmans and C. Bijvoet (2007), "The value of supply security: The costs of power interruptions: Economic input for damage reduction and investment in networks", *Energy Economics*, Vol. 29/2, pp. 277-295, http://dx.doi.org/10.1016/J.ENECO.2006.05.022. [72]

DECC (2013), *Reliability Standard Methodology*, Department of Energy & Climate Change, https://assets.publishing.service.gov.uk/government/uploads/system/uploads/attachment_data/file/223653/emr_consultation_annex_c.pdf (accessed on 27 June 2019). [71]

Deemer, B. et al. (2016), "Greenhouse Gas Emissions from Reservoir Water Surfaces: A New Global Synthesis", *BioScience*, Vol. 66/11, pp. 949-964, http://dx.doi.org/10.1093/biosci/biw117. [43]

Department of Energy (2017), *Quadrennial energy review: Transforming the nations's electricity system*, https://www.energy.gov/sites/prod/files/2017/01/f34/QER%20Transforming%20the%20Nations%20Electricity%20System%20Full%20Report.pdf (accessed on 5 February 2019). [68]

Dugoua, E., R. Kennedy and J. Urpelainen (2018), "Satellite data for the social sciences: measuring rural electrification with night-time lights", *International Journal of Remote Sensing*, Vol. 39/9, pp. 2690-2701, http://dx.doi.org/10.1080/01431161.2017.1420936. [80]

EEA (2019), *About E-PRTR*, https://prtr.eea.europa.eu/#/static?cont=about (accessed on 21 February 2019). [84]

EEA (2019), *Up-to-date air quality data*, https://www.eea.europa.eu/data-and-maps/explore-interactive-maps/up-to-date-air-quality-data (accessed on 26 June 2019). [87]

Eichhorn, M. et al. (2019), "Spatial Distribution of Wind Turbines, Photovoltaic Field Systems, Bioenergy, and River Hydro Power Plants in Germany", *Data*, Vol. 4/1, p. 29, http://dx.doi.org/10.3390/data4010029. [91]

Electricity Map (2019), *electricityMap | Live CO2 emissions of electricity consumption*, https://www.electricitymap.org/?page=map&solar=false&remote=true&wind=false (accessed on 14 June 2019). [50]

ENTSO-E and ENTSOG (2018), *Power to Gas-A Sector Coupling Perspective*, https://docstore.entsoe.eu/Documents/Publications/Position%20papers%20and%20reports/ENTSOs_position_on_Sector_Coupling_final_Madrid_Forum.pdf (accessed on 21 June 2019). [38]

EPA (2019), *Inventory of U.S. Greenhouse Gas Emissions*, Environmental Protection Agency, https://www.epa.gov/sites/production/files/2019-04/documents/us-ghg-inventory-2019-chapter-3-energy.pdf (accessed on 26 June 2019). [42]

EPA (2016), *2014 National Emissions Inventory, version 1: Technical Support Document*, https://www.epa.gov/sites/production/files/2016-12/documents/nei2014v1_tsd.pdf (accessed on 21 February 2019). [17]

EPA (2011), *Air Quality Modeling Technical Support Document: EGU Mercury Analysis*, Environmental Protection Agency, https://www3.epa.gov/ttn/atw/utility/epa-454_r-11-008.pdf (accessed on 26 June 2019). [88]

EPA (1997), *Mercury Study Report to Congress Volume I: Executive Summary*, https://www.epa.gov/sites/production/files/2015-09/documents/volume1.pdf (accessed on 21 February 2019). [18]

Epstein, P. et al. (2011), "Full cost accounting for the life cycle of coal", *Annals of the New York Academy of Sciences*, Vol. 1219/1, pp. 73-98, http://dx.doi.org/10.1111/j.1749-6632.2010.05890.x. [20]

ESMAP (2018), *Policy Matters: Regulatory Indicators For Sustainable Energy*, World Bank Group. [40]

European Commission (2019), *EU Energy Poverty Observatory*, https://www.energypoverty.eu/ (accessed on 5 June 2019). [64]

European Commission (2018), *Study on the quality of electricity market data of transmission system operators, electricity supply disruptions, and their impact on the European electricity markets*, https://ec.europa.eu/energy/sites/ener/files/documents/dg_ener_electricity_market_data_-_final_report_-_22032018.pdf (accessed on 5 February 2019). [12]

Eurostat (2019), *EU-Statistics on Income and Living Conditions (EU-SILC)*, https://ec.europa.eu/eurostat/web/income-and-living-conditions/data (accessed on 5 June 2019). [65]

Eurostat (2019), *Household Budget Survey*, https://ec.europa.eu/eurostat/web/microdata/household-budget-survey (accessed on 5 June 2019). [66]

Facebook (2019), *Predictive model for accurate electrical grid mapping - Facebook Code*, https://code.fb.com/connectivity/electrical-grid-mapping/ (accessed on 19 March 2019). [81]

Flues, F. and K. van Dender (2017), "The impact of energy taxes on the affordability of domestic energy", *OECD Taxation Working Papers*, No. 30, OECD Publishing, Paris, https://dx.doi.org/10.1787/08705547-en. [62]

Foley, J. (2005), "Global Consequences of Land Use", *Science*, Vol. 309/5734, pp. 570-574, http://dx.doi.org/10.1126/science.1111772. [89]

Gasparatos, A. et al. (2017), "Renewable energy and biodiversity: Implications for transitioning to a Green Economy", *Renewable and Sustainable Energy Reviews*, Vol. 70, pp. 161-184, http://dx.doi.org/10.1016/J.RSER.2016.08.030. [27]

Goel, P. (2006), *Water pollution : causes, effects and control*, New Age International, https://books.google.fr/books?hl=en&lr=&id=4R9CYYoiFCcC&oi=fnd&pg=PA2&dq=Water+Pollution+-+Causes,+Effects+and+Control&ots=fJgxD-_Taw&sig=3wD2VBMxl1ZBqsN34KLbEAwRh9k#v=onepage&q=Water%20Pollution%20-%20Causes%2C%20Effects%20and%20Control&f=false (accessed on 16 March 2019). [22]

Government of Canada (2018), *Notice with respect to the substances in the National Pollutant Release Inventory for 2018 and 2019*, Canada Gazette Part I, http://gazette.gc.ca/rp-pr/p1/2018/2018-01-20/pdf/g1-15203.pdf#page=4 (accessed on 21 February 2019). [85]

Grandell, L. et al. (2016), "Role of critical metals in the future markets of clean energy technologies", *Renewable Energy*, Vol. 95, pp. 53-62, http://dx.doi.org/10.1016/j.renene.2016.03.102. [28]

GWS, DLR and DIW (2018), *Ökonomische Indikatoren des Energiesystems*, https://www.bmwi.de/Redaktion/DE/Publikationen/Studien/oekonomische-indikatoren-und-energiewirtschaftliche-gesamtrechnung.html. [98]

Hertwich, E. et al. (2014), "Integrated life-cycle assessment of electricity-supply scenarios confirms global environmental benefit of low-carbon technologies", *Proceedings of the National Academy of Sciences*, Vol. 112/20, pp. 6277-6282, http://dx.doi.org/10.1073/pnas.1312753111. [92]

Holland, S. and E. Mansur (2008), "Is Real-Time Pricing Green? The Environmental Impacts of Electricity Demand Variance", *Review of Economics and Statistics*, Vol. 90/3, pp. 550-561, http://dx.doi.org/10.1162/rest.90.3.550. [52]

IAEA (2005), *Energy Indicators for sustainable development: Guidelines and Methodologies*, http://www.iaea.org/Publications/index.html (accessed on 21 February 2019). [39]

IAEA, WHO and UN (2005), *Chernobyl's Legacy: Health, Environmental and Socia-Economic Impacts and Recommendations to the Governments of Belarus, Russian Federation and Ukraine*, https://www.who.int/ionizing_radiation/chernobyl/chernobyl_digest_report_EN.pdf (accessed on 16 March 2019). [23]

IEA (2019), *Global Energy and CO2 Status Report*, International Energy Agency. [13]

IEA (2019), "OECD - Electricity and heat generation", *IEA Electricity Information Statistics* (database), https://dx.doi.org/10.1787/data-00457-en (accessed on 21 June 2019). [33]

IEA (2019), *The Future of Hydrogen: Seizing today's opportunities*, OECD, Paris Cedex 16, https://dx.doi.org/10.1787/1e0514c4-en. [37]

IEA (2019), *Tracking Clean Energy Progress: Energy Integration*, https://www.iea.org/tcep/energyintegration/demandresponse/ (accessed on 19 June 2019). [57]

IEA (2019), *Tracking Clean Energy Progress: Informing Energy Sector Transformations*, https://www.iea.org/tcep/ (accessed on 27 February 2019). [5]

IEA (2018), *Energy Efficiency 2018: Analysis and outlooks to 2040*, International Energy Agency, Paris, https://dx.doi.org/10.1787/9789264024304-en. [53]

IEA (2018), *Market Report Series: Energy Efficiency 2018*, IEA, Paris, https://webstore.iea.org/market-report-series-energy-efficiency-2018 (accessed on 14 February 2019). [32]

IEA (2018), "OECD - Electricity/heat supply and consumption (Edition 2018)", *IEA Electricity Information Statistics* (database), https://dx.doi.org/10.1787/b0a629f0-en (accessed on 27 June 2019). [46]

IEA (2018), *Status of Power System Transformation 2018: Advanced Power Plant Flexibility*, International Energy Agency, Paris, https://dx.doi.org/10.1787/9789264302006-en. [31]

IEA (2018), *World Energy Outlook 2018*, International Energy Agency, Paris, https://dx.doi.org/10.1787/weo-2018-en. [7]

IEA (2018), *World Energy Statistics 2018*, OECD Publishing, Paris, https://dx.doi.org/10.1787/world_energy_stats-2018-en. [54]

IEA (2017), *Digitalization & Energy*, International Energy Agency, Paris, https://dx.doi.org/10.1787/9789264286276-en. [35]

IEA (2017), *Energy Technology Perspectives 2017: Catalysing Energy Technology Transformations*, IEA, Paris, https://dx.doi.org/10.1787/energy_tech-2017-en. [34]

IEA (2017), *Status of Power System Transformation 2017: System integration and local grids*, International Energy Agency, Paris, https://dx.doi.org/10.1787/9789264278820-en. [8]

IEA (2017), *WEO-2017 Special Report: Energy Access Outlook*, http://www.iea.org/t&c/. [77]

IEA (2017), *World Energy Outlook 2017*, OECD Publishing, Paris/International Energy Agency, Paris, https://dx.doi.org/10.1787/weo-2017-en. [47]

IEA (2015), *Making the energy sector more resilient to climate change*. [75]

IEA et al. (2019), *Tracking SDG 7: The Energy Progress Report*, http://www.worldbank.org (accessed on 3 June 2019). [9]

IPCC (2018), *Global Warming of 1.5 °C: Summary for Policy Makers*, http://report.ipcc.ch/sr15/pdf/sr15_spm_final.pdf (accessed on 30 October 2018). [6]

IPCC (2014), "Climate Change 2014: Synthesis Report. Contribution of Working Groups I, II and III to the Fifth Assessment Report of the Intergovernmental Panel on Climate Change [Core Writing Team, R.K. Pachauri and L.A. Meyer (eds.)]. IPCC, Geneva, Switzerland". [1]

IPCC (2014), "Energy Systems", in *Climate Change 2014: Mitigation of Climate Change. Contribution of Working Group III to the Fifth Assessment Report of the Intergovernmental Panel on Climate Change*, Cambridge University Press, Cambridge, https://www.ipcc.ch/pdf/assessment-report/ar5/wg3/ipcc_wg3_ar5_chapter7.pdf. [3]

IPCC (2006), *2006 IPCC Guidelines for National Greenhouse Gas Inventories*, https://www.ipcc-nggip.iges.or.jp/public/2006gl/vol2.html. [44]

ISO (2006), "14040: Environmental Management - Life Cycle assessment". [86]

ITF (2019), *ITF Transport Outlook 2019*, OECD Publishing, Paris, https://dx.doi.org/10.1787/transp_outlook-en-2019-en. [36]

Jain, A. and J. Urpelainen (2016), *Measuring Energy Access in India Insights from applying a multi-tier framework in cooking energy and household electricity*. [79]

Jairaj, B. et al. (2018), *The Future Electricity Grid: Key Questions and Considerations for Developing Countries*, World Resource Institute, https://www.wri.org/sites/default/files/The_Future_Electricity_Grid.pdf (accessed on 18 September 2018). [30]

Kleijn, R. et al. (2011), "Metal requirements of low-carbon power generation", *Energy*, Vol. 36/9, pp. 5640-5648, http://dx.doi.org/10.1016/j.energy.2011.07.003. [95]

Linares, P. and L. Rey (2013), "The costs of electricity interruptions in Spain. Are we sending the right signals?", *Energy Policy*, Vol. 61, pp. 751-760, http://dx.doi.org/10.1016/J.ENPOL.2013.05.083. [10]

London Economics (2013), *The Value of Lost Load (VoLL) for Electricity in Great Britain*. [74]

McCully, P. (2001), *Silenced rivers : the ecology and politics of large dams*, Zed Books, https://www.press.uchicago.edu/ucp/books/book/distributed/S/bo20852228.html (accessed on 18 February 2019). [2]

Meldrum, J. et al. (2013), "Life cycle water use for electricity generation: a review and harmonization of literature estimates", *Environmental Research Letters*, Vol. 8/1, p. 015031, http://dx.doi.org/10.1088/1748-9326/8/1/015031. [93]

Mirabile, M. and J. Calder (2018), "Clean power for a cool planet: Electricity infrastructure plans and the Paris Agreement", *OECD Environment Working Papers*, No. 140, OECD Publishing, Paris, https://dx.doi.org/10.1787/2dc84376-en. [14]

NASEO and EFI (2019), *The 2019 U.S. Energy and Employment Report*, https://www.usenergyjobs.org/ (accessed on 5 June 2019). [99]

National Research Council (2010), *Hidden Costs of Energy: Unpriced Consequences of Energy Production and Use*, National Academies Press, Washington, D.C., http://dx.doi.org/10.17226/12794. [19]

OECD (2019), *Good Governance for Critical Infrastructure Resilience*, OECD Reviews of Risk Management Policies, OECD Publishing, Paris, https://dx.doi.org/10.1787/02f0e5a0-en. [76]

OECD (2017), "Air emissions by source (Edition 2017)", *OECD Environment Statistics* (database), https://dx.doi.org/10.1787/f974fae7-en (accessed on 22 July 2019). [105]

OECD (2017), *Investing in Climate, Investing in Growth*, OECD Publishing, Paris, https://dx.doi.org/10.1787/9789264273528-en. [29]

OECD (2000), *PRTR Implementation: Member Country Progress*, http://www.oecd.org/officialdocuments/publicdisplaydocumentpdf/?doclanguage=en&cote=env/epoc(2000)8/final (accessed on 21 February 2019). [82]

OECD (1996), *Pollutant Release and transfer registries (PRTRS): Guidance Manual for Governments*, OECD Publishing, Paris, http://www.oecd.org/officialdocuments/publicdisplaydocumentpdf/?cote=ocde/gd(96)32&doclanguage=en (accessed on 21 February 2019). [83]

OECD/IEA (2016), *Energy and Air Pollution*, OECD/IEA, https://www.iea.org/publications/freepublications/publication/WorldEnergyOutlookSpecialReport2016EnergyandAirPollution.pdf (accessed on 20 September 2018). [15]

OFGEM (2016), *Aggregators-Barriers and External Impacts*. [59]

Ofgem (2011), *Electricity Capacity Assessment: Measuring and modelling the risk of supply shortfalls*, http://www.ofgem.gov.uk (accessed on 26 February 2019). [70]

Pavel, C. et al. (2017), "Substitution strategies for reducing the use of rare earths in wind turbines", *Resources Policy*, Vol. 52, pp. 349-357, http://dx.doi.org/10.1016/j.resourpol.2017.04.010. [96]

Rademaekers, K. et al. (2016), *Selecting Indicators to Measure Energy Poverty*, European Commission/Trinomics , Rotterdam, https://ec.europa.eu/energy/sites/ener/files/documents/Selecting%20Indicators%20to%20Measure%20Energy%20Poverty.pdf (accessed on 20 September 2018). [63]

Reliability Panel AEMC (2018), *2017 Annual Market Performance Review*, https://www.aemc.gov.au/sites/default/files/2018-03/Final%20report.pdf (accessed on 19 March 2019). [67]

SE4A and ESMAP (2015), *Beyond Connections, Energy Access Redefined.* [78]

SEDC (2017), *Explicit Demand Response in Europe: Mapping the Markets 2017*, Smart Energy Demand Coalition, http://www.smartenergydemand.eu (accessed on 7 June 2019). [61]

Sharma, T. et al. (2016), "Of pilferers and poachers: Combating electricity theft in India", *Energy Research & Social Science*, Vol. 11, pp. 40-52, http://dx.doi.org/10.1016/j.erss.2015.08.006. [101]

SRU (2017), *Start coal phaseout now*, https://www.umweltrat.de/SharedDocs/Downloads/EN/04_Statements/2016_2020/2017_10_statement_coal_phaseout.pdf;jsessionid=EFD43F4CD76D0DF5D337F8273C1BD8B3.2_cid284?__blob=publicationFile&v=4. [97]

Steinhauser, G., A. Brandl and T. Johnson (2014), "Comparison of the Chernobyl and Fukushima nuclear accidents: A review of the environmental impacts", *Science of The Total Environment*, Vol. 470-471, pp. 800-817, http://dx.doi.org/10.1016/J.SCITOTENV.2013.10.029. [25]

Tabassum-Abbasi, M. et al. (2014), "Wind energy: Increasing deployment, rising environmental concerns", *Renewable and Sustainable Energy Reviews*, Vol. 31, pp. 270-288, http://dx.doi.org/10.1016/j.rser.2013.11.019. [4]

Tranberg, B. et al. (2018), *Real-Time Carbon Accounting Method for the European Electricity Markets*, https://arxiv.org/pdf/1812.06679.pdf (accessed on 11 February 2019). [49]

Vanclay, F. (2017), "Impact Assessment and Project Appraisal Project-induced displacement and resettlement: from impoverishment risks to an opportunity for development?", http://dx.doi.org/10.1080/14615517.2017.1278671. [103]

Wilmsen, B., M. Webber and Y. Duan (2011), "Involuntary Rural Resettlement", *The Journal of Environment & Development*, Vol. 20/4, pp. 355-380, http://dx.doi.org/10.1177/1070496511426478. [104]

Winemiller, K. et al. (2016), "Balancing hydropower and biodiversity in the Amazon, Congo, and Mekong", *Science*, Vol. 351/6269, pp. 128-129, http://dx.doi.org/10.1126/science.aac7082. [26]

World Economic Council (2019), *Energy Trilemma Index*, https://trilemma.worldenergy.org/ (accessed on 21 July 2019). [41]

WRI (2015), *GHG Protocol Scope 2 Guidance: An amendment to the GHG Protocol Corporate Standard*, https://ghgprotocol.org/sites/default/files/standards/Scope%202%20Guidance_Final_0.pdf (accessed on 11 February 2019). [45]

Yakubu, O., N. Babu C. and O. Adjei (2018), "Electricity theft: Analysis of the underlying contributory factors in Ghana", *Energy Policy*, Vol. 123, pp. 611-618, http://dx.doi.org/10.1016/j.enpol.2018.09.019. [102]

Zachariadis, T. and A. Poullikkas (2012), "The costs of power outages: A case study from Cyprus", *Energy Policy*, Vol. 51, pp. 630-641, http://dx.doi.org/10.1016/J.ENPOL.2012.09.015. [11]

Notes

[1] Creating two-way alignment between climate action and the broader goals of human well-being and sustainable development means that: i) action in non-climate policy areas should support, rather than undermine, the pursuit of climate change mitigation goals; and ii) climate change mitigation will be more attractive when it also meets other important societal goals (e.g. clean air and improvements in health) that are likely to materialise over a shorter timescale.

[2] For example, between 1990 and 2016, power-related SO_X emissions in OECD countries fell by more than 75 %, whereas NO_X emissions fell by almost 50% (OECD, 2017[105]).

[3] Forced resettlements due to (coal) mining and large hydro dams can lead to significant emotional pain as displaced people lose the places to which they are attached (Vanclay, 2017[103]). For example, according to recent estimates, the Three Gorges Dam in China is estimated to have displaced more than one million people (Wilmsen, Webber and Duan, 2011[104]).

[4] Transmission and distribution losses are typically measured as the residual between total electricity generation and total electricity consumption. They can be divided into technical and non-technical losses. Technical losses refer to the energy lost in the transport of electricity, which can be reduced by upgrading transmission lines or power transformers, or by improving operational practices. The major reason for non-technical losses, notably in developing and emerging economies, is power theft, which constitutes a severe problem for utilities' financial sustainability (Sharma et al., 2016[101]). Lack of electricity access and problems of affordability are major drivers for power theft (Yakubu, Babu C. and Adjei, 2018[102]).

[5] Similarly, electricity consumers can use this information to improve their carbon footprint by shifting demand over time. Shifting demand from a high to a low carbon-intense hour would result in CO_2 emission savings.

[6] These data can be complemented by satellite data to derive a better understanding of pollution levels at different locations. For example, NASA and the Copernicus Atmospheric Modelling Service provide air-pollution data on an hourly basis, with grid cells as small as 10 km by 10 km.

3 Moving to sustainable industrial production

This chapter applies a well-being lens to the heavy industry sector. The first part discusses a number of priorities beyond the provision of products that align the sector to wider well-being and sustainability goals. It then explains how shifting towards a net-zero, circular and resource-efficient production is necessary to deliver the policy priorities identified. The second part proposes a set of indicators that will enable policy makers to track this shift while assessing the synergies and trade-offs between climate and other priorities in the sector.

The statistical data for Israel are supplied by and under the responsibility of the relevant Israeli authorities. The use of such data by the OECD is without prejudice to the status of the Golan Heights, East Jerusalem and Israeli settlements in the West Bank under the terms of international law.

In Brief

Moving to sustainable production by heavy industry

For the last century, heavy industry has been maximising production to meet the demands of a growing global population, rising standards of living and increasing urbanisation. In this sense, it touches on nearly every facet of our lives since it produces nearly all the materials and chemicals in use (e.g. iron and steel, cement, aluminium). The world is producing billions of tons of primary materials annually, more than twice as fast as population growth.

The problem, however, is that **current industrial production is damaging our health and that of the planet, polluting the air we breathe, contaminating soil and water, using up the planet's resources, and in the midst, exacerbating climate change.** The heavy industry sector emitted approximately 36% of global energy-related CO_2 emissions in 2016 including electricity and heat.

The choices made today, with respect to building or retrofitting plants, will be in place for the next 20 to 40 years, locking in heavy industry into either sustainable or unsustainable production until mid-century. However, only a subset of heavy industry processes can be cheaply and directly electrified; hence, new processes will be required to decarbonise. Many of the existing options are expensive or technically difficult. Demonstration and deployment to establish the commercial viability of such new technologies is vital, since the next few decades will bring more people, increased urbanisation, and higher standards of living.

Sustainable production means decarbonising heavy industry and adopting circular and resource-efficient production processes. Firms will need to modify plants to become more energy efficient, shut down especially "dirty" ones, use more recycled materials, and develop and deploy new production processes since decarbonising some material and chemical processes presents unresolved challenges. Many of these options not only reduce greenhouse gases, but also improve environmental quality and help to sustainably manage the planet's resources. For example, for some materials, like steel, using more scrap means less energy, water, and land usage, in addition to less GHGs. To realise these possibilities, governments will need to shift away from the linear economy – where raw materials are extracted, processed, consumed and disposed – and mainstream decarbonisation, circularity and resource efficiency across the entire economy.

For this shift to happen, the sector will need to pursue sustainable productivity that incorporates social and environmental impacts into decision-making, thereby broadening its policy priorities. This can be done, for instance, by using indicators that show whether production is increasing at the expense of air, land, water, soil and materials pollution and GHGs. These and other indicators capturing the diverse impacts of heavy industry on well-being will need to be used systematically.

Policy packages to decarbonise heavy industry should encompass a set of *core policies* like carbon pricing, and *enabling policies* like enhancing the availability of scrap for heavy industry. *Policies that attenuate any adverse impacts on well-being,* such as active labour management programmes and revenue recycling, will also be needed. Targeted RD&D will be necessary to develop new processes, and resource efficiency programmes will be important. Overall, shifting the mind-sets of policy makers to consider wider social and environmental impacts will help accelerate the deployment of these policies, since, for instance, shifting to a notion of productivity that accounts for the environment can make the case for decarbonisation as a way to catalyse productivity gains.

Infographic 3.1. Moving to sustainable production by heavy industry

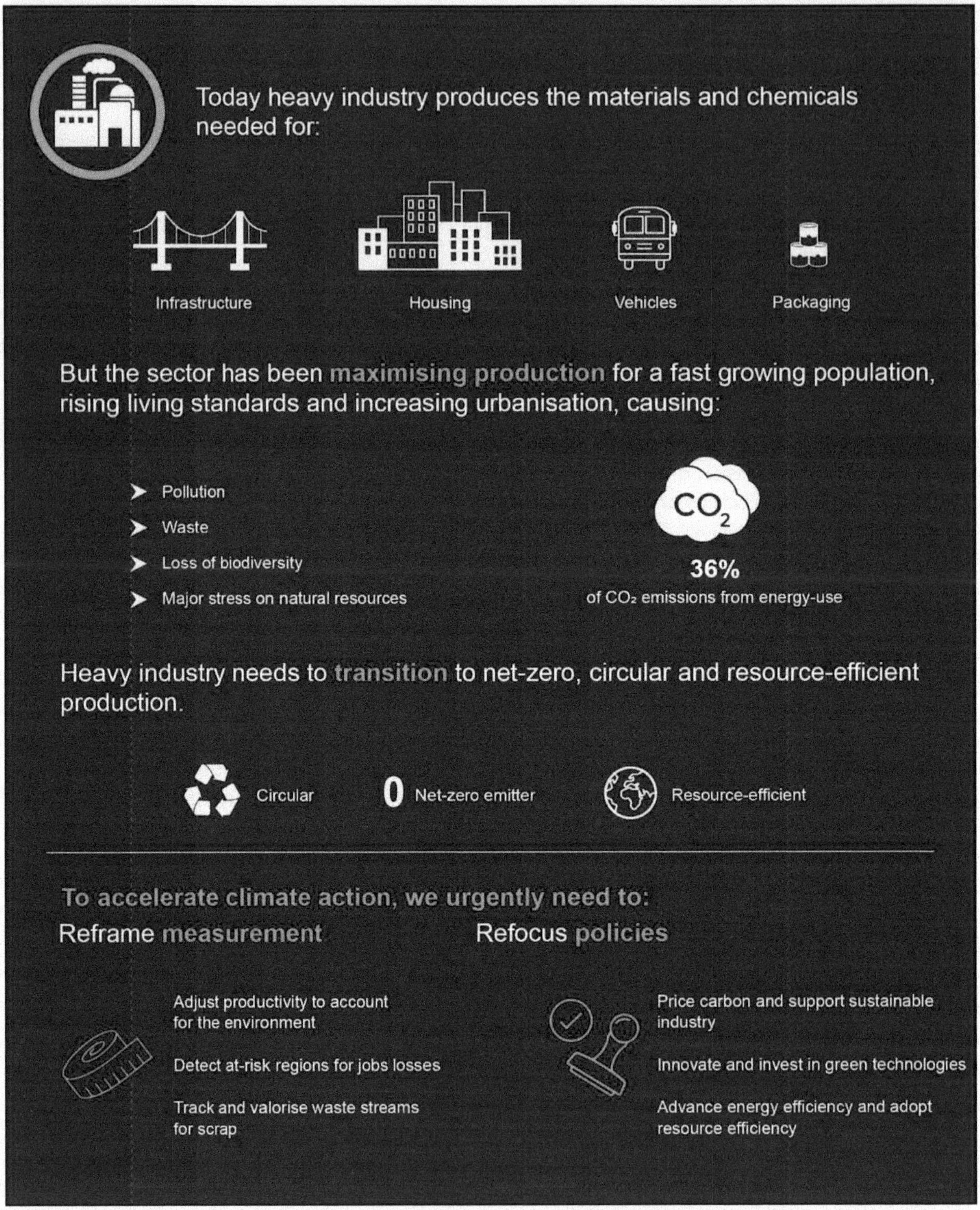

3.1. Introduction

This report proposes adopting a **well-being lens** as a framework for mitigation policies. Its first component is to define societal goals in terms of well-being and systematically reflect these goals in decision-making across the economy, putting people's well-being at the centre of policy making. Its second component is to ensure that policymakers consider multiple well-being objectives, rather than focusing on a single issue (or a few issues) across sectors. The final component of the well-being lens is to acquire a thorough understanding of the system in which a policy intervenes, in order to grasp the broader interactions between different facets of well-being. Using this lens helps identify and design policies that can deliver **two-way alignment** between climate change mitigation and other well-being priorities, so that these goals are mutually reinforcing rather than antagonistic. This chapter applies a well-being lens to heavy industry, which comprises energy-intensive trade-exposed industries. It focuses on iron and steel, cement, non-ferrous metals (e.g. aluminium), pulp and paper, and chemicals (e.g. ammonia). It does not discuss refineries, which are touched upon in other chapters.

Heavy industry links to nearly every aspect of current and future well-being. It transforms the planet's raw materials into products for society. Over the last century, the planet has experienced unprecedented urbanisation, rising standards of living and a larger population than ever before, all of which has led to increasing demand for products from heavy industry. In 1970, the world produced 22 billion tonnes of primary raw materials (i.e. materials sourced from mining or extraction in their raw form that are entering the economy for the first time) globally. This volume has grown to 70 billion tonnes by 2010,[1] twice as fast as population growth during the same period (OECD, 2019[1]). Driven by living standards, population growth and urbanisation, the major focus of heavy industry has been on maximising production to meet these growing demands profitably. This meant increasing output while reducing costs, typically through improvements in production efficiency, understood as minimising inputs – labour, capital, energy and other intermediate inputs – for every unit of production.

While heavy industry has successfully met this growing demand for materials and chemicals, it has done so in a way that makes a major contribution to climate change. Heavy industry requires high temperatures for materials production, chemical feedstocks and other specialised process chemistries, rendering it very energy and emission-intensive. It is responsible for roughly 36% of annual global carbon dioxide (CO_2) emissions (compared to only 5.5% for the rest of industry) (IEA, 2019[2]); these emissions are rising significantly faster than total global CO_2 (Hoesly et al., 2018[3]).

The heavy industry sector emits roughly 36% of global CO_2 annually (compared to only 5.5% for the rest of industry) (IEA, 2019[2]); these emissions are growing significantly faster than total global CO_2 (Hoesly et al., 2018[3]).

In terms of broader well-being, the extraction and processing of raw materials can irreversibly alter ecosystems through physical alteration of the landscape, waste and other by-products. Some of these ecosystem changes may even subsequently alter local climate conditions, as seen with rising local temperatures caused by deforestation from mining (Wolff et al., 2018[4]). Pollution of the surrounding air, water and soil damages biodiversity and threatens human life. Thus, heavy industry's dependence on the planet's resources (i.e. energy, land, water and raw materials) poses challenges for sustainability because of the growing competition between agriculture, energy and industry sectors. The extent of such competition depends on the speed and direction these sectors innovate.

There exists a risk of perpetuating or even worsening these well-being losses into the future. If current trends continue, models project a doubling of demand for materials in the next 50 years from 89 Gt in 2017 to 160 Gt in 2060 across all major categories of materials – metallic ores, non-metallic ores, biomass and fossil fuels (OECD, 2019[1]). In light of the well-being impacts outlined above, this calls not just for innovation but also for reassessment of heavy industry's priorities, and further reflection on the use of resources to deliver materials and chemicals to society.

The inadequacy of the extract-process-consume-dispose economy (otherwise known as the "linear economy") is quickly apparent when adopting a well-being lens. Heavy industry can only promote well-being if the broader economy shifts to a net-zero, circular and resource-efficient model. These broader changes will, in turn, enable heavy industry to reach net-zero, circular and resource-efficient production.

This report focuses on mitigation. It highlights a number of different strategies to decarbonise heavy industry on both the supply and demand sides (IPCC, 2018[5]). Options include improving energy efficiency; increasing the use of low-carbon electricity; using more recycled materials; modifying the existing processes to employ carbon capture, utilisation and storage (CCUS); identifying alternative heat sources for existing processes; and even switching fuels completely (e.g. through direct or indirect electrification, bio feedstocks, or hydrogen) (Bataille et al., 2018[6]; Davis et al., 2018[7]). There is limited time to meet stringent climate change mitigation goals. The multi-decadal life of industrial facilities means all new industrial facilities must be net-zero by 2030 to 2055 to achieve the 1.5° to 2°C temperature goal (Bataille et al., 2018[6]). Facilities' investment cycles typically last 20 to 40 years, meaning firms are only one – or at most two – investment cycles away from the middle of the century (Wyns, Robson and Khnadekar, 2018[8]).

Nonetheless, compared to other end-use sectors like transport, only a subset of heavy industry processes can be cheaply and directly electrified; hence, new processes (e.g. new cement chemistries) will be required. Many of the existing options are expensive (e.g. the HIsarna process for steel) or technically difficult (Bataille et al., 2018[6]; Davis et al., 2018[7]). However, the technological possibilities for decarbonising are constantly evolving at the frontier of innovation; demonstration and deployment to establish the commercial viability of such new technologies are also vital. Reducing demand for products from heavy industry through greater materials efficiency will be just as important as supply-side measures, but caution should be exercised with regard to prioritisation. Concentrating on the demand-side can slow the deployment of low-carbon production technologies, and therefore, the rate of reduction in the emission intensity of materials production (OECD/IEA, 2019[9]).

The methods used to decarbonise heavy industry will have great implications for other dimensions of well-being, which cannot be ignored. On the one hand, the sensitivity of heavy industry to increased production costs adds an extra dimension of complexity to competitiveness. Most of heavy industry operates at intermittent profitability and is usually highly exposed to trade, with little capacity to hand down costs to consumers (1-5% at most). Hence, extra costs linked to decarbonisation often lead to concerns over competitiveness, which in turn could lead to job losses and the "death" of communities, since heavy industry tends to be located in rural and remote areas. On the other hand, various pathways to decarbonisation can help manage the planet's resources, by using less energy or better managing water consumption; others can help reduce pollutants and waste to maintain a healthy and safe environment. Moving forward, governments will need to navigate this tangled web of interests and unknowns with carefully crafted policy packages that create two-way alignment between all of these well-being priorities.

This chapter analyses the impacts of heavy industry on well-being, now and in the future. Section 3.1 calls for expanding policy priorities to guide decisions in the sector in a way that can secure wider well-being positive impacts, as well as anticipate and avoid potential trade-offs. Section 3.2 proposes a set of indicators to monitor the delivery of these various priorities and help countries effectively prioritise action to ensure progress in attaining them. It shows how these indicators can complement the Sustainable Development Goals (SDGs) and the OECD Framework for Measuring Well-being and Progress (henceforth the OECD well-being framework).

3.2. Shifting perspective: Beyond maximising production

Despite its relatively small share of global gross domestic product (GDP), heavy industry underpins the current economy, processing almost all materials and chemicals presently in use (Wyns, Robson and Khnadekar, 2018[8]). Hence, countries often consider heavy industry strategic to economic development (Silva and Mattera, 2018[10]). Steel, in particular, is considered key not only for the economy, but also for defence. Securing domestic sources of steel is therefore often an important consideration for policy makers (Silva and Mattera, 2018[10]).

Heavy industry faces very high fixed costs upfront, leading these industries to maximise output even in periods of low demand (Silva and Mattera, 2018[10]). Rising standards of living, increasing urbanisation and population growth are also creating increasing demand for products. These combined factors provide an even greater push to increase output and improve efficiency to reduce costs, i.e. minimising inputs for every unit of output. As Figure 3.1 shows, such inputs are human – e.g. workers and their expertise (red box); natural – e.g. water, land and raw materials (blue box); and produced – e.g. energy and machinery (yellow box). In return, heavy industry creates the processed materials and chemicals needed by society (yellow box), along with wages for those workers (red box), as well as other less desirable by-products, such as pollution, waste and greenhouse gases (GHGs) (blue box).

Figure 3.1. Inputs and outputs of heavy industry production

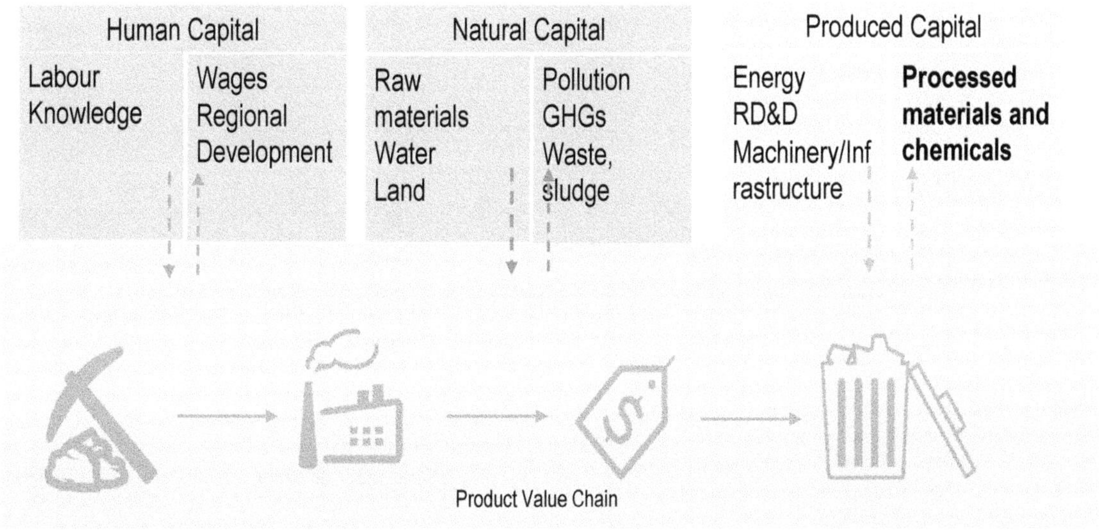

Heavy industry is keeping up with the pace of demand. Primary aluminium production nearly doubled over the last decade, from 38 971 Mt in 2008 to 64 336 Mt in 2018, driven mainly by increased production in China (OECD, 2019[1]). Likewise, crude steel production increased from 1.3 billion metric tonnes in 2008 to 1.8 billion metric tonnes in 2018 (Mercier and Mabashi, 2019[11]). Ramping up production worldwide is adding jobs and developing regions worldwide. Even though these jobs account for a relatively small share of employment globally, they link indirectly to sectors across the economy. For example, steel employs only 6 million people globally, but links indirectly to 42 million jobs (World Steel Association, 2019[12]).

Nevertheless, automation is gradually replacing these jobs; similarly to automakers, heavy industry is shifting towards automating processes (Kherat, 2019[13]). Industrial robots will likely replace nearly 20 million manufacturing jobs (approximately 8.5%) globally by 2030 (Oxford Economics, 2019[14]). The declining costs and growing capabilities of robots (using artificial intelligence), combined with ever-increasing demand for goods, is prompting major producers like China to invest heavily in automation (Oxford Economics, 2019[14]). Since 2000, the European Union has lost 400 000 jobs to automation, China

550 000, the United States 260 000, and South Korea 340 000 (Oxford Economics, 2019[14]). The need to care for displaced workers to avoid entrenching social inequalities is increasingly recognised, as low-income and rural sparsely populated areas will be the most vulnerable to job losses from automation and the low-carbon transition (Oxford Economics, 2019[14]). The latter is an issue addressed by the 2015 ILO guidelines for a just transition (ILO, 2015[15]).

Despite this trend, heavy industry – and industrial policy – are maximising production, to the detriment of other aspects of current and future well-being. The growth in production by heavy industry over the last few decades substantially increased energy-related GHG emissions, further exacerbating climate change. Heavy industry emitted 11.8 $GtCO_2$ (36% of global CO_2) in 2016, plus 3.1 $GtCO_2$ (9%) for fossil-fuel production (which is traditionally counted within heavy industry), making it the single-largest emitting sector when allocating CO_2 emissions from electricity to consuming sectors (blue arrow in Figure 3.1) (IEA, 2019[2]). Iron and steel (31%), and cement and concrete (19%), are the top two emitters from heavy industry (see Figure 3.2 for a further breakdown).

Figure 3.2. Breakdown of energy-related CO_2 emissions by sub-sector

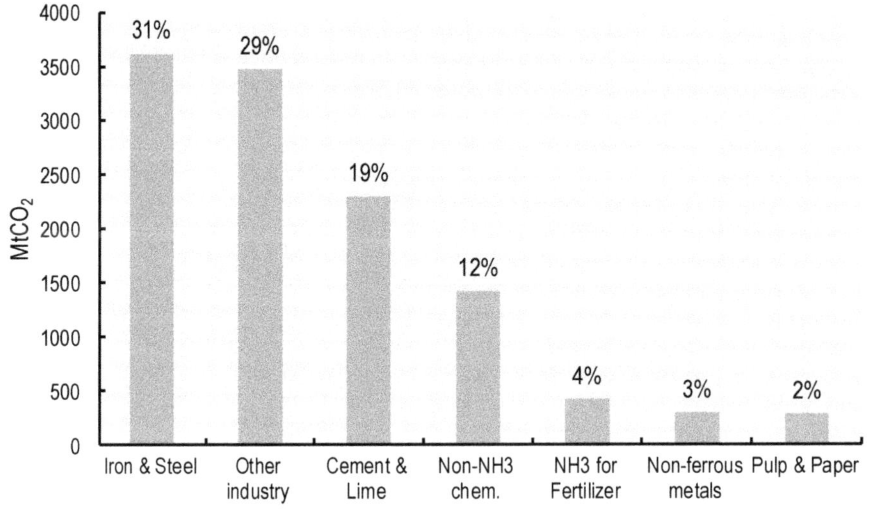

Source: (IEA, 2019[2]).

StatLink https://doi.org/10.1787/888933993047

By-products from heavy industry – i.e. waste, sludge and dust (blue arrow in Figure 3.1) – in some parts of the world may pollute the air, water and soil, damaging biodiversity through water acidification, eutrophication, and aquatic and terrestrial ecotoxicity (OECD, 2019[1]). This exposure can persist over time, e.g. sulphuric acid rain from burning coal persisted over much of North-eastern United States until the 1990s. It can also be very acute, as shown by the collapses of the Brumadinho dam in 2019 and the Mariana dam 2015, which released millions of litres of waste from mining iron ore in Brazil, killing people and destroying biodiversity. This pollution may then harm human health directly and indirectly, by contaminating food and water (Table 3.1). The use of the planet's resources, i.e. land, water and raw materials (blue box), and energy (yellow box) – could pose future sustainability problems, owing to increasing competition for these resources between heavy industry, agriculture and energy (OECD, 2017[16]). In January 2018, Cape Town faced the stark reality of running out of water in three months; the city resolved this crisis by cutting off industry's access to consumable water. These types of choices will become increasingly common in our future: total global water demand (i.e. the amount of water withdrawn from freshwater sources) is projected to grow by 23% between 2015 and 2060; industry accounts for 38%

of this demand (OECD, 2017[16]). How to meet this increasing demand in the context of potential resource scarcity in the future is unclear.

Table 3.1. Examples of heavy industry's impact on well-being

By-products from heavy industry	Effect on well-being	Examples
Water pollution	Biodiversity losses.	Copper (e.g. used in the electromechanical parts of construction) will have the largest impact on acidification in the next 50 years (OECD, 2019[1]) leading to freshwater aquatic ecotoxicity and killing many algal species, soft-bodied animals, insects and fish (e.g. high risk of losses for salmon, trout and roach) (Tang et al., 2014[17]).
Soil pollution		Non-ferrous metals release toxic substances in ecosystems, causing terrestrial ecotoxicity. Impacts on insects include egg loss, reduced fitness of offspring and impaired behaviour, leading to a general reduction in population sizes and species diversity at contaminated sites. Declining insect populations, in turn, could disrupt ecosystem services – and, for example, food production (Mogren and Trumble, 2010[18]).
Air pollution	Unhealthy for humans.	Heavy industry, especially in emerging economies, emits excessive amounts of pollutants rich in sulphur dioxide and particulate matter, the ingredients of smog. In China, the health effects of smog are felt very quickly (for example, tightness in the chest 10 or 15 minutes after breathing it in), leading to long-term problems like asthma, premature deaths and birth defects.
Wastewater sludge and residues		The wastewater, residues and sludge from heavy industry (e.g. iron and other non-ferrous metals) threaten health even at very low levels of contamination (Gunatilake SK, 2015[19]). Metal-contaminated wastewater leads to cancer, organ damage, nervous-system damage and in extreme cases, death for humans. It also reduces children's growth and development, e.g. through the contamination of drinking water and food, as observed in India (Gunatilake SK, 2015[19]).
Dust		Exposure to heavy metals in dust through either ingestion, inhalation or absorption through the skin, e.g. in China (Leung et al., 2008[20]; Zheng et al., 2010[21]), India and Pakistan (Farooq, Anwar and Rashid, 2008[22]), results in damage to central and peripheral nervous systems, blood composition, lungs, kidneys and the liver, even resulting in death (Leung et al., 2008[20]).
Water usage	Loss of natural resources.	Total global water demand (e.g. the amount of water withdrawn from freshwater sources) is projected to increase by 23% over 2015-60. Industry accounts for 38% of this increase (OECD, 2017[20]). As water becomes scarcer in places where heavy industry manufactures its products, wasteful production methods present a danger to operations, particularly if local governments turn off the tap or impose large surcharges on water use and pollution.
Land usage		Occupation of land area by heavy industry, as well as landfills, absorb land needed for other purposes (Giam, Olden and Simberloff, 2018[23]).

Demand for materials and chemicals from heavy industry will rise in the coming decades; exactly how much it will rise will depend on society's response to the challenges ahead. For example, if trends continue globally (and if the economic structure remains roughly the same), growth of primary and secondary metal production – e.g. aluminium, copper, iron and steel – will most likely continue at the same rates over the next 50 years (OECD, 2019[1]). According to projections, a continuation of present trends would double demand for *primary* materials (from extracted raw materials) between 2017 and 2060, primarily from emerging and developing countries (OECD, 2019[1]). Although this could bring jobs and regional development, the extent to which jobs materialise will depend on advancements in automation and speed of adoption. Nevertheless, there would also be a near doubling of environmental impacts from primary material production – e.g. GHGs, acidification, eutrophication, land use, and aquatic and terrestrial toxicity (see Table 3.1) (OECD, 2019[1]). This would also place the Paris goals out of reach, undermining the prospects of well-being for future generations.

Avoiding these losses in well-being – and a future where mistakes from the last century are repeated – entails a readjustment of heavy industry's priorities. Heavy industry will still need to maintain production while caring for workers, but this should not occur at the expense of other aspects of well-being, notably limiting climate change; maintaining a healthy and safe environment; and sustainably using the planet's resources, such as energy, land, water and raw materials.

The priorities outlined above are unattainable for heavy industry in the context of the present emission-intensive linear economy. A holistic shift towards a net-zero, circular and resource-efficient economy is essential. Such an economy aims to reach net-zero GHG emissions by the middle of the century, and "to keep products, components and materials in the economy for as long as possible, trying to eliminate waste and virgin resource inputs," (McCarthy, Dellink and Bibas, 2018[24]). Crucially, each of these shifts is imperative and additive: decarbonisation of production is needed *in addition to* circularity and resource efficiency. Transforming the economy will take a lot of time, since the behaviour of billions of consumers and producers – as well as end-use sectors for industrial products (e.g. construction standards) – will need to change. Moreover, the downgrading of recycled material brings qualitative and quantitative losses, requiring additional primary materials to meet increasing demand (e.g. airplanes require purer aluminium than food cans). In addition, some materials presently in use are not immediately available for re-use and recycling (e.g. buildings have life cycles lasting decades). New primary materials will therefore continue to be needed to satisfy continual demand (van Ewijk, 2018[25]), meaning that heavy industry needs to decarbonise production.

A number of routes exist on both the demand and supply sides to decarbonise heavy industry. With respect to the two most intensive sectors, i.e. iron/steel and concrete/cement, the Energy Transitions Commission (Energy Transitions Commission, 2018[26]) estimates that:

- Up to 38% of iron and steel emissions could be reduced through demand management (greater and better scrap recycling, redesigning products for materials efficiency and circularity); up to 20% through improvements in energy efficiency (re-use of high-pressure gas to power other equipment, coke dry quenching, closure of inefficient plants); and up to 100% through decarbonisation technologies (scrap-based electric arc furnaces, contingent on the availability of low-GHG electricity; natural gas-based direct reduced iron (transition); hydrogen-based direct reduced iron; carbon capture and storage [CCS]; and direct molten oxide electrolysis of iron ore).
- Up to 34% of CO_2 emissions from cement and concrete could be reduced through demand management (i.e. designing buildings more efficiently, recycling un-hydrated concrete, re-using concrete and substituting timber for concrete); 10% through energy efficiency (e.g. switching to dry kilns, multistage cyclone heaters and decreasing the clinker-to-cement ratio); and the rest from decarbonisation technologies (e.g. gas, biomass/waste heat generation and kiln electrification).

In a scenario consistent with a 2°C goal, projected emissions from power generation will decrease by around 90% relative to 2010, compared to only around 50% from industry. Consequently, most of the additional emission reductions required to meet a 1.5°C goal, rather than a 2°C goal, would require more challenging emission reductions from industry and other demand sectors (buildings and transport), which are likely to have much higher marginal costs (Luderer et al., 2018[27]).

Nevertheless, changing the course of production brings a very real, short-term loss of well-being for some individuals, i.e. heavy industry employees. If all regions of the world implemented a carbon tax of 50 USD (US dollars) per tonne today, the mining and fossil-fuel sector would lose about 8% jobs in OECD countries and 6% in non-OECD countries, while construction, chemicals and other heavy industries would lose less than 5% globally (Chateau, Bibas and Lanzi, 2018[28]). In absolute terms, the total number of jobs lost in such a scenario would only amount to 21 million, on par with the expected 30 million global job losses from automation by 2030. The bigger threat to these communities is automation rather than decarbonisation, yet jobs will also be added by this shift in production. For example, almost 6 million jobs can be created globally by moving away from the linear economy to embrace the recycling, re-use, remanufacture, rental and longer durability of goods (ILO, 2018[29]).

Even though a relatively small number of jobs may be lost from this transition and it may even be possible to reallocate workers, real people work directly in these emission- and resource-intensive industries. In a typical myopic focus on mitigation, changing production often means confronting a reality where these people are out of work and communities are potentially unravelling. The key of the well-being lens lies in carefully designed policies and the right measurement tools that inform the design of these policies addressing these workers and communities. The well-being lens prompts decision makers to evaluate these costs, identifies these communities and establishes proper measures to monitor and improve policies. The next section provides an example of an indicator that can signal "at-risk" communities.

Other priorities for heavy industry – maintaining production while caring for workers, increasing resource efficiency or reducing pollution – can help limit climate change and achieve two-way alignment. For example, Kalundborg Symbiosis, the first functioning example of industrial symbiosis (i.e. greater resource efficiency), includes several (public and private) facilities that exchange energy, water and materials in closed loops. In 2015, Kalundborg reduced its use of drinking water by 3.6 million m^3 and 87 000t of materials (gypsum, fly ash, sulphur, sand and ethanol), while reducing emissions by 635 $MtCO_2$ (equivalent to the per capita CO_2 of 75 000 Danes) (Ellen MacArthur Foundation, 2017[30]). Table 3.2 explains further how these other priorities can align with climate change mitigation, and how potential trade-offs with climate change mitigation may arise when pursuing these other priorities.

Table 3.2. Potential two-way alignment benefits from applying the well-being lens to heavy industry

Other policy priority	Contributing to limiting climate change	
	Generating synergies	Avoiding/reducing trade-offs
Maintaining production while caring for workers	Removing market distortions and import bans on scrap enhances market efficiency for heavy industry products. This helps close inefficient emission-intensive plants and enables greater use of scrap in production, lowering direct emissions (e.g. electric arc furnace [EAF] in steel making vs. blast furnace-basic oxygen furnace [BF-BOF).	Active labour-market policies will help transition towards other opportunities for jobs and communities whose livelihood centres on inefficient emission-intensive plants in heavy industry, to prevent protecting jobs at the expense of mitigation.
Maintain a healthy and safe environment	Maintaining a healthy and safe environment to decrease air, water and soil pollution from heavy industry by using CCS, improving the energy efficiency of plants and electrification (e.g. EAF with low-carbon energy), and identifying alternative heat sources also reduces GHGs.	Appropriately assessing the costs and benefits of different technologies to reduce air pollution can prevent options that reduce pollution but exacerbate CO_2,, and vice versa. For example, building CCS facilities where the production, processing and transport of iron, steel, aluminium, cement, etc., and construction of buildings to build the facility outweigh the benefits.
Sustainably manage the planet's resources	Increasing resource efficiency through industrial symbiosis (e.g. Kalundborg) re-uses waste and by-products from one process in another (e.g. fly ash from iron and steel in cement) reducing waste, and requires fewer resources (e.g. water, energy). All of this leads to better management of the planet's resources, while lowering emissions.	Reintegrating informal waste pickers into institutionalised solid-waste management avoids competition between informal recycling and solid-waste management, ensuring access to scrap. In turn, greater use of scrap in heavy industry (e.g. EAF in steelmaking vs BF-BOF) lowers emissions.

3.3. Indicators for monitoring heavy industry's contribution to well-being

Section 3.2 called for expanding heavy industry's priorities beyond **maintaining production and caring for workers**. Failure to do so creates a risk of perpetuating – and even worsening – future losses of well-being. This expanded set of priorities includes **limiting climate change**, **maintaining a healthy and safe environment**, and **sustainably using the planet's resources**. Achieving these priorities means the upcoming era needs net-zero, circular and resource-efficient production. In this shift, policy makers need indicators to track whether heavy industry actually attains these priorities and is producing what society needs, without undermining well-being, limiting climate change, etc.

Although this report is far from the first to propose a set of indicators that depict a fuller picture of well-being, it is one of the first to do so at a sectoral level. The SDGs and the OECD well-being framework laid the groundwork for **well-being priorities and indicators at level of the whole economy**. In fact, the priorities defined here noticeably link with those in these existing frameworks. Table 3.3 lists these priorities, mapping them to relevant goals in the OECD well-being framework and SDGs. This section walks through these well-being priorities for heavy industry step by step and proposes **indicators that can help translate these goals into measurable outcomes**. It also discusses the relationship between the indicators proposed and the existing indicators in both the SDGs and the OECD well-being framework. This list of indicators is not exhaustive; rather, it suggests the types of indicators that could be useful and the type of data enhancements needed.

The present section differs from a traditional industrial mitigation report. The indicators proposed do not provide detailed measures for drivers of emissions, which would simply repeat many years of work performed by other institutions. Instead, the section focuses on indicators that can measure outcomes relative to different policy goals to grasp the interactions between different facets of well-being, along with their impacts. Using these types of indicators – especially simultaneously – will help, for instance, identify opportunities for two-way alignment, by better capturing the potential positive and negative impacts of different decarbonisation pathways on multiple well-being priorities.

Table 3.3. Policy priorities for heavy industry and their link to the SDGs and the OECD well-being framework

Policy priority	SDG goal and target	OECD Well-being domain	OECD Well-being dimension
Maintain production while caring for workers	8.5. By 2030, achieve full and productive employment and decent work for all women and men.	Future well-being: resources.	Economic capital.
	9.2. Promote inclusive and sustainable industrialization and, by 2030, significantly raise industry's share of employment and gross domestic product, in line with national circumstances, and double its share in least developed countries.		
	12.2. By 2030, achieve the sustainable management and efficient use of natural resources.	Material quality.	Jobs and earnings.
Limit climate change	13. Take urgent action to combat climate change and its impacts.	Future well-being: resources.	Natural capital.
Maintain a healthy and safe environment	3.9. By 2030, substantially reduce the number of deaths and illnesses from hazardous chemicals and air, water and soil pollution and contamination.	Future well-being: resources.	Natural capital.
	9.2. Promote inclusive and sustainable industrialization and, by 2030, significantly raise industry's share of employment and gross domestic product, in line with national circumstances, and double its share in least developed countries.		
	15.5. Take urgent action to reduce the degradation of natural habitats.	Future well-being: resources.	Economic capital.
Sustainable management of the planet's resources	6.4. By 2030, substantially increase water-use efficiency across sectors.	Future well-being: resources.	Natural capital.
	8.4. Improve progressively, through 2030, global resource efficiency in consumption and production.		
	12.5. By 2030, substantially reduce waste generation through prevention, reduction, recycling and re-use.		
	15.3. By 2030, strive to achieve a land degradation-neutral world.		

3.3.1. Maintaining production while caring for workers

The previous section called for heavy industry to shift towards net-zero, circular and resource-efficient production. This is echoed in SDG 9.2, "promote inclusive and sustainable industrialization and, by 2030, significantly raise industry's share of employment and gross domestic product, in line with national circumstances, and double its share in least developed countries", and the OECD well-being framework dimension on "future resources", which includes economic and natural capital (Table 3.3). To incentivise "sustainable industrialisation", current measures of success need to be adjusted (as argued in Chapter 1). Productivity measures need to value environmental quality and environmental inputs explicitly, which would create two-way alignment (at least in terms of measurement) between the goals of production on the one hand, and limiting climate change, sustainably using the planet's resources, and maintaining a healthy and safe environment on the other hand. Historically, increases in productivity lead to significant increases in CO_2 and other pollutants (Empora and Mamuneas, 2011[31]; Kalaitzidakis, Mamuneas and Stengos, 2018[32]), signalling that productivity measures do not fully capture well-being.

Neither the SDGs nor the OECD well-being framework offers a viable indicator as an alternative to traditional measures of productivity. The key indicator for SDG 9.2, value added of manufacturing as a proportion of GDP, measures a given industry's contribution to the economy using the System of National Accounts, although there is ongoing effort to adequately account for the environment in this through the System of Environment and Economic Accounts. However, there exists an incongruity in the existing SDG framework between the stated goal of SDG 9.2 and the chosen indicator. Therefore, if this indicator is used in decision-making, it will lead to unsustainable choices that perpetuate losses of well-being. The OECD well-being framework does not propose an alternative measure of productivity.

The environmentally adjusted multifactor productivity (EAMFP) indicator in the Green Growth Database (covering 51 countries since 1990) fills gaps in existing frameworks and addresses the shortcomings of existing measures. Traditionally, multifactor productivity (also known as total factor productivity) measures the share of output that cannot be explained by either labour or capital inputs. Economists view this as a measure of efficiency, i.e. technological innovation, even though it has been criticised. By contrast, the EAMFP indicator measures the share of output that cannot be attributed to a given set of inputs, while accounting for the consumption of natural resources and environmental outputs (Cárdenas Rodríguez, Haščič and Souchier, 2018[33]). EAMFP is not the only indicator that adjusts productivity measures; it is merely an example of the types of indicators that could be useful.

First, the EAMFP indicator includes the private cost to firms to *extract* the natural capital (by including resource rents) of 14 subsoil assets of fossil fuels (hard coal, soft coal, gas, oil) and minerals (gold, iron ore, lead, nickel, phosphate, bauxite, copper, silver, tin and zinc), encompassing many of the key raw materials used by heavy industry. Valuing the extraction of raw materials enables policy makers to compare the costs of primary materials versus secondary materials more accurately, leading to better management of finite natural resources. Using this valuation, it is feasible to calculate the amount of GDP growth due to the extraction of natural capital. As a result, the indicator helps manage the planet's resources sustainably, fostering two-way alignment between these priorities. Other forms of natural capital, such as land or water, could also be included. Cárdenas Rodríguez, Haščič and Souchier (Cárdenas Rodríguez, Haščič and Souchier, 2018[33]) provide further details on methodology.

Additionally, the EAMFP indicator values undesirable outputs such as air emissions, including three GHGs – CO_2, CH_4, N_2O – and five air pollutants – sulphur oxides, nitrogen oxides, PM_{10}, carbon monoxide and non-methane volatile organic compounds. Calculating a shadow price of the number of foregone units needed to reduce one unit of pollution allows an estimation of pollution-adjusted GDP growth, a critical facet of maintaining a healthy and safe environment, and limiting climate change. This contrasts with traditional measures of multifactor productivity, which do not explicitly value pollution or emissions because these frequently unpriced.

If productivity measures fully value environmental quality and the natural environment, then production will shift away from emission-intensive and resource-intensive facilities, and jobs will be lost. Therefore, an accompanying indicator to the EAMFP – or similar measures – identifies regions at risk of "losing" from sustainable production to better target policies aiming to help these communities and workers. The indicators for SDG 8.5 (relative to the unemployment rate) and SDG 9.2 (relative to the share of employment in manufacturing) lack the granularity to evaluate effectively which policies should be used to gauge the impacts of net-zero, circular and resource-efficient production. One indicator to track this is the U.S. Cluster Mapping Project, a national initiative that amalgamates over 50 million open-data records on industry clusters in the United States. Led by Harvard University, the U.S. Department of Commerce and the U.S. Economic Development Administration, the project groups industries into clusters, e.g. Biopharmaceutical cluster (US Cluster Mapping, 2019[34]). A Cluster Dashboard provides data on economic performance, geographic presence, and sub-cluster and industry composition. The geographic presence of any sub-cluster can be shown at the level of the state, economic areas, metro/micropolitan areas and counties. The economic indicators include level of specialisation, absolute level of employment, employment growth rate, job creation, annual wage, annual wage growth rate, number of establishments, establishment growth rate, establishment formation, patent count (indicator for innovation) and patent growth rate. Figure 3.3 is an example of changes in employment (number of jobs) between 2010 and 2016 for iron and steel forging (a sub-cluster of upstream metals manufacturing) in the United States, by state using data from US Cluster Mapping.

Figure 3.3. Changes in employment from 2010 to 2016 by state in iron and steel mill forging

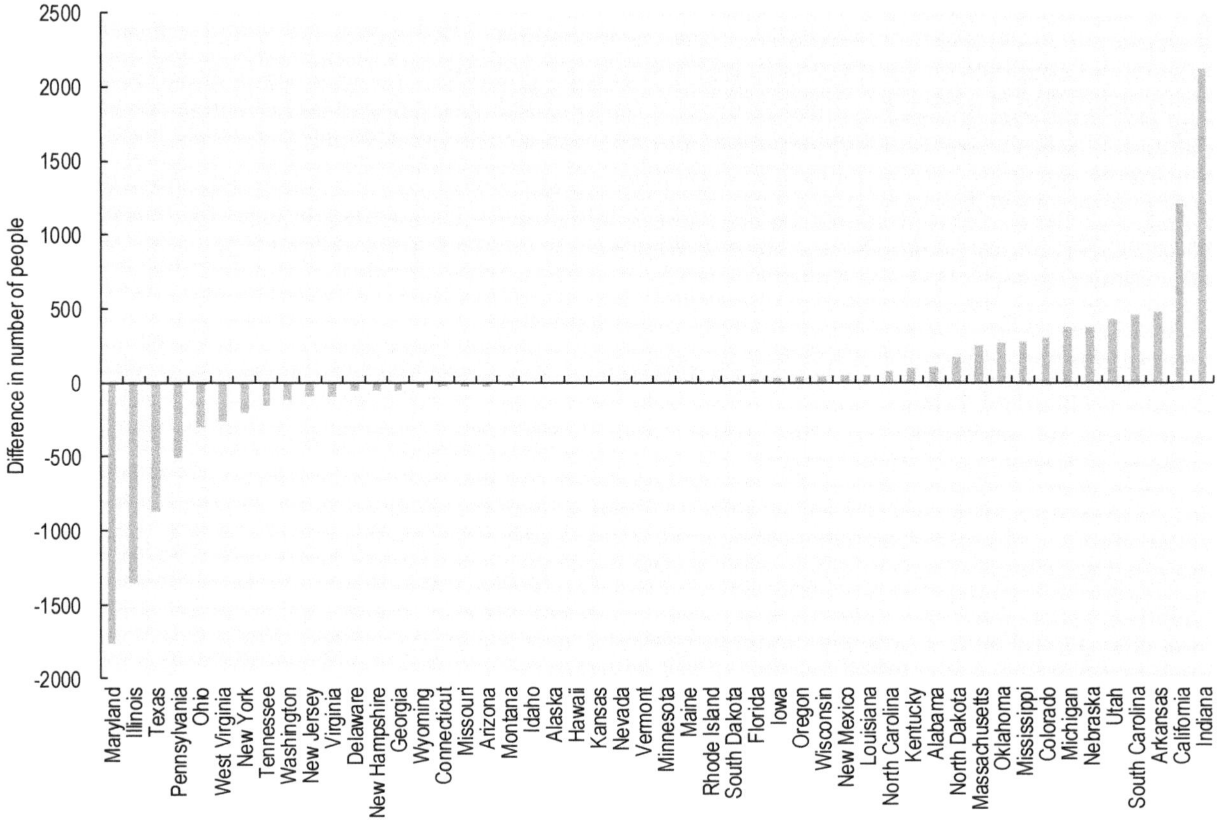

Source: (US Cluster Mapping, 2019[34])

StatLink https://doi.org/10.1787/888933993066

Table 3.4 summarises the key points from the section above. The blue columns show the well-being priority for heavy industry, the corresponding SDGs, and the well-being dimension and domain (introduced in Table 3.3), as well as the indicators attached to these frameworks, to reveal how the EAMFP indicator and the Cluster Map can complement them.

Table 3.4. Summary table: Indicators for monitoring progress in maintaining production while carrying for workers and links to SDGs and OECD well-being framework

Policy priority	Proposed indicators	SDG goal and target	SDG indicators	OECD Well-being domain/dimension	OECD Well-being indicators
Maintaining production while caring for workers	EAMFP (from the Green Growth Indicators).	9.2. Promote inclusive and sustainable industrialisation.	9.2.1. Manufacturing value added.	Future well-being: resources. Economic capital.	No measure of productivity included.
		12.2. By 2030, achieve the sustainable management and efficient use of natural resources.	12.2.1. Material footprint. 12.2.2. Domestic material consumption.		
	Jobs, revenue and number of facilities in geographical clustering of heavy industries.	8.5. By 2030, achieve full and productive employment and decent work for all women and men.	8.5.1. Average hourly earnings. 8.5.2. Unemployment rate.	Material quality. Jobs and earnings.	Employment rate.

3.3.2. Limiting climate change

Heavy industry needs to reach net-zero emissions by the middle of the 21st century. This is echoed in the framework for SDG 13, "take urgent action to combat climate change and its impacts", and the OECD well-being framework, which includes natural capital under the "future resources" dimension. Neither of these frameworks provides indicators on emissions from heavy industry. This section, therefore, suggests indicators of emissions from: a) energy use; and b) the processes used in the chemical and physical transformations undertaken by heavy industry. As a complement, a vast line of work explores the drivers of heavy industry emissions (which lies outside the scope of this chapter), e.g. *Tracking Industrial Energy Efficiency and CO_2 Emissions* (OECD/IEA, 2007[35]).

Estimating process emissions is challenging, since they vary according to the technology used during production and the plant's location. To calculate process GHGs per unit of GDP for each sub-sector and/or unit of physical output, the Intergovernmental Panel on Climate Change (IPCC) presents three methodologies: Tier 1, Tier 2 and Tier 3; accuracy increases with each tier. Tier 1 and Tier 2 use an output-based methodology of multiplying production volumes with emission factors. Tier 1 uses the default emission factors of the IPCC (IPCC, 2006[36]); Tier 2 adjusts these emission factors to country-specific values. Tier 3 is an input-based methodology that calculates emissions based on carbon inputs; this is a more demanding task, as it requires a material flow analysis of the entire production supply chain. Total GHGs per unit of physical output per industry helps gauge whether its emission intensity is decreasing over time. If possible, breaking emissions into non-CO_2 and CO_2 gases per unit of output would be valuable, given their different lifetime in the atmosphere (for further explanation, see Box 1.2, Chapter 1).

Emissions from energy use can be calculated based on electricity use per unit of GDP for each sub-sector and/or physical output (percentage of end-use energy if fossil-fuel data are lacking), multiplied by the emission intensity of electricity production (e.g. tonnes of GHG per kWh).

Even in isolation, the electricity use per unit of GDP for each sub-sector and/or physical output is useful to identify industries that are vulnerable to loss of competitiveness owing to increasing electricity prices. This indicator is also useful for utilities to balance demand response: it allows groups to collect information on existing prevention and control techniques, while integrating variable renewables into the grid and the electrification of end uses (e.g. heating and transport). Any significant imbalance between consumption and generation could cause grid instability or severe voltage fluctuations, and failures within the grid, affecting well-being (discussed in detail in Chapter 2 on electricity). The electricity consumption of heavy industry is already a useful tool to help balance consumption and generation needs.

Table 3.5 summarises the key points from the section above: the well-being priority for heavy industry, its corresponding SDGs, and the well-being dimension and domain (introduced in Table 3.3), as well as the indicators attached to these frameworks.

Table 3.5. Summary table: Indicators for monitoring progress in limiting climate change and links to SDGs and OECD well-being framework

Policy priority	Proposed indicators	SDG goal and target	SDG indicators	OECD Well-being Domain/ dimension	OECD Well-being indicators
Limiting climate change	GHGs from production (energy and process), CCUS rate.	13.2. Integrate climate change measures into national policies, strategies and planning.	13.2.1. Number of countries that have communicated the establishment or operationalisation of an integrated policy/strategy/plan.	Future well-being: resources. Natural capital	GHGs from domestic production

3.3.3. Maintaining a healthy and safe environment

A future well-being priority for heavy industry will be to maintain a healthy and safe environment in order to protect human health and biodiversity. This aligns with SDG 3.9, "substantially reduce the number of deaths and illnesses from pollution and contamination"; SDG 15.5, "take action to reduce the degradation of natural habitats, SDG 9.2; "promote inclusive and sustainable industrialization"; and SDG 12.4, "ensure the environmentally sound management of chemicals". The indicators for these SDGs and the OECD well-being framework measure mortality rates from pollutants or the absolute levels of pollution. Their drawback is the missing link to heavy industry – e.g. how much pollution comes from which facilities? This section proposes additional indicators to assess the quality of heavy industry facilities and their contribution pollution.

Best available techniques (BATs, not to be confused with best available technology) are a key tool to prevent and control pollution from industrial facilities. A growing number of governments use BATs to establish legally binding emission-limit values in industrial permits for emissions to air, water and soil. BATs are state-of-the-art techniques for emission prevention and control, developed at a scale that allows implementation under technically and economically viable conditions. A BAT-based approach to environmental permitting for industrial installations allows setting conditions for environmental permits that are rooted in evidence and based on participatory decision-making, and are thus more likely to result in a high level of human health and environmental protection. To establish BATs, governments typically set up sector-specific technical working groups involving stakeholders from government, industry and environmental non-governmental organisations. The groups collect information on existing prevention and control techniques, and conduct a thorough assessment of these techniques according to environmental, economic and technical criteria. This process results in a set of BATs and associated emission levels (presented as a range), which are published in best available techniques reference documents (BREFs). The key information contained in the BREFs serves as a basis for setting emission-limit values and other permit conditions for individual industrial installations (OECD, 2018[37]), measuring the level of compliance with BAT-based emission-limit values for a given heavy industry by monitoring the percentage of industrial facilities that meet these values. The assumption is that these values are stringent. For further information, see *Measuring the Effectiveness of BAT Policies* (OECD, 2019[38]) and *Best Available Techniques for Preventing and Controlling Industrial Pollution* (OECD, 2018[37]).

The next set of indicators measures the pollutants from heavy industrial facilities. The EU Pollutant Release and Transfer Register (E-PRTR)[2] is a front runner in this respect. Facilities must report annual data to a national repository; these data are then recorded in the E-PRTR. The database includes more than 30 000 industrial facilities, covering 65 economic activities within 9 industrial sectors: energy, production and processing of metals, mineral industry, chemical industry, waste and wastewater management, paper and wood production and processing, animal and vegetable products from the food and beverage sector, and other activities. The register tracks 91 pollutants released into air and water, including GHGs and other gases, heavy metals, pesticides, chlorinated organic substances, other organic substances and inorganic substances. This granularity helps identify particular facilities that harm the environment, and potentially harm human health and biodiversity indirectly, signalling where to target policies.

Table 3.6 summarises the key points from the section above: the well-being priority for heavy industry, its corresponding SDGs, and the well-being dimension and domain (introduced in Table 3.3), as well as the indicators attached to these frameworks.

Table 3.6. Summary table: Indicators for monitoring progress in maintaining a healthy and safe environment and links to SDGs and OECD well-being framework

Policy priority	Proposed indicators	SDG goal and target	SDG indicators	OECD Well-being Domain/ dimension	OECD Well-being indicator
Maintain a healthy and safe environment	Annual pollution by facility of air, water, soil by facility.	3.9. By 2030, substantially reduce the number of deaths and illnesses from hazardous chemicals and air, water and soil pollution and contamination.	3.9.1. - 3.9.3. Mortality rate attributed to household and ambient air pollution; water; unintentional poisoning.	Future well-being: resources. Natural capital.	Exposure to $PM_{2.5.}$
		15.5. Take urgent action to reduce the degradation of natural habitats.	15.5.1. Red List Index.		
	% of facilities meeting BATs.	9.2. Promote inclusive and sustainable industrialisation.	n/a	Future well-being: resources. Economic capital.	n/a

3.3.4. Sustainable management of the planet's resources

Heavy industry is one among many users of the planet's resources, including raw materials, land, water and energy. Indicators on heavy industry's use of these resources is beneficial, on the one hand to avoid competition between sectors in a future of scarce resources, and on the other hand to improve the circularity and resource efficiency of production. These ambitions overlap with the goals of the existing frameworks and more specifically SDG 8.4, "improve progressively, through 2030, global resource efficiency in consumption and production", and the OECD well-being framework's "natural capital" domain under the "future resources" dimension. This subsection proceeds by resource to fill in gaps in these existing frameworks.

Materials usage – raw, primary and secondary

Part of the shift that needs to occur in heavy industry is to decrease the use of raw materials as much as possible (SDG 8.4) while recognising it will not drop to zero in the near future, and increase the use of secondary materials (SDG 12.5, "by 2030, substantially reduce waste generation through prevention, reduction, recycling and re-use"). Producing outputs based on secondary materials is less emission-intensive than outputs from primary materials, which explains why secondary materials are candidates for decarbonisation (as mentioned in the previous section). In addition, processing of secondary materials causes less pollution, maintaining environmental quality and creating two-way alignment across heavy industry's priorities (OECD, 2019[1]). While the indicators adequately assess the use of raw materials and the production of waste, they do not capture the circularity of resources, or whether some waste could be repurposed.

A number of institutions, including UN Environment, the OECD and the European Union, collect data for indicators related to material flow analysis, expanding on the indicators already proposed for SDG 8.4. The aim is to describe the interaction of the domestic economy with the natural environment in terms of the flow of materials, seen as material "inputs" and "outputs". The Global Material Flows Database[3] produced by UN Environment's International Resource Panel calculates a set of indicators, definitions and existing data. The exhaustiveness of these (readily available) datasets extends beyond domestic material consumption and the material footprint.

SDG 12.5.1 uses indicators for the national recycling rate and tonnes of material recycled. However, none of these indicators tell us whether waste is being re-used (a measure of circularity in the economy); what kinds of waste are being produced, and by whom (e.g. heavy industry); or whether some waste that is being disposed of could be re-used for other purposes.

A novel indicator used by the European Union is the circular material use (CMU) rate,[4] which is "the share of material recovered and fed back into the economy – thus saving extraction of primary raw materials – in overall material use" on an annual basis. This indicator can be further disaggregated by material. It is especially valuable as it actually evaluates the capacity of the economy to re-use these materials and signals which heavy industries use more scrap (since there is disaggregation by material).

Indicators on the quantity and type of waste produced could help heavy industry and other industries minimise and re-use waste. A best practice is California's Department of Resources Recycling and Recovery (CalRecycle), which runs a database[5] that expands on the SDGs by measuring disposal amounts (e.g. landfilled, imported, exported) over time at varying levels of disaggregation at the county, facility and jurisdiction levels. The database also measures exports of recycled materials and biomass.

In addition, CalRecycle tracks what exactly characterises the waste, to understand what various actors could re-use. The "Waste Characterisation Tool"[6] helps jurisdictions understand the types and amounts of materials disposed in and diverted from California's waste stream. The State of California collects waste samples from three sources – residential, commercial/industrial and self-hauled – that would have been put in landfills. It then sorts samples into components in order to understand what is actually being thrown away. These data are then used to *estimate* the potential disposal and diversion rate (for recycling) by business group, material type and residence. Material types include several originating from heavy industry, including metal (e.g. aluminium, other ferrous, other non-ferrous); special waste (e.g. ash); inert and other (e.g. concrete, gypsum board, other wood waste); household hazardous waste (e.g. batteries, vehicle and equipment materials); glass; electronics; and paper. After characterising the waste streams, jurisdictions can try to divert this waste into secondary material usage for heavy industry, when applicable.

Water

Heavy industry uses water, which could be problematic in a resource-scarce future. For example, during a drought in South Africa, local municipalities cut off industries from the local water supply, which prompted these facilities to pursue greater resource and explore alternative ways to access and re-use water. To ensure a steady supply of materials and fuels, and sustainably use the planet's resources, indicators tracking water consumption can signal industries where greater resource efficiency is needed. This aligns with SDG 6.4, which aims by 2030, substantially increase water-use efficiency across sectors by tracking two indicators: change in water-use efficiency and percentage of freshwater withdrawal as a proportion of resources. A valuable indicator from the Food and Agricultural Organization is the value added divided by the water used (USD per m^3) over time by ISIC code.[7]

Land

In the future, sectors will increasingly compete for land: energy needs land for solar panels and wind farms, agriculture needs it to feed our rising populations and for bioenergy crops, and industry – and extractive industries – need it to produce materials and fuels. Extractive industries – which provide the inputs for heavy industry – use land for different purposes. A particular concern is their conversion of forested land (e.g. to extract Bauxite in Malaysia), since this exacerbates climate change by both the resulting direct emissions and by removing a carbon sink.

Table 3.7 summarises the key points from the section above: the well-being priority for heavy industry, its corresponding SDGs, and the well-being dimension and domain (introduced in Table 3.3), as well as the indicators attached to these frameworks.

Table 3.7. Summary table: Indicators for monitoring progress in sustainable management of the planet's resources and links to SDGs and OECD well-being framework

Policy priority	Proposed indicators	SDG goal and target	SDG indicators	OECD Well-being Domain/dimension	OECD Well-being indicators
Sustainable management of the planet's resources	• Material flow indicators. • CMU rate. • Disposal rates by jurisdiction, year and actor. • Waste characterisation indicators. • % of water resources abstracted for industrial use. • % land use driven by raw materials extraction.	8.4. Improve progressively, through 2030, global resource efficiency in consumption and production.	8.4.1. Material footprint 8.4.2. Domestic material consumption.	Future well-being: resources. Natural capital.	Forest area.
		12.5. By 2030, substantially reduce waste generation through prevention, reduction, recycling and re-use.	12.5.1. National recycling rate, tonnes of material recycled.		
		6.4. By 2030, substantially increase water-use efficiency across sectors.	6.4.1. Change in water-use efficiency 6.4.2 % freshwater withdrawal as a proportion of resources.		
		15.3. By 2030, strive to achieve a land degradation-neutral world.	15.3.1. Proportion of land that is degraded over total land area.		

3.4. Conclusion and looking ahead

This chapter argued that heavy industry should broaden its priorities to safeguard current and future well-being. It should maintain production while addressing the needs of workers and communities, limiting climate change, ensuring a healthy and safe environment, and sustainably managing the planet's resources. To achieve these priorities, heavy industry needs to adopt net-zero, circular and resource-efficient production. The last section identified a number of indicators – e.g. the EAMFP and the CMU rate – that reflect these multiple priorities, in order to evaluate the synergies and trade-offs of different actions and strategies.

The foundation of any policy package for decarbonisation is the creation of transition plans, set within the context of wider economic transformations and progress towards a net-zero, resource-efficient and circular economy. Constructing these plans with relevant stakeholders from heavy industry builds on their expertise to identify *feasible* pathways towards this (Bataille et al., 2018[6]; Davis et al., 2018[7]). These transition plans can then direct needed policies and further investments to facilitate heavy industry's transition. However, to do this, they must be built on a set of core policies, including carbon pricing; targeted research, design and development; and resource efficiency programmes. Finally, they must be accompanied by a number of enabling policies, including removal of market distortions and trade barriers, and better classifications of trade, BATs and waste management/reduction.

References

Bataille, C. et al. (2018), "A review of technology and policy deep decarbonization pathway options for making energy-intensive industry production consistent with the Paris Agreement", *Journal of Cleaner Production*, Vol. 187, pp. 960-973, http://dx.doi.org/10.1016/J.JCLEPRO.2018.03.107. [6]

Cárdenas Rodríguez, M., I. Haščič and M. Souchier (2018), "Environmentally Adjusted Multifactor Productivity methodology and empirical results for oecd and G20 countries", *OECD Green Growth Papers*, No. 2018/02, OECD, Paris, http://www.oecd.org/greengrowth (accessed on 13 March 2019). [33]

Chateau, J., R. Bibas and E. Lanzi (2018), "Impacts of Green Growth Policies on Labour Markets and Wage Income Distribution: A General Equilibrium Application to Climate and Energy Policies", *OECD Environment Working Papers*, No. 137, OECD Publishing, Paris, https://dx.doi.org/10.1787/ea3696f4-en. [28]

Davis, S. et al. (2018), "Net-zero emissions energy systems.", *Science*, Vol. 360/6396, http://dx.doi.org/10.1126/science.aas9793. [7]

Ellen MacArthur Foundation (2017), *Effective Industrial Symbiosis*, https://www.ellenmacarthurfoundation.org/case-studies/effective-industrial-symbiosis. [30]

Empora, N. and T. Mamuneas (2011), *The Effect of Emissions on U.S. State Total Factor Productivity Growth*, https://ideas.repec.org/a/ren/journl/v3y2011i2p149-172.html. [31]

Energy Transitions Commission (2018), *Reaching zero carbon emissions from Steel*, Energy Transitions Commission, http://www.energy-transitions.org/sites/default/files/ETC_MissionPossible_FullReport.pdf. [26]

Farooq, M., F. Anwar and U. Rashid (2008), "Appraisal of heavy metal contents in different vegetables grown in the vicinity of an industrial area", *Pakistan Journal Botany*, Vol. 40/5, pp. 2099-2106, https://s3.amazonaws.com/academia.edu.documents/30910209/PJB40%285%292099.pdf?AWSAccessKeyId=AKIAIWOWYYGZ2Y53UL3A&Expires=1550489659&Signature=IE5KHGez%2FwCDRul0tMRrLShA1dc%3D&response-content-disposition=inline%3B%20filename%3DAppraisal_of_heavy_metal_co (accessed on 18 February 2019). [22]

Giam, X., J. Olden and D. Simberloff (2018), "Impact of coal mining on stream biodiversity in the US and its regulatory implications", *Nature Sustainability*, Vol. 1/4, pp. 176-183, http://dx.doi.org/10.1038/s41893-018-0048-6. [23]

Gunatilake SK (2015), *Methods of Removing Heavy Metals from Industrial Wastewater*, http://www.jmess.org (accessed on 18 February 2019). [19]

Hoesly, R. et al. (2018), "Historical (1750–2014) anthropogenic emissions of reactive gases and aerosols from the Community Emissions Data System (CEDS)", *Geoscientific Model Development*, Vol. 11/1, pp. 369-408, https://doi.org/10.5194/gmd-11-369-2018. [3]

IEA (2019), *World Energy Balances Database*, https://www.iea.org/statistics/balances/. [2]

ILO (2018), *World Employment and Social Outlook 2018 – Greening with jobs*, ILO , Geneva, http://www.ilo.org/publns. (accessed on 13 March 2019). [29]

ILO (2015), *Guidelines for a just transition towards environmentally sustainable economies and societies for all*, http://www.ilo.org/publns (accessed on 8 August 2019). [15]

IPCC (2018), *Global Warming of 1.5°C. An IPCC Special Report on the impacts of global warming of 1.5°C above pre-industrial levels and related global greenhouse gas emission pathways, in the context of strengthening the global response to the threat of climate change, sustainable development, and efforts to eradicate poverty*, IPCC, https://report.ipcc.ch/sr15/pdf/sr15_spm_final.pdf. [5]

IPCC (2006), *Emission Factor Database*, IPCC, https://www.ipcc-nggip.iges.or.jp/EFDB/find_ef.php?ipcc_code=2&ipcc_level=0. [36]

Kalaitzidakis, P., T. Mamuneas and T. Stengos (2018), "Greenhouse Emissions and Productivity Growth", *Journal of Risk and Financial Management*, Vol. 11/3, p. 38, http://dx.doi.org/10.3390/jrfm11030038. [32]

Kherat, S. (2019), "The Future of AI in Heavy Industry – Agriculture, Construction, Mining, and Beyond", https://emerj.com/ai-podcast-interviews/future-ai-in-heavy-industry/. [13]

Leung, A. et al. (2008), "Heavy Metals Concentrations of Surface Dust from e-Waste Recycling and Its Human Health Implications in Southeast China", *Environment, Science and Technology*, Vol. 42/7, http://dx.doi.org/10.1021/es071873x. [20]

Luderer, G. et al. (2018), "Residual fossil CO2 emissions in 1.5–2 °C pathways", *Nature Climate Change*, Vol. 8/7, pp. 626-633, http://dx.doi.org/10.1038/s41558-018-0198-6. [27]

McCarthy, A., R. Dellink and R. Bibas (2018), "The Macroeconomics of the Circular Economy Transition: A Critical Review of Modelling Approaches", *OECD Environment Working Papers*, No. 130, OECD Publishing, Paris, https://dx.doi.org/10.1787/af983f9a-en. [24]

Mercier, F. and D. Mabashi (2019), "Steel Market Developments", *STI Working Paper Series*, OECD, http://dx.doi.org/JT03447063. [11]

Mogren, C. and J. Trumble (2010), "The impacts of metals and metalloids on insect behavior", *Entomologia Experimentalis et Applicata*, http://dx.doi.org/10.1111/j.1570-7458.2010.00967.x. [18]

OECD (2019), *Best Available Techniques (BAT) for Preventing and Controlling Industrial Pollution Activity 3: Measuring the Effectiveness of BAT Policies*, OECD, https://www.oecd.org/chemicalsafety/risk-management/measuring-the-effectiveness-of-best-available-techniques-policies.pdf. [38]

OECD (2019), *Global Material Resources Outlook to 2060: Economic Drivers and Environmental Consequences*, OECD Publishing, Paris, https://dx.doi.org/10.1787/9789264307452-en. [1]

OECD (2018), *Best Available Techniques for Preventing and Controlling Industrial Pollution*, OECD, https://www.oecd.org/chemicalsafety/risk-management/approaches-to-establishing-best-available-techniques-around-the-world.pdf. [37]

OECD (2017), *The Land-Water-Energy Nexus: Biophysical and Economic Consequences*, OECD Publishing, Paris, https://dx.doi.org/10.1787/9789264279360-en. [16]

OECD/IEA (2019), *Material efficiency in clean energy transitions*, OECD/IEA, https://webstore.iea.org/material-efficiency-in-clean-energy-transitions. [9]

OECD/IEA (2007), *Tracking Industrial Energy Efficiency and CO2 Emissions*, International Energy Agency, Paris, https://www.iea.org/publications/freepublications/publication/tracking_emissions.pdf. [35]

Oxford Economics (2019), *How robots change the world: what automation really means for jobs and productivity*, Oxford Economics, http://resources.oxfordeconomics.com/how-robots-change-the-world. [14]

Silva, F. and G. Mattera (2018), "State enterprises in the steel sector", *OECD Science, Technology and Industry Policy Papers*, No. No. 53, OECD, Paris, https://www.oecd-ilibrary.org/docserver/2a8ad9cd-en.pdf?expires=1556613534&id=id&accname=guest&checksum=723964F9DAF5593087A0F61553ADD591 (accessed on 30 April 2019). [10]

Tang, W. et al. (2014), "Heavy metal accumulation by periphyton is related to eutrophication in the Hai River Basin, Northern China.", *PloS one*, Vol. 9/1, http://dx.doi.org/10.1371/journal.pone.0086458. [17]

US Cluster Mapping (2019), *Iron and Steel Mills and Forging Subcluster*, https://clustermapping.us/cluster/upstream_metal_manufacturing/subclusters/upstream_metal_manufacturing_iron_and_steel_mills_and_forging (accessed on 21 May 2019). [34]

van Ewijk, S. (2018), "An Introduction to Resource Efficiency: Concepts and Definitions", in Flachenecker, F. and J. Rentschler (eds.), *Investing in Resource Efficiency*, Springer International Publishing, http://dx.doi.org/10.007/978-3-319-78867-8. [25]

Wolff, N. et al. (2018), "Impacts of tropical deforestation on local temperature and human well-being perceptions", *Global Environmental Change*, Vol. 52, pp. 181-189, http://dx.doi.org/10.1016/j.gloenvcha.2018.07.004. [4]

World Steel Association (2019), "Working in the steel industry", World Steel Association, https://www.worldsteel.org/en/dam/jcr:597ab555-3b9e-4177-bcd3-604e4d6e5a2b/fact_Employment_2019.pdf. [12]

Wyns, T., I. Robson and G. Khnadekar (2018), *A Bridge Towards a Carbon Neutral Europe*, Institute for European Studies, https://www.ies.be/files/Industrial_Value_Chain_25sept.pdf. [8]

Zheng, N. et al. (2010), "Health risk assessment of heavy metal exposure to street dust in the zinc smelting district, Northeast of China", *Science of The Total Environment*, Vol. 408/4, pp. 726-733, http://dx.doi.org/10.1016/J.SCITOTENV.2009.10.075. [21]

Notes

1 https://www.resourcepanel.org/reports/global-material-flows-and-resource-productivity-database-link.

2 https://prtr.eea.europa.eu/#/static?cont=about.

3 http://www.resourcepanel.org/global-material-flows-database.

4 https://ec.europa.eu/eurostat/web/products-datasets/-/cei_srm030.

5 https://www.calrecycle.ca.gov/datacentral.

6 https://www2.calrecycle.ca.gov/WasteCharacterization/.

7 http://www.fao.org/nr/water/aquastat/data/query/index.html?lang=en.

4 Building sustainable dwellings, neighbourhoods and communities

This chapter analyses the residential sector from a well-being perspective and proposes a number of policy priorities that are consistent with wider well-being and sustainability goals. It explores several indicators that can improve policy makers' ability to monitor progress in delivering these priorities in the sector, as well as guide decisions to capture the benefits of a two-way alignment between climate and wider well-being goals, while also managing trade-offs. The chapter examines the relationship between the proposed indicators and the indicators used by the Sustainable Development Goals and the OECD Framework for Measuring Well-being and Progress.

The statistical data for Israel are supplied by and under the responsibility of the relevant Israeli authorities. The use of such data by the OECD is without prejudice to the status of the Golan Heights, East Jerusalem and Israeli settlements in the West Bank under the terms of international law.

In Brief

Building sustainable dwellings, neighbourhoods and communities

The residential sector is central to the low-emissions transition and also to public health, safety, security, comfort, affordability and equity outcomes. Buildings generated some 28% of global GHG emissions in 2017, and the residential sector accounted for 60% of these. The provision of services within buildings is a central driver of energy demand and emissions, mainly from space and water heating, cooling and cooking. These services are linked to other aspects of well-being, including clean energy access (SDG 7), which is necessary to prevent health risks. But many other characteristics of housing are also relevant. Its location, the availability and connections to services and opportunities (e.g. education, jobs), the surrounding environment (e.g. green spaces), and the form of a city (e.g. whether it is compact and fosters mixed land-use) all play a role in the sector's wider contribution to well-being and GHG emission reductions. These conditions help in particular to avoid sprawl, car dependence and transport emissions.

Decision-makers often have limited visibility across multiple scales or may pursue their goals in silos. Consequently, inappropriate policies create numerous unintended effects and miss important opportunities to improve quality of life and make ambitious contributions to climate change mitigation. Policies addressing housing affordability are often focused solely on dwellings, overlooking the availability of nearby opportunities and the affordability of other services (e.g. transport, energy, health care). This can perpetuate social segregation while increasing car dependency and transport emissions. At the city scale, densification strategies can overlook implications at the dwelling and neighbourhood level. Some examples are space reductions beyond minimum standards, limitations in water and transport infrastructure, or reductions in green space across the city. This could lead to detrimental impacts to well-being (e.g. health, equity) as well as off-setting any GHG emission reductions from densification.

By better capturing GHG mitigation, health, and equity benefits, a well-being approach can make a stronger case for solutions that align climate and other goals. For instance housing developments that are transit-friendly, and redevelopment projects that modernise and green deprived neighbourhoods, provide educational, leisure and employment facilities, and safer streets.

Developing new indicators to track progress and guide decisions is a key step towards redefining "good sustainable housing". Measuring accessibility from housing to different opportunities and mainstreaming it into decisions is crucial to developing a holistic view of equity and affordability that can unlock synergies between equity and climate goals. Moreover, there is a need to develop indicators that can help measure and monitor urban ecosystem services, as well as tools for eco-positive thinking and design, to support planning of nature-based solutions (NBS).

Policies, including stringent building standards and better schemes for building refurbishment, can encourage a move from marginal improvements to the use of best available practices, avoiding locking-in future emission levels that are incompatible with global climate goals. Equally important are actions at the level of neighbourhoods (e.g. eco-districts) and cities (e.g. land-use regulations and fiscal policies), which can have significant reinforcing effects, both positive and negative, with respect to one another and with respect to dwellings.

Infographic 4.1. Building sustainable dwellings, neighbourhoods and communities

The residential sector is central to a climate neutral future. But we need to look **beyond buildings** to ensure wider societal benefits such as public health, safety, comfort and security.

A well-being approach can make a stronger case for **sustainable solutions** like:

- Transit-friendly developments
- Safer streets
- Greening neighbourhoods

To accelerate climate action, we urgently need to:

Reframe measurement

- Incorporate accessibility and neighbourhood quality when defining "good housing"
- Expand monitoring of urban ecosystem services
- Create tools for eco-positive thinking and design

Refocus policies

- Shift from marginal improvements to best available practices
- Prioritise nature-based solutions
- Link dwelling-, neighbourhood- and city-level actions

4.1. Introduction

This report argues that a change in perspective – referred to as applying a **well-being lens** to policy making – is central to identifying, assessing and managing the synergies and trade-offs of policy actions, thus achieving a **two-way alignment** between climate and broader well-being objectives. Adopting a well-being lens implies first, that societal goals are defined in terms of well-being outcomes (including the risks and impacts of climate change) and are systematically reflected in decision-making across the economy. Second, it entails that decision-making considers multiple well-being objectives, rather than seeking to resolve a single issue (or a very narrow range of issues). Third, it requires a thorough understanding of the interrelations between the different elements of the system in which a policy intervenes (and thus between sectors in the economy), as well as of the flows and feedback loops within systems. This chapter explains how a well-being lens can be applied to the residential sector. It discusses policy goals that would be coherent with this approach and the type of measurement system (i.e. indicators for tracking progress and setting decision-making criteria) that would support it.

The built environment, i.e. "human-modified places such as homes, schools, workplaces, parks, industrial areas, farms, roads and highways" (Srinivasan, O'Fallon and Dearry, 2003[1]), affects well-being in several ways. On the one hand, it provides significant benefits, allowing human beings to be housed, to work and to carry out all kinds of daily activities. On the other hand, it can generate significant costs, including through pressures on ecosystems and the environment, which in turn jeopardise current and future human well-being. When it is degraded or has poor functional or aesthetic quality, the built environment can also significantly compromise well-being through its effects on physical and mental health, security and safety, etc. Buildings are an important part of the built environment and the residential or housing sector[1], the focus of this chapter, covers 70% of the total land use in cities (UN-Habitat, 2016[2]).

Access to housing has significant implications for well-being; thus, ensuring housing supply and access to housing has become an important policy focus. Nonetheless, housing can promote or hinder the attainment of wider sustainable goals in many other ways.

In 2017, the building sector was responsible for some 28% of global GHG emissions.[2] The residential sector accounted for some 60% of these emissions; the building sectors' main energy demand was related to space and water heating (34% and 19%) and cooking (20%) (IEA, 2018[3]) Energy demand for space cooling is rapidly growing and could triple if no further developments in energy efficiency are made (IEA, 2018[3]). In the residential sector, 35% of GHG emissions were direct, and 65% indirect; by contrast, 74% of emissions from commercial buildings were indirect, owing to electricity use (IEA, 2019[4]).

Housing affordability and stability are related to levels of stress and other mental health conditions (Robinson and Adams, 2008[5]). The quality of housing (i.e. a dwelling's internal and external physical structure), as well as its internal environment (e.g. adequate ventilation, moisture levels, internal air quality), are also key to human physical health and security. For instance, the use of fossil fuels for cooking and heating is linked to premature deaths stemming from poor indoor air quality, child poisoning and severe burns (WHO, 2018[6]). Overcrowding, for its part, is linked to risks of respiratory (and other) infections in children, as well as mental stress (Krieger and Higgins, 2002[7]). Moreover, the low energy efficiency levels of heating technologies could contribute to fuel poverty, i.e. the inability to maintain minimum standards of thermal comfort and safety (WHO, 2007[8]).

According to the Intergovernmental Panel on Climate Change (IPCC)'s Fifth Assessment report (AR5), energy use and related emissions from buildings could double or even triple by the middle of the century, driven by several different factors (Lucon et al., 2014[9]). Yet significant potential exists to reduce both energy use and emissions, producing substantial benefits in other dimensions of well-being – constrained, however, by strong barriers. Addressing these barriers could improve energy security, affordability and health, in addition to providing workplace productivity and new employment opportunities (Lucon et al., 2014[9]).

The residential sector's impacts on well-being (including climate change mitigation) are even broader when looking beyond building and house's characteristics and the internal services provided. Urban form,[3] as well as access to nearby opportunities (e.g. employment, health and education), neighbourhood characteristics (e.g. the quality of services, public space and infrastructure), and the transport connections between a given dwelling and different areas of a city all have relevant impacts on GHG emissions, health, safety, comfort, equity and overall well-being. For instance, planned housing as part of more compact and mixed land-use development, integrated with high-quality public and non-motorised transport facilities, can avoid sprawl and car dependence, reducing GHG emissions and air pollution, and improving quality of life.

The rest of this chapter is structured as follows: Section 4.2 argues that applying a well-being lens to the residential sector implies shifting towards a comprehensive perspective when defining "good housing". On the one hand, policy priorities should duly consider the multiple impacts on current and future well-being. On the other hand, considering the spatial implications of housing – from the micro and local scale of individual dwellings and homes, to the meso scale of neighbourhoods, the macro scale of cities, the regional scale and the wider ecosystems in which the urban agglomerations are embedded – is also crucial.

Section 4.3 argues that an adequate measurement system to guide policies and track progress is central to a holistic perspective of "good housing". Such a system is key to revealing synergies and trade-offs across policy priorities at different spatial scales. The section discusses a number of limitations of commonly used indicators for policy making. It suggests some potential changes and alternatives, and provides examples of potential use where possible.

4.2. Adopting a vision of "good housing" based on multiple priorities and spatial scales

The residential sector has a direct and indirect impact on overall well-being and the Sustainable Development Goals (SDGs), notably those related to public health, safety, security and comfort. Just having access to housing is key to human well-being, yet ensuring universal access to housing is still challenging across countries. Improving access to housing is therefore a widely shared policy priority, even in the richest countries (Salvi Del Pero, Adema and Ferraro, 2014[10]). Population growth and the rapid pace of urbanisation have been driving the continuous expansion of urban areas in developing countries, particularly the construction of residential buildings in cities. This is reflected in the fact that the overall area dedicated to buildings worldwide expanded at an even faster pace than global population between 2010 and 2017[4] (UNEP, 2018[11]). Despite this, 1 out of every 8 people (i.e. around 1 billion) in the world still lives in a slum[5] (UN Habitat, 2015[12]). In the OECD area, the growth of urban land area has not exceeded urban population growth since the early 2000s, a reflection that these countries have already undergone rapid urbanisation. However, the lack of regular access to housing is also a persistent problem across the OECD area, where 1-8 people out of 1 000 lack regular access to housing (Salvi Del Pero, Adema and Ferraro, 2014[10]).

Nonetheless, the importance of housing for well-being goes well beyond simply ensuring access to shelter. Indeed, policy decisions solely based on providing access to a dwelling can miss important opportunities to produce wider benefits, and may even create significant unintended negative effects (often resulting in higher GHG emissions). For example, several OECD countries have established access to affordable housing as one of the main priorities for the sector (Salvi Del Pero, Adema and Ferraro, 2014[10]) However, the policy instruments used (e.g. rental assistance for low-income families) often tend to ignore to what degree different dwellings have access to quality services and opportunities nearby, or at locations within easy reach. They also ignore the cost burden households face if living in different neighbourhoods. Thus, beneficiaries are frequently priced out of areas that offer higher quality of services and opportunities, and are better connected to the rest of the city (Acevedo-Garcia et al., 2016[13]). Also, the cost of housing in certain "lower-opportunity" neighbourhoods can be lower than in "higher-opportunity neighbourhoods", but the spending per family on associated services, e.g. health care, energy and transport, can still be higher (Gan, 2017[14]). Hence, the support provided could ultimately not be helping to household's overall affordability issues. In addition, the higher costs related to transport services, for instance, are often associated with increased car use if the more affordable (in terms of housing costs only) neighbourhoods are in more remote locations and have lower accessibility to goods, services and jobs through sustainable modes (ITF, 2017[15]). As a result, these situations can create important trade-offs between improving access to affordable housing and increasing or perpetuating social segregation, while in many cases also generating higher GHG emissions.

Securing wider current and future benefits from the residential sector, therefore, requires policy makers to define "good housing" in terms of multiple well-being dimensions and priorities. These include contributing to limiting climate change; providing equitable access to opportunities, ensuring a healthy and safe living environment; and enhancing the efficient use and conservation of natural resources and ecosystems.

At the same time, considering the different spatial implications of housing when analysing and implementing policy and investment decisions is key to expanding the sector's role in mitigating climate change and delivering on other priorities listed above. Table 4.1 summarises different impacts of the residential sector on well-being at different spatial scales, including elements from the ecosystem in which urban areas are embedded and highlighting the need for consideration and planning for nature-based solutions (NBS). The concept of NBS captures measures that utilise natural systems to support the delivery of ecosystem services and wider societal benefits (Nesshöver et al., 2016[16]). Ecosystem services are defined as benefits provided by ecosystems to people (Nesshöver et al., 2016[16]). NBS are therefore "green" interventions that seek to use the properties of natural systems to address a set of challenges. As such, NBS can produce multiple ecological, economic, social and urban-planning benefits simultaneously (Cohen-Shacham et al., 2016[17]). NBS can be a complement or alternative to conventional methods of urban planning and development, which mainly deploy purely engineered or "grey infrastructure" (Nesshöver et al., 2016[16]). Ecosystem services and NBS are more present in discussions regarding non-urban territories. Nonetheless, their importance is increasingly acknowledged when addressing management and development of urban areas, as "the future of cities and the future of ecosystem services are inter-dependent" (Ravetz, 2015[18]).

Policy decisions solely based on providing access to a dwelling can miss important opportunities for bringing wider benefits, and even create significant negative effects. Securing wider current and future benefits requires policy makers to define "good housing" in terms of multiple well-being dimensions and priorities, and to consider different spatial implications.

Table 4.1. Well-being impacts from the residential sector across different spatial scales

Dwelling		Neighbourhood/community (including natural ecosystems)	
Characteristics	**Well-being Impacts**	**Characteristics**	**Well-being impacts**
Quality of the physical structure and internal environment, including basic services (electricity, water and sanitation)	• Poverty, equity: ensuring basic facilities (water, electricity, energy) is linked to ensuring minimum conditions for all population, and reducing poverty and inequality between groups. Access to electricity is also linked to education performance, itself key to reducing income and social inequalities. • Health: ensuring access to basic services is also linked to good health (e.g. basic sanitation facilities).	Green space and surfaces.	• Climate change mitigation: green space and surfaces have potential for carbon sequestration and storage, and for altering energy use in buildings (Box 4.1). • They can also encourage walking and cycling, with potential reductions in car trips and related emissions (see Chapters 5 on transport). • Health: green space promotes physical activity, reduces air pollution, noise and the incidence of respiratory diseases; it can also reduce urban heat island effects and thermal stress during periods of high temperatures (climate change adaptation measure). • Other environmental impacts: Reduction of flood risks (climate change adaptation purposes), improved biodiversity.
Sustainable construction materials	• Climate change mitigation: use of less carbon-intensive materials (e.g. cement, steel) or materials (e.g. wood) that store carbon. These could also support decarbonisation of the industry sector, as well as create less demand and hence less need for energy-intensive resource extraction. • Health: less disease caused by hazardous materials.	Brownfield/infill development.	• Natural ecosystem protection: limiting expansion of urban footprint. • Climate change mitigation: avoids sprawl and can lead to less car dependence and reduced GHG emissions from transport.
Type of fuels used inside the dwelling and energy efficiency levels	• Climate change mitigation: increasing use of cleaner fuels reduces GHG emissions. Also, the use of more-efficient technologies (e.g. for cooling) can help offset growing energy demand due to space cooling and other uses, and related emissions. • Health and comfort: clean and efficient provision of services (e.g. cooling, heating), coupled with high-performance building envelopes and enhanced ventilation, allow access to cooling/heating access while reducing heating and cooling demand, thereby improving comfort and indoor air quality. • Safety: cleaner fuels also reduce risk of accidents (e.g. from cooking with gas).	Compact and mixed-use development, especially around major transit hubs.	• Climate change mitigation: avoiding sprawl, long-distance and car-based trips (as opposed to the consequences of single-use development) can be key to reducing emissions, especially from transport. • - It can also put stress on infrastructure and cause dis-benefits (e.g. congestion, water shortages) if not well managed.

Dwelling		Neighbourhood/community (including natural ecosystems)	
Characteristics	**Well-being Impacts**	**Characteristics**	**Well-being impacts**
	• Affordability and equity: more-efficient dwellings and appliances reduce energy demand, and therefore fuel poverty (which, in turn, also reduces physical and mental health risks).		
Optimal space standards	• Health: lower risk of respiratory infections. Optimal living space is also relevant to mental health.	Improved access to key services and opportunities (e.g. education, health, transport, jobs) in the neighbourhood and wider community.	• Poverty, equity: improved access to key services and opportunities (e.g. education facilities, jobs) reduces inequalities. • Health: connection to health facilities is key to improvements in health and management of chronic conditions. • Better life satisfaction. • Climate change mitigation: if linked through quality infrastructure for sustainable transport.
Efficient water use for internal use	• Climate change mitigation: reducing energy use for water provision. • Health: better hygiene. • Climate adaptation: use of collected water for non-consumptive use reduces pressures on centralised water supply.	Water management system with use for energy recovery.	• Climate change mitigation potential: systems that use water for thermal storage (heat and cold) can further reduce GHG emissions.
Waste management in the home	• Material and resource efficiency supports circular approaches. • Health: less disease transmission. • Natural ecosystem protection: reducing food waste and improving management reduces disposal in surrounding areas.	Waste management system with use for energy production.	• Climate change mitigation potential: if the system uses waste for energy production. • Material and resource efficiency supporting circular approaches.
Affordability related to the dwelling	• Poverty, affordability and equity: affordable housing is a key pillar to bridge equity gaps. • Health: ensuring affordable and stable housing is linked to reducing stress and mental health problems.	Affordability beyond the dwelling (i.e. affordability of services, such as transport due to location or lack of affordability in high-quality neighbourhoods).	• Poverty, affordability and equity: costs of services (e.g. food, transport, education) that go beyond those direct costs of housing and internal services (e.g. water, energy, etc.) also have an impact on a household's disposable income. • Health: overall affordability of living, rather than only affordability of the dwelling, have an influence on stress and mental health.
		Neighbourhood quality.	• Equity: the number and quality of (environmental, economic and social) opportunities in a neighbourhood can make an important difference. • Reduced violence and crime: good-quality neighbourhood infrastructure (as opposed to degraded built environments) is associated with reduced violence and crime rates.

Source: Authors, based on (International Energy Agency, 2018[19]); (International Energy Agency, 2019[20]); (OECD, 2018[21]); (WHO, 2018[6]) .

The need to adopt this more holistic approach (i.e. one that systematically considers multiple well-being priorities and spatial scales) has been put forward in academic discussions, which highlight that "housing is a bundled good: it includes the housing unit but also the amenities associated with its location" (Acevedo-Garcia et al., 2016[13]). This is consistent with (Chapman, Preval and Howden-Chapman, 2017[22]), which highlights that "rather than seeing housing policy options as focused only on optimizing household welfare for a given time and place, it is more helpful to view housing policies as part of a set of government choices regarding outcomes from the urban built and social environment, with both short and longer term consequences for such outcomes". The World Resources Institute also emphasises that adopting a broader approach to housing policies can help address relevant challenges when aiming to provide adequate, secure and affordable urban housing; this is especially true in developing countries, where informal housing (such as slums) is a common feature in cities (King et al., 2017[23]). With this vision, governments could prioritise upgrading slums and promoting rental housing rather than pursue radical relocation measures that generally move people to areas outside the city without adequate infrastructure and services delivery, social networks and employment opportunities (King et al., 2017[23]).

Along the same lines, the OECD is developing a housing strategy across different parts of the Organisation, which will be delivered by the end of 2020. A key objective of this project is to evaluate policies and objectives across policy dimensions, to support whole-of-government and holistic policy approaches.

Work carried out by the World Health Organization (WHO) also adopts this approach. It defines healthy housing as drawing on four interlinked levels: i) the feeling of *home*, and provision of a place that is a protective, safe and intimate refuge where people can develops a sense of identity and attachment; ii) the adequacy of the physical structure and the dwelling in ensuring physical health, security and comfort; iii) the presence of a community, and the quality of the neighbourhood and its relation to social interaction, sense of trust and collective efficacy; and iv) the nature of the immediate housing environment, such as the quality of urban design, including green spaces, services and public transport choices (WHO, 2018[6]).

In 2016, the United Nations adopted the New Urban Agenda (NUA), which outlines that cities and human settlements should be the places where all inhabitants enjoy equal rights and opportunities in just, healthy, affordable and sustainable areas (United Nations, 2017[24]). According to the NUA, adequate housing is embedded in broader considerations, which include: i) ensuring adequate social functions and standard of living that ensure access to basic services such as drinkable water, public goods, and quality services for food and security; ii) fostering inclusiveness and gender equality; iii) promoting civic engagement; iv) leveraging urbanisation to support the transition to a sustainable and formal economy; v) fostering territorial integration and development; vi) enhancing efficient and sustainable urban mobility, as well as improving accessibility; and (vii) protecting ecosystems and natural habitat, and promoting sustainable consumption and production" (United Nations, 2017[24]).

Figure 4.1 offers a framework for understanding different potential policy outcomes in the context of this more holistic perspective and depending on the changes created in terms of climate change mitigation (x-axis) and other well-being objectives (y-axis). It also captures the interdependencies or reciprocal relations between the three scales of the residential sector (dwelling, neighbourhood, and the wider city and regional community[6]). It builds on previous work done by (Turcu, 2010[25]), (Turcu, 2012[26]) and (Brandon and Lombardi, 2005[27]), looking at the relationships between the various scales of the built environment and complex concepts such as sustainability and develops these ideas.

Figure 4.1. Comprehensive view of synergies and trade-offs in the residential sector

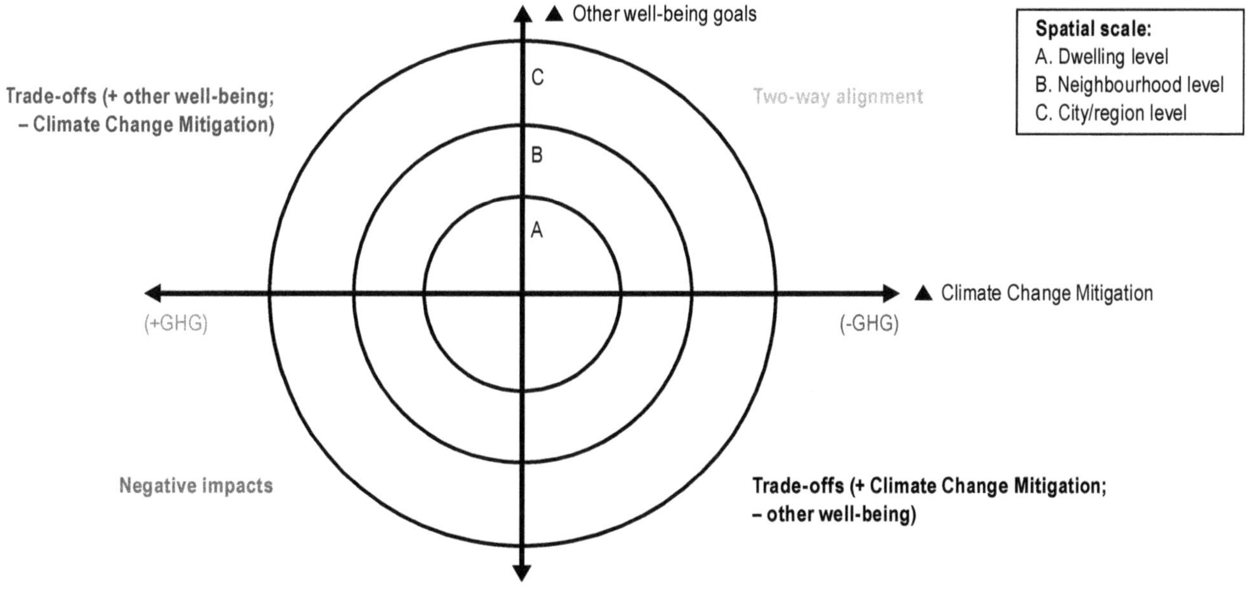

Policy outcomes in the upper-right quadrant of Figure 4.1 would fall into the so-called **two-way alignment** (i.e. the ideal situation where synergies between climate and well-being goal are achieved), while policy outcomes in the bottom-left quadrant would be detrimental to both climate change mitigation and other policy goals. Policies with outcomes falling in the upper left-hand and bottom right-hand quadrants would present trade-offs between climate goals and wider well-being. The upper left-hand quadrant shows benefits in terms of other policy priorities that are detrimental to climate, while the bottom right-hand quadrant creates the opposite effect. Changes in climate change mitigation are indicated in terms of increases (left-hand quadrants) or reductions (right-hand quadrants) in GHG emissions. Different points of reference could be set to divide left and right quadrants (e.g. current emissions, a baseline scenario, etc.). The different circles (A, B, C) represent different spatial scales in which policies can intervene.

Figure 4.2 illustrates, by using some policy examples, the complexity of combined climate and other well-being outcomes across spatial scales, and emphasises the need for this broader perspective to achieve better outcomes.

Figure 4.2. Different policy outcomes for different set of actions

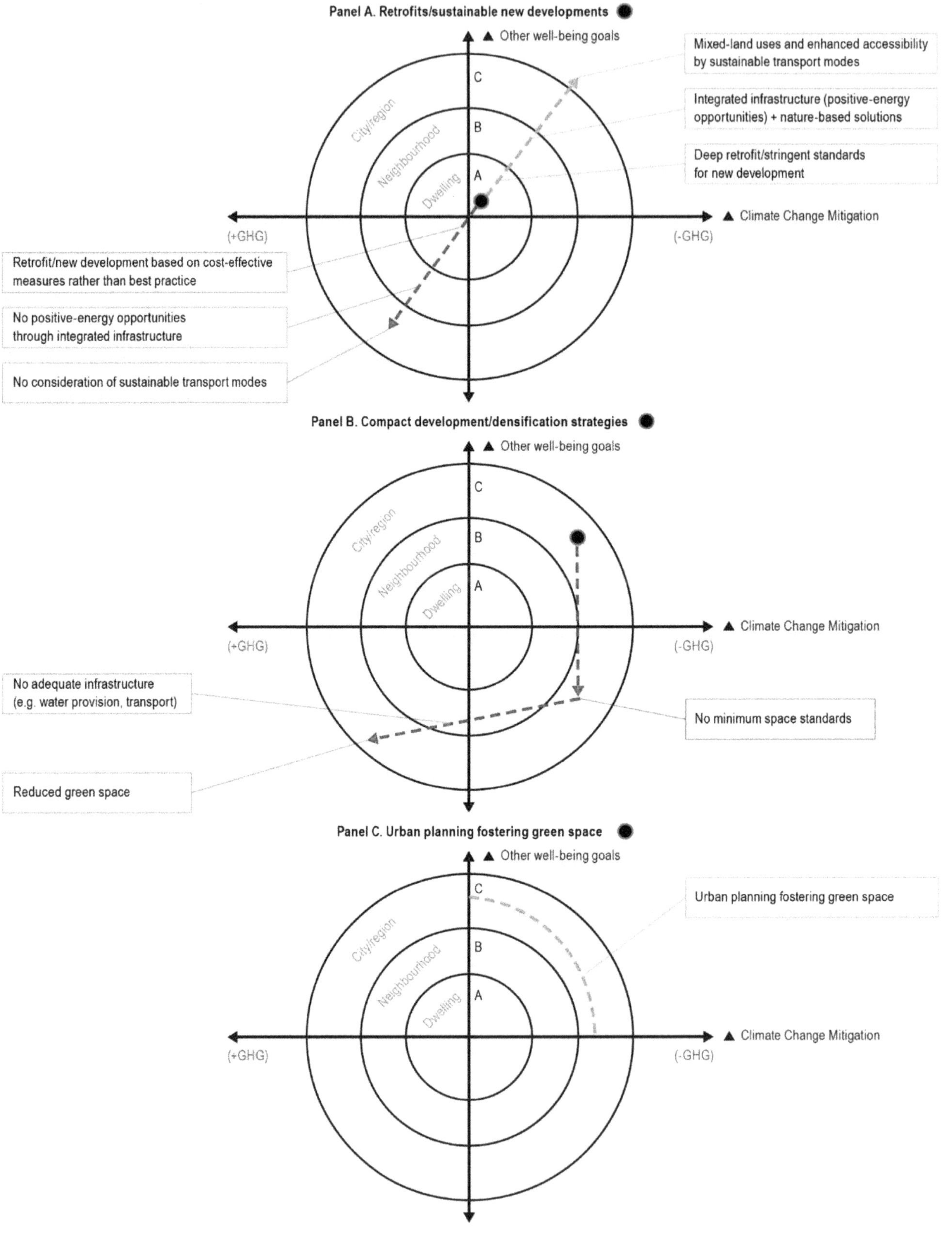

Panel A shows the example of retrofits and new housing developments that aim to be sustainable (e.g. using low-carbon materials and being built along design principles that foster energy efficiency). In principle, these retrofits and new developments would bring both climate and other benefits (e.g. health, reduction in fuel poverty) at the scale of the dwellings involved. Nevertheless, the wider impacts (depending on a number of considerations at different scales) could end up being incrementally positive (both in terms of climate change mitigation and other benefits), creating different trade-offs between them, or they could also even be detrimental, in terms of both climate and other priorities in the longer-run.

For example, whether these are deep retrofits and developments with ambitious targets (based on best practice, rather than only considering the most cost-effective set of measures) will make an important difference overtime in avoiding infrastructure lock-in to energy and emission levels that are far higher than those needed to meet global climate goals (Urge-Vosatz et al., 2013[28]). In addition, whether these projects are planned as part of integrated infrastructure systems and design that enables energy-positive development can also help determine the GHG emission reductions and wider benefits. The term energy-positive refers to buildings that produce more energy from renewable sources than what they consume, while maintaining adequate comfort levels. The definition can englobe however different cases. For instance, those where construction is also taken into account (zero-energy foot-print buildings), or those where all energy loads are included (all energy positive buildings) (Global Buildings Performance Network, 2013[29]). Finally, the location, the availability of different activities and services nearby (i.e. whether housing is developed under mixed land-use principles), and the connections to the wider city through sustainable modes can make an important difference in the transport-related costs borne by dwellers, the wider transport-related GHG and other pollutant emissions, and whether health and social exclusion issues are created. **Panel A** shows two opposite and extreme potential paths, but different combinations of the elements addressed could play a role in creating other scenarios that would fall in either of the two trade-off quadrants

Panel B shows the example of densification strategies, which are targeted at the city level and thus have potential impacts at this scale. As shown by the figure, these strategies can have an important potential to reduce GHG emissions as well as to bring other benefits. For instance, several urban services – e.g. public transport – are more feasible to provide if minimum densities are created (Aguilar Jaber and Glocker, 2015[30]). Less sprawl can also bring less pollution and more health benefits. Nonetheless, without taking into account minimum living-space standards, many dwellers could suffer from overcrowding as the city densifies, harming their well-being by reducing their physical and mental health. Overcrowding is associated with risks of respiratory (and other) infections in children and mental stress in adults (Krieger and Higgins, 2002[31]). All of this would bring potential outcomes towards the lower right-hand quadrant, by creating a trade-off between climate and health outcomes.

In addition, without considering criteria on the necessary infrastructure (e.g. water, transport) required to sustain such densities, or the need to integrate nature-based solutions (e.g. ensure green space), as discussed above, climate change mitigation and other benefits could also be reduced, taking policy outcomes towards the bottom left-hand quadrant. For instance, densifying areas with low water availability can increase the energy (and related GHG emissions) needed to ensure the water supply, increasing water stress. Densifying areas without sufficient levels of transport accessibility, particularly through sustainable transport modes, can increase congestion (especially in adjacent neighbourhoods), increasing GHG emissions and pollution, and reducing life quality. Likewise, densification policies that do not ensure minimum green space in urban areas can be a missed opportunity for contributing to climate change mitigation and resilience-by reducing urban heat islands- through nature-based negative-emission approaches (see Box 4.3). This could also reduce the physical and mental health of inhabitants, since the availability of accessible green spaces[7] in neighbourhoods is associated, for instance, with improved mental and physical health (e.g. reduced anxiety and depression, and increased physical activity) (Wentworth and Clarke, 2016[32]); (Power et al., 2009[33]).

Finally, **Panel C** shows the example of urban green space strategies, showing that these could expand the potential for achieving both climate and other policy related objectives. As shown and discussed in Box 4.1, studies estimating the potential carbon sequestration capacity of urban green space have found the potential reduction in carbon emissions to be relatively small when compared to fossil-fuel related emissions in cities. However, a number of studies have found net reductions in emissions from the development of urban green space (especially when adequately designed), and some have estimated positive related economic value. Several other studies show that these strategies can have a number of other potential benefits in terms of storm-water management and surface temperature moderation (Rogers, Jaluzot and Neilan, 2012[34]), as well as improved mental and physical health (Wentworth and Clarke, 2016[32]); (Power et al., 2009[33]). Thus, these strategies can support governments in delivering multiple well-being goals, in addition to contributing (even moderately) to climate change mitigation (as shown in **Panel C**).

Table 4.2 presents a number of two-way alignment opportunities, including but also going beyond those depicted in Figure 4.2, discussed above. An important consideration is that approaches focused on part of the diagram above (i.e. only at some spatial scales and a restricted number of well-being priorities) will not only ignore a number of synergies and trade-offs, but will also overlook the ways in which different stakeholders and authorities would need to co-ordinate in order to overcome governance challenges. This is particularly relevant as different infrastructure and policies are managed by different levels of government and/or ministries and departments, increasing the incidence of uncoordinated policies and policy outcomes. Level A (dwelling or building) in Figure 4.1 and Figure 4.2, for instance, is generally addressed by architects, designers, developers, building contractors and clients of individual structures, as well as housing ministries and authorities. Level B (neighbourhood) would involve actors in Level A, as well as decision-making authorities in charge of planning, ministries and authorities in charge of different policies and infrastructure at the local government level, and in some cases, some entities from the national government. Level C (city/region) involves all of Levels A and B actors, plus the wider civil society.

A number of governance arrangements and instruments, e.g. national urban policies (OECD, 2017[35]) and metropolitan transport authorities (ITF, 2017[15]), have been recognised for their value in helping authorities overcome such challenges. While the governance of the residential sector is outside the scope of this chapter, the development of a shared vision across relevant actors on the need to define "good housing" in terms of the wider perspective proposed will help move the process forward. Moreover, the use of indicators like those discussed in the next section can help establish shared goals and criteria for decision-making across different ministries, authorities and government levels, and articulate actions towards ensuring "good housing" within this wider perspective.

The use of better indicators can help establish shared goals and criteria for decision-making across different ministries, authorities and levels of governments, and articulate actions towards ensuring "good housing" in terms of this wider perspective.

Box 4.1. Urban green space and climate change mitigation

Nature-based negative emissions from carbon sequestration and storage potential in trees

Green space areas, particularly trees, have the potential to sequester carbon. Nevertheless, trees in urban areas pose different challenges than those situated in non-urban areas. Urban green areas entail important costs and emissions, linked to their construction and maintenance. Like trees in non-urban areas, they also pose challenges in terms of mortality rates as dead trees decompose, releasing GHGs. For these reasons, conducting careful and comprehensive life-cycle assessment is key to assessing the climate change mitigation potential of urban green areas. The city of Leipzig in Germany has conducted such an analysis, illustrating the importance of considering the carbon footprint of construction and maintenance (Strohbach, Arnold and Haase, 2012[36]). In construction, the delivery of trees and excavation for planting these were found to have the largest carbon dioxide (CO_2) emission contribution (Strohbach, Arnold and Haase, 2012[36]). The analysis also highlights the relevance of developing reliable methodologies to estimate tree growth and mortality when predicting potential GHG emission reductions. Overall, with high tree mortality rates, emissions from construction and maintenance make a relevant share of total positive emissions that must be accounted for when looking at the net impact of urban green space on GHG emissions. These tend to weight more in the case of parks, which have a lower total sequestration potential than other green space populated more densely with trees (Strohbach, Arnold and Haase, 2012[36]).

Green space design (including diversity of tree population, and the share and distribution of open space relative to tree-covered space) has proven important for increasing the potential of carbon sequestration (Strohbach, Arnold and Haase, 2012[36]) (Hutchings, Lawrence and Brunt, 2012[37]) (Nero et al., 2017[38]). The next section discusses some of the most important indicators related to urban tree coverage. There is also potential for below-ground carbon storage, i.e. carbon storage in soil and root biomass, but not many studies have estimated this potential, due to lack of available data. A study in Ghana quantified the carbon pool from urban green space in the city of Kumasi (3 758 Gigagrams of carbon stored below and above ground). The study found that soil, roots and above-ground vegetation contributed respectively to 42%, 6% and 52% of carbon storage (Nero et al., 2017[38]).

Studies show that the potential reduction in carbon emissions from carbon sequestration and storage of green urban areas is relatively small when compared to fossil-fuel related emissions in cities. Nonetheless, several of these studies conclude that these strategies contribute to carbon neutrality, with several other positive benefits. One of the main conclusions of the study conducted in Leipzig (Strohbach, Arnold and Haase, 2012[36]) highlights the potential opportunity derived from greening brownfield sites although it also underlines the strong competition for redeveloping urban land for industrial, residential, and commercial uses. The study in Ghana also emphasises the need to account for the contribution of urban green spaces through carbon sequestration in national and regional estimates of carbon stocks (Nero et al., 2017[38]). Other studies have also estimated and monetised benefits from urban green space in terms of CO_2 sequestration and storage. Estimations in a report developed for a Business Improvement District project in London (United Kingdom) find that trees in Victoria remove 1.2 tonnes of pollutants, store 847.08 tonnes and sequester 18.35 tonnes of CO_2 per year (Victoria Business Improvement District, 2015[39]). The report estimates annual pollution-removal benefits at 85 149 GBP (pounds sterling), estimating the value of the carbon storage at almost 44 895 GBP and the value of carbon drawdown at 972.55 GBP yearly.

Source: based on (Strohbach, Arnold and Haase, 2012[36]); (Hutchings, Lawrence and Brunt, 2012[37]); (Nero et al., 2017[38]); (Victoria Business Improvement District, 2015[39]).

Table 4.2. Potential two-way alignment benefits from applying the well-being lens to the residential sector

Other policy priority	Contributing to limiting climate change	
	Generating synergies	Avoiding/reducing trade-offs
Offering affordable housing and contributing to more equitable access to opportunities and services.	Governments can reduce fuel poverty and the day-to-day cost of living for vulnerable groups by promoting efficient energy and water use in housing. This also has important benefits for climate (and health). Increasing infrastructure integration across buildings, energy and transport systems can reduce the cost of living, as well as the cost of maintaining the infrastructure – and in some cases, of developing housing. This can also lead to more-efficient and less carbon-intensive (sometimes zero or negative-carbon) housing, as well as less carbon-intensive behaviour (e.g. when housing is linked to quality public transport). Going for a broader view of equity (beyond socio-economic characteristics strongly focused on incomes) can highlight the relevance of unequal access to environmental and other opportunities (e.g. access of housing to green spaces). This can bring attention to the relevance of developing greenspace requirements for housing projects (especially those which have very limited access) while also resulting in GHG emission reductions.	Placing stricter climate-related regulations for the development of buildings and surrounding infrastructure can affect overall housing prices, making them less affordable for lower-income groups. Nonetheless, monitoring the changes in affordability of housing across income groups, and taking into account neighbourhood quality and services (e.g. sustainable transport connections or energy efficiency of buildings), can help identify the need for complementary policies/compensation. It can also help design policies, programmes and projects that can better reconcile climate change mitigation and equity benefits.
Promoting the efficient use and conservation of natural resources and ecosystems.	Protecting forest and biodiversity is an important incentive for brownfield development and implementing planning regulations to limit urban sprawl. It can also lead to relevant reductions in GHG emissions (through carbon sequestration from trees, avoided emissions from land-use change, etc.).	Monitoring green space availability can help prevent the reduction of green space ratios as a consequence of densification and infill strategies to mitigate climate change.
Ensuring a healthy and safe living environment.	Estimating the health benefits of energy-efficient programmes (e.g. retrofit, new buildings, eco-districts and eco-cities) can importantly reduce payback time and improve projects' cost-benefit ratio). In many cases tipping the balance towards more sustainable development. The increase of green and blue spaces in neighbourhoods and cities has an important health rationale; while also having potential to reduce CO_2 emissions (i.e. lower air temperatures and more less ground-level ozone, with more trees and plants to clean the air and provide oxygen). More stringent standards for cooling and heating, and the increasing deployment for renewables, foster the diffusion of more-efficient and clean appliances, bringing benefits in terms of air quality, comfort and health, while reducing energy demand and GHG emissions. Sustainable building design (improved natural ventilation, orientation, day light, etc.) can provide health benefits by bringing thermal comfort and reducing respiratory diseases that could arise from mould or particulate matter, while reducing energy needs and hence GHG emissions (World Health Organization, 2011[40]).	Enhanced insulation and thermal efficiency of dwelling envelopes and use of health-damaging insulation materials can lead to inadequate ventilation, reducing indoor air quality and causing respiratory diseases or cancer. Accounting for potential health risks, can lead to using construction materials and technologies that can prevent health damages while improving inhabitants' internal comfort and reducing emissions (World Health Organization, 2011[40]). Densification policies lead to more compact urban areas, with smaller units. Reduced habitable surface can lead to overcrowding and negatively affect mental health. Monitoring and regulating minimum adequate standards for given characteristics (number of inhabitants per square metre, living space) can avoid negative health impacts, while improving comfort and mental health. More stringent standards for cooling or heating can lead to affordability issues for low-income households in the short term if appliances become more expensive. Tackling affordability by allowing multiple actors and technologies in these appliance markets promotes innovation and competition, and therefore lower prices for appliances. Natural ventilation without air filtration (e.g. windows and doors with screens) can increase exposure to outdoor air pollution and vector-borne illnesses (World Health Organization, 2011[40]). Taking actions to reduce external air pollution, and promoting the use of household filters, can help avoid these negative impacts while improving public health.

Note: This table builds on work cited throughout the chapter as well as some additional sources. Where the latter is the case, these are indicated in the table.

4.3. Indicators for monitoring the residential sector's contribution to well-being

As stated in Chapter 1, a change in the measurement system is key to implementing a shift in perspective for policy making. Important efforts have been made to develop indicators sets that can support sustainable development. The SDGs and the OECD Framework for Measuring Well-being and Progress (henceforth the OECD well-being framework) incorporate a number of indicators, used throughout this report as references. Winston and Eastaway (2008[41]) explore a number of international indicator sets, analysing in particular to what extent they incorporate indicators for sustainable housing and pointing out that many challenges remain. First, housing, and its related indicators, are often still absent or barely addressed in overall sustainability measurement efforts. Second, housing-related indicators are often biased towards one of the pillars of sustainability (economic, social and environmental), while failing to capture the range of aspects that are key to other pillars, hence a general need for more comprehensive sets of indicators. Third, it is difficult to choose indicators sets reflecting the multiple aspects of housing, e.g. location, design and use. Moreover, as the highlighted indicators also need to gain political commitment to be influential (Winston and Eastaway, 2008[41]), developing these tools needs to strike a balance between multiple characteristics, including scientific validity, reliability, guiding vision, holistic perspective and relevance. They also should be easy to understand and have a practical focus.

This section discusses a number of indicators that can both improve policy makers' ability to monitor progress in applying a well-being lens to the residential sector and guide decisions to capture the benefits of two-way alignment between climate and wider well-being priorities, while managing potential trade-offs. The section is structured according to the different priorities identified in Section 4.2 as key to promoting wider well-being goals in the sector, as follows: limiting climate change; offering affordable and good-quality housing, and contributing to more equitable access to opportunities and services; ensuring healthy and safe environments; and fostering efficient use and conservation of natural resources and ecosystems. Systematically looking at indicators that reflect simultaneously outcomes related to different well-being objectives is necessary to identify and manage potential synergies and trade-offs. In other words, it is key to achieving a two-way alignment between climate change mitigation and other well-being policy priorities. Examples of how the type of indicators discussed can be – and have been – used to achieve greater two-way alignment are provided where these are known and available. Table 4.3 summarises the relation between the different policy priorities, the SDG goals and targets, and the domains and dimensions in the OECD well-being framework. Summary tables showing the indicators proposed for tracking progress and setting criteria towards each of the priorities are provided in each subsection. They also summarise the links between the indicators proposed and those already offered by the SDGs and the OECD well-being framework.

Table 4.3. Policy priorities for the residential sector and their link to the SDGs and the OECD well-being framework

Other policy priorities	SDG goal and target	OECD Well-being domain	OECD Well-being dimension
Limiting climate change	13. Climate action.	Future well-being: resources.	Natural capital.
	11.6. By 2030, reduce the adverse per capita environmental impact of cities.		
Offering affordable and good-quality housing, and contributing to more equitable access to opportunities	1.2. By 2030, reduce at least by half the proportion of men, women and children living in poverty.	Current well-being: material conditions.	Income and wealth.
	1.4. By 2030, ensure that all men and women have equal rights to economic resources.		
	3.8. Achieve universal health coverage.		Jobs and earnings.
	4.2. By 2030, ensure that all girls and boys have access to quality early childhood development, care and pre-primary education.		
	7.1. By 2030, ensure universal access to affordable, reliable and modern energy services.		Housing.
	10.2. By 2030, empower and promote the social, economic and political inclusion of all.	Current well-being: quality of life.	Work balance.
			Health status.
			Education and skills.
			Social connections.
	11.1. By 2030 eradicate extreme poverty for all people.	Future well-being: resources.	Human capital.
	11.2. By 2030 provide access to safe, affordable, accessible and sustainable transport systems for all.		
	11.7. By 2030, provide universal access to safe, inclusive and accessible, green and public spaces.		Social capital.
			Economic capital.
Ensuring a healthy and safe living environment	1.4. By 2030, ensure that all men and women have equal rights to economic resources.	Current well-being: material conditions.	Housing.
	3.4. By 2030, reduce by one third premature mortality from non-communicable diseases and promote mental health and well-being.		
	3.9. By 2030, substantially reduce the number of deaths and illnesses from hazardous chemicals and air, water and soil pollution and contamination.	Current well-being: quality of life.	Health status. Personal security.
	6.1. By 2030, achieve universal and equitable access to safe and affordable drinking water for all.		
	6.2. By 2030, achieve access to adequate and equitable sanitation and hygiene for all.		
	6.3. By 2030, improve water quality by reducing pollution, eliminating dumping and minimising release of hazardous chemicals and materials, halving the proportion of untreated wastewater.	Future well-being: resources.	Social capital.
Promoting the efficient use and conservation of natural resources and ecosystems	6.4. By 2030, substantially increase water-use efficiency across all sectors.	Current well-being: quality of life.	Environmental quality.
	11.3. By 2030, enhance inclusive and sustainable urbanisation.		
	11.6. By 2030, reduce the adverse per capita environmental impact of cities.		
	12.5. By 2030, substantially reduce waste generation		
	15.1. By 2020, ensure the conservation, restoration and sustainable use of terrestrial and inland freshwater ecosystem.	Future well-being: resources.	Natural capital.
	15.5. Take urgent and significant action to reduce the degradation of natural habitats.		

The indicators included in this section are not exhaustive. Rather, the analysis is suggestive and intended to stimulate further discussion while highlighting data limitations and potential data enhancements, as well as illustrating good practice where improved indicators are already proving valuable. The entire section mentions indicators focusing on the dwelling, but as these tend to already be widely used, the discussion focuses on indicators relating to the neighbourhood and wider city level, and those that provide information on different elements of ecosystems. The analysis in this section emphasises that taking a more comprehensive view expands the alignment between the sector and wider goals. For instance, only by taking a holistic view of equity and affordability (e.g. including physical access to health services) does the link with SDG Target 3.8 (coverage of essential health services) become evident. Transport and energy-related indicators can play a central role in determining what is "good housing" and monitoring progress in the sector. While these indicators are mentioned in this section, more detailed analysis on these tools can be found in Chapter 5 (transport-related indicators) and Chapter 2 (indicators for monitoring energy poverty).

4.3.1. Limiting climate change

Indicators for monitoring GHG emissions in the residential sector provide information of the sector's contribution to SDG 13, "take urgent action to combat climate change and its impacts" (the SDG framework does not have a specific indicator or target on GHG emissions). These indicators also help track and understand performance in relation to SDG 11 ("Make cities and human settlements inclusive, safe, resilient and sustainable"). Information is important to track specifically the sector's contribution to SDG Target 11.6, which calls for reducing the adverse per capita environmental impact of cities (again, without any indicator reflecting GHG emissions). In terms of the OECD well-being framework, indicators for understanding and tracking GHG emissions from the residential sector are also linked to the "resources for future well-being" domain and the "natural capital" dimension of well-being. GHG indicators for the residential sector would provide sector-specific data to complement the economy-wide indicators used by this framework[8]. The rest of this subsection describes data limitations and recommendations regarding the type of GHG emission indicators that would be important for the sector (summarised in Table 4.4).

GHG emissions coming directly from buildings and dwellings are relatively well understood. They comprise both direct (i.e. burning gas/oil for heating) and indirect emissions (i.e. from electricity consumption). However, one challenge is that GHG emissions related to the residential sector are amalgamated in many statistical sets with those from the commercial and service sector. Even when residential GHG emissions are shown separately from other emissions, the indicators used suffer from a number of limitations.

First, statistics on "carbon [dioxide] emissions in tonnes per household", a widely used measure for decision-making in the climate change arena, are typically only available at a national scale, and using simple averages. Hence, there is limited understanding of GHG emissions from the residential sector at the neighbourhood and city levels, or across territories. This may inhibit well-targeted, cost-effective action. Second, even where available, such data are not always disaggregated according to households' characteristics, such as household type, housing tenure and dwelling type. Many countries carry out income-expenditure surveys that track household expenditures over time, and could provide some insights on their behaviour and carbon footprint. However, few countries make disaggregated data easily available and public; and some countries have expenditure divisions that are not adequate for estimating carbon-related emissions. For instance, transport-related expenses from households do not always cover all modes of transport (ITF-OECD, 2017[42]).

Household energy consumption has shown a significant and positive link to income (Hargreaves et al., 2013[43])). Nonetheless, significant correlations between GHG emission levels and socio-economic characteristics beyond income – such as household size and location, housing tenure, the number of workers per household, employment status, socio-economic group and age – have also been found relevant (Hargreaves et al., 2013[43])). The study carried out by (Hargreaves et al., 2013[43]) not only focused on CO_2 emissions from energy consumption in homes, but also analysed differences in emissions from transport (private cars, public transport and international aviation). Overall, the study concluded that household characteristics such as the number of bedrooms, the number of occupants and the property type were more relevant for determining energy use in the home. By contrast, transport-related emissions are highly dependent on variables such as income, location, and the number of workers in the household. On average, emissions were the highest for households in villages, hamlets and isolated locations, and the lowest for households in urban environments (Hargreaves et al., 2013[43]).

This type of results confirms that having data on household characteristics and emissions could help policy makers better identify carbon-intensive population sectors, and target policies accordingly e.g. guiding retrofit programmes toward specific areas and targeting the most carbon-intensive type of dwellings, or improving the design of demand-management strategies by adjusting them to the specific behavioural trends identified. It also emphasises the relevance of land-use policy decisions, which play an important role in the type of development and dwelling choices, as well as the location of housing, and therefore the impact on transport-related emissions. In the same lines it also highlight the importance of incorporating criteria related to transport accessibility – particularly sustainable transport modes – to definitions of "good housing", and systematically linking transport emissions to the residential sector and land-use policies rather than treating them in isolation (see Chapter 5 on transport).

Another important point would be to distinguish between the impact and relevance of different GHGs. For instance, pollutants affecting human health such as black carbon and methane are emitted when using solid fuels, such as wood or biomass for cooking, heating or lighting purposes. An estimated 25% of total black carbon emissions come from households burning solid fuels and 1-3 tonnes of CO_2eq per stove could be saved every year if replaced by clean and efficient stoves (Usaid, 2017[44]). Keeping track of the extent of the deployment of clean and efficient stoves is important for both climate change mitigation and health, and for actions to address both goals simultaneously.

Table 4.4. Summary table: Indicators for monitoring progress in limiting climate change and links to SDGs and OECD well-being framework

Policy priority	Proposed indicators	SDG goal and target	SDG indicators	OECD Well-being dimension/domain	OECD well-being indicators
Limiting climate change	GHG emissions : Total and disaggregated by household and individual characteristic (e.g. type, tenure, dwelling type, income), including emissions from energy production and use beyond the dwelling, differentiated between gases (e.g. CO_2, methane, black carbon).	13.	The framework does not provide a data-specific indicator on GHG emissions.	Future-well-being: resources. Natural capital.	GHG emissions from domestic production. CO2 emissions from domestic consumption.
		11.6.	No indicators that are related to GHG emissions are used, but the target calls for reducing the overall environmental impacts of cities.		

4.3.2. Offering affordable housing and contributing to more equitable access to opportunities and services

Ensuring access to good-quality and affordable housing links to well-being in multiple ways (e.g. poverty, physical and mental health). Housing costs tend to account for the largest share of household expenditures (Guerra and Kirschen, 2016[45]); (ITF-OECD, 2017[42]). Thus, housing affordability has an impact on a number of SDG targets (summarised in Table 4.6) related to poverty (SDG 1) and the reduction of inequality (SDG 10). Sustainable cities (SDG 11) uses the proportion of population living in slums, which is also related to the affordability of formal housing services. The OECD well-being framework specifically tracks housing affordability. In addition, housing affordability is also related to household income, another indicator used by the framework.

Box 4.2 provides some examples of different indicators that can be used to measure housing affordability.The examples provided highlight the need to consider costs beyond those directly linked to housing (i.e. rent and mortgage costs). For instance, the U.S. Department of Housing and Urban Development (HUD) includes in its analysis interest on mortgage payments, property taxes and utility costs (electricity, water, gas and sewer). Chapter 2 presents related measures to track energy poverty, which can also complement analysis on affordability. The OECD Affordable Housing Database includes the share of households experiencing difficulties in keeping the dwelling warm at different points of the income distribution (OECD, 2019[46]).

Taking into account other costs, for instance transport, is also relevant, as households often face important trade-offs between housing quality and improved transport conditions. Chapter 5 fully develops this discussion, also describing in detail the use of an indicator, the Housing plus Transport (H+T®) Affordability Index. Nonetheless, this indicator is also relevant for policy decisions regarding the residential sector, as transport expenses are importantly linked to housing location and often constitute the second-largest expenditure for households (ITF-OECD, 2017[42]). As shown in Chapter 5, there exists evidence that households living in more affordable neighbourhoods (in terms of both housing and transport) also tend to have lower car-related emissions as they generally have better public transport connections, offering a more sustainable and less expensive way for travel. Thus, capturing transport costs and other costs (such as utility charges) provides a more comprehensive picture of the affordability of different housing options and can support decision-makers in achieving two-way alignment between climate and equity goals.

Another important point is the need to account for wealth. The relative and absolute situation of different households can vary significantly when including housing wealth in income calculation (see (Forrest, 2013[47])and (Hamnett, 1991[48])).The housing tenure of different groups implies important divides between owners and renters, and outright and mortgage owners. These contribute to a growing polarisation of society (Forrest, 2013[47]) and need to be taken into account when analysing affordability. Housing wealth is not easy to measure. Different methods and data (usually information on house prices and housing stock) can be used, and the size of housing wealth varies significantly across information sets and methods (Berge, 2006[49]). For example, methods can be based on: a) total housing stock (measured in square metres); or b) the value of housing capital in fixed prices, as calculated in the national accounts on the basis of cumulated gross investment in housing (Berge, 2006[49]).[9]

Box 4.2. Housing affordability indicators

Housing costs as proportion of income or expenditure

Affordable housing is measured as the "ratio between average house price and average household income": the higher the ratio, the less affordable the housing. A common threshold used is the 30/40 rule, i.e. a household is considered to lack affordable housing if it is in the bottom 40% of income distribution and spends more the 30% of its income on housing (Yates and Milligan, 2007[50]).

In many cases, a simple percentage of income spent on total housing costs is used for the income-cost indicator, regardless of the level of household income. In the OECD Affordable Housing Database, for example, the cost of housing includes mortgage (i.e. principal and interest repayments) and rent costs (i.e. private and market-subsidised rent) (OECD, 2019[51]). The OECD also uses the percentage of housing costs from total household expenditure. Other countries also use this indicator. For instance, HUD includes interest on mortgage payment, property taxes and utilities (electricity, water, gas, and sewer) when calculating housing costs, providing a more comprehensive picture of housing affordability. HUD applies two thresholds: 30% and 50% of income to identify households with a housing cost burden and with a severe housing cost burden respectively (Jewkes and Delgadillo, 2009[52]).

These indicators are easy to compute (since data are relatively available) and understand. The data can also be easily estimated at different territorial scales, contributing to spatial analysis and allowing comparisons over time (Jewkes and Delgadillo, 2009[52]) . Nonetheless, the indicator does not account for differences in living costs across different housing markets or in housing quality (size, location, etc.). Also, the ratio is often used as reflecting household's ability to pay, while many factors (including wealth) are not captured. It is also based on present income, while permanent income (i.e. income over time) is more relevant (Jewkes and Delgadillo, 2009[52]) . Finally, being based on average prices, it can misrepresent the situation for new entrants, as there is usually a gap between rents for new and long-term tenants.

The Housing Wage measure

This indicator was developed by the National Low Income Housing Coalition, an advocacy group focusing on affordability issues in the United Sates. It uses the fair market rent (FMR) as a base. The FMR is an estimate of what the net rent (base rent plus essential utilities, such as electricity and gas) of a dwelling with a specific size and in a specific neighbourhood costs.[10] The housing wage measure is then calculated, providing the hourly full-time wage a household would need to earn in order to afford a dwelling of a certain type without exceeding the 30% income threshold (Jewkes and Delgadillo, 2009[52]) .

The housing wage indicator discussed above can be used to analyse the situation of both renters and owners. Nonetheless, the Housing Wage measure provides specific insights on the situation of renters (Jewkes and Delgadillo, 2009[52]) , who generally include a higher proportions of low-income dwellers than owners. Another important advantage is that by using the FMR estimate, the indicator encompasses differences in wages and housing costs in different areas and for diverse housing types, instead of using simple averages (Jewkes and Delgadillo, 2009[52])

The ability-to-repay rule

This indicator was developed and is strongly used by the National Association of Realtors in the United States. It measures whether a typical family, i.e. a family earning the median gross family income reported by the U.S. Bureau of the Census, would be able to qualify for a mortgage loan on a typical home, i.e. a single-family home with the median-price calculated by the National Association of Realtors. The index is expressed as a percentage of the assets the family should have in order to qualify for the mortgage. Therefore, it provides information on the extent to which a household is under- or over-qualified, rather than using a binary measure (Jewkes and Delgadillo, 2009[52]) . This indicator is relatively easy to compute, providing median housing prices and incomes are available. It can therefore be easily calculated at both the national and local levels. It also considers mortgage interest rates, which are not usually included in the price-income ratio (Jewkes and Delgadillo, 2009[52]) .

Source: based on (Jewkes and Delgadillo, 2009[52]) .

Beyond housing affordability, the sector can also improve equity and wider well-being by promoting more equitable access to opportunities, ensuring that housing offers quality services and opportunities nearby, and is well connected to the wider community. Land-use and housing decisions are key to creating proximity to opportunities and transport services, and hence need to be at the centre of priorities. In line with this, the indicators proposed in this chapter also focus on the accessibility of housing to jobs and services. This, in turn, is linked to a number of other goals and indicators in the SDG and OECD well-being frameworks that track unemployment, access to health and education, educational attainment, and access to public and green spaces. Having accessible opportunities nearby can also reduce commuting times, which is linked to other goals monitored by the OECD-well-being framework (e.g. time off, under "work and life balance" in the well-being domain). Chapter 5 on transport provides detailed analysis on transport accessibility indicators and their use in linking housing and transport decisions, to reduce transport-related GHG emissions. However, as with the H+T® Affordability Index, these indicators should be used to define housing quality, particularly to evaluate and design social and/or affordable housing programmes (ITF-OECD, 2017[42]).

In addition, the Childhood Opportunity Index (COI), also proposed for this policy priority, aims to track neighbourhood quality and can therefore be used to discuss equity (and the role of housing) in terms that go beyond income inequality. The COI is a newly developed measure and a powerful policy tool created by Diversitydatakids.org and the Kirwan Institute for the Study of Race and Ethnicity at the Ohio State University. Its aim is to address residential inequalities in US metropolitan areas by measuring whether children have an equal chance to achieve healthy development groups (Acevedo-Garcia et al., 2016[53]) .

The COI incorporates 19 individual indicators grouped under 3 domains: educational, health and environmental, and social and economic opportunities. An important objective of the COI is to contribute to broadening equity conversations beyond socio-economic conditions. In addition, it seeks to provide data that can support authorities in developing and implementing policy initiatives to improve children's neighbourhood environments and reduce opportunity gaps between groups (Acevedo-Garcia et al., 2016[53]).

The COI methodology also offers particular indicators for each of the three domains covered, which can be useful for conducting particular analysis on different types of opportunities. Table 4.5 summarises the indicators used by the COI methodology to measure social, economic and educational opportunity.Table 4.8 features the indicators used for the health and environment category under the corresponding policy priority.

As suggested in (Acevedo-Garcia et al., 2016[13]), the COI can also be used in combination with the location affordability index (LAI).[11] The LAI reflects the predicted cost burden a household with a certain composition would incur when living in a specific location. It builds on eight representative household profiles (according to the number of family members, income and number of commuters). Specific household profiles were defined for different metropolitan areas or rural counties. The LAI is expressed as the percentage of cost (relative to income), just like the income-price ratio (featured in Box 4.2). Nonetheless, unlike the income-price ratio, this indicator uses both housing and transport costs (just as the H+T® Affordability Index discussed in Chapter 5 on transport) (Acevedo-Garcia et al., 2016[13]).

Table 4.5. Indicators for measuring the educational, and social and economic domains in the COI methodology

Domain	What is measured	Precise indicator
Educational opportunity	Adult educational attainment.	Percentage of adults age 25 and older with a college education.
	Student (school) poverty rate.	Percentage of students receiving free or reduced-price lunches, calculated as the average for the three nearest in-district schools.
	Reading proficiency rate.	Fourth-grade reading proficiency rate, calculated as the average for the three nearest in-district schools.
	Math proficiency rate.	Fourth-grade math proficiency rate, calculated as the average for the three nearest in-district schools.
	Early childhood education neighbourhood participation patterns.	Ratio of the number of children (three years and older) attending preschool/nursery school.
	High school graduation rate.	Percentage of students who graduated from high school on time.
	Proximity to high-quality (accredited by the National Association for the Education of Young Children early childhood education centres).	Number of early childhood education providers of any type located within the census tract or within a reasonable walking distance (1/2 mile).
Social and economic opportunity	Neighbourhood foreclosure rate.	Ratio of estimated number of foreclosures.
	Poverty rate.	Percentage of people below poverty.
	Unemployment rate.	Percentage of the civilian labour force who are unemployed.
	Public assistance rate.	Percentage of people receiving public assistance.
	Proximity to employment.	Average number of employees in zip codes within 5 miles.

Source: (Diversitydatakids and Kirwan Institute for the Study of Race and Ethnicity, 2016[54]).

When combined with indicators that can measure neighbourhood opportunities (such as the COI), the LAI can provide relevant insights on the potential facing trade-offs low-income families between neighbourhood opportunity and housing affordability. Combining the COI and LAI in the criteria used by programmes providing rental assistance to low-income families (e.g. housing vouchers) would allow authorities to ensure that the resources used improve the quality of the neighbourhood in which children develop (Acevedo-Garcia et al., 2016[13]). This can move analysis and policy beyond poverty rates and rent levels, towards a more comprehensive vision of housing affordability. On the one hand, this approach could cover both housing and transport costs (Acevedo-Garcia et al., 2016[13]); it could align sustainable transport and affordable housing strategies, and would even be more comprehensive if it incorporated the cost of utility services. On the other hand, a useful approach would include the quality of the wider environment in which different households can afford to live, as well as the connection between the housing they can afford and different types of opportunities (Acevedo-Garcia et al., 2016[13]). The opportunities addressed include environmental opportunities (such as green space), which can bring a number of ecosystem services (as discussed in Section 4.1). Therefore, incorporating this type of analysis in policy decisions can bring important opportunities for aligning equity and environmental priorities (including climate change mitigation).

Table 4.6. Summary table: Indicators for monitoring affordable housing and contribution to more equitable access to opportunities and links to the SDGs and OECD well-being framework

Policy priority	Proposed indicators	SDG goal and target	SDG Indicators	OECD well-being dimension/domain	OECD well-being Indicator
Offering affordable and good-quality housing, and contribute to more equitable access.	• Housing costs as a proportion of income or expenditure. • H+T® Affordability Index (see Chapter 5). • Energy poverty indicators (see Chapter 2). • Housing wage measure. • Ability-to-repay ratio. • Location affordability index. • COI. • Housing accessibility by different transport modes to key services and activities (see Chapter 5).	1.2.	Proportion of men, women and children of all ages living in poverty in all its dimensions, according to national definitions.	Current well-being: material conditions. Income and wealth.	• Household income. • Household net wealth.
		1.4.	Proportion of adults with secure tenure rights to land.	Current well-being: material conditions. Jobs and earnings.	• Employment • Earnings. • Long-term unemployment.
		3.8.	Coverage of essential health services.	Current well-being: material conditions. Housing.	• Housing affordability.
		4.2.	• Children participation rate in organised learning. • Adult participation rate in formal and non-formal education.	Current well-being: quality of life. Work balance.	• Working hours. • Time off.
				Current well-being: quality of life. Health status.	• Perceived health.
				Current well-being: quality of life. Education and skills	• Educational attainment.
		7.1.	• Proportion of population with access to electricity. • Proportion of population with primary reliance on clean fuels and technology.	Current well-being: quality of life. Social connections.	• Social support.
		10.1 - 10.2.	• Growth rates of household expenditure or income per capita among the bottom 40% of the population and the total population. • Proportion of people living below 50% of median income, by age, sex and persons with disabilities.	Future well-being: resources. Human capital.	• Young adult educational attainment. • Educational expectancy.
		11.1 - 11.3.	• Proportion of urban population living in slums, informal settlements or inadequate housing. • Proportion of population that has convenient access to public transport.	Resources for future well-being. Social capital.	• Trust in others.
		11.7.	• Average share of the built-up area of cities that is open space for public use for all, by sex, age and persons with disabilities.	Resources for future well-being. Economic capital.	• Household debt.

4.3.3. Ensuring a healthy and safe living environment

As discussed in Section 4.1, the characteristics of housing quality, such as lack of basic housing facilities, can result in diminished health, e.g. through the use of unsafe water and sanitation alternatives. These issues overlap with equity and poverty (addressed above), as a persistent problem is that the poorest population is generally subject to lower-quality housing. For example, in most OECD countries (except for Japan and Malta), the level of overcrowding is higher among residents in the lowest income quintiles. Similarly, the share of households that lack access to basic facilities (e.g. an indoor flushing toilet) or cannot afford to keep their home warm is higher among the poorest; these shares are particularly high in some OECD countries (Salvi Del Pero, Adema and Ferraro, 2014[10]).[12] The OECD well-being framework uses the "number of dwellings without basic facilities such as drinking water, sanitation, and heating" as a key indicator. Overcrowding, usually measured in terms of average rooms or floor space per person can also diminish health, safety and comfort. Different countries set their own minimum living-space standards; the WHO recommends at least 9 m^2 per capital. The OECD Housing Affordability database provides available data for OECD countries on overcrowding and the availability of other basic services (e.g. percentage of households living without an indoor flushing toilet). These types of indicators are relevant to track progress in the sector in promoting a healthy and safe living environment; both the SDG and the OECD well-being frameworks have a number of detailed indicators that go in this direction.

Indoor air pollution in a dwelling is also determinant to securing housing health and is measured in terms of the concentration of particulate matter (PM10 or PM2.5) in homes. It can be determined by heating, cooking, smoking, cleaning, and even furnishings or building materials, which can be important indoor sources of gaseous pollutants and particles – and hence, hazardous for human health (HE, 2004[55]); (Isaxon et al., 2015[56])). PM2.5 and PM10 concentrations are not only dangerous for human health, but are also directly correlated to carbon emissions through residential combustion of wood, and the impact on air quality at the local and regional scales, especially during the winter (heating) period (Guerreiro et al., 2016[57]). Monitoring indoor air pollution is key to tracking the sector's contribution to wider sustainable and well-being goals. It is directly linked to one of the indicators used to track SDG Target 3.9 (mortality rate attributed to household and ambient air pollution) and brings important information to understand the role of the sector on the OECD well-being framework indicator tracking life expectancy. Monitoring outdoor air pollution would also be important as a component of neighbourhood quality, supporting the case for quality building envelopes.

In addition, giving poor populations the possibility to inhabit more liveable and pleasant neighbourhoods is desirable in itself, and provides better life opportunities. Not only do poor people systematically face lower-quality housing in terms of basic services, low-income areas are also often associated with lower-quality education, less access to good-quality green space, and a lower quality of the dwelling itself (Wentworth and Clarke, 2016[32]). Safer environments will also elicit greater use of low-carbon and active modes of transport (walking, cycling, etc.). Thus, redevelopments aiming to modernise and green low-quality neighbourhoods while providing educational, leisure and employment facilities also need to make streets safer and homes more secure, and to redirect youth towards productive activities. Monitoring indicators that measure property crime can help track the progress of inclusive climate change policies and developments in a country or neighbourhood. These indicators are also linked to indicators in the OECD well-being framework, which track, for example, trust in others (as part of tracking the evolution of social capital). In Scotland, the Scottish Crime and Justice Survey measures, among other things, the property crime rate across Scotland, by conducting household surveys and public perception of fear or crime. In 2016-17, 6 000 adults living in private households took part on the survey (Scottish Government, 2019[58]). The results highlight, for example, that people were more likely to experience crime in deprived zones, highlighting the relevance of tracking such an indicator when establishing policies for upgrading or modernising neighbourhoods in order to monitor improvements (Scottish Government, 2019[58]). Thus, a number of opportunities exist to create synergies (and avoid trade-offs) between health, equity, safety and climate, but data and indicators that monitor these impacts at different spatial scales are key.

The COI uses several indicators to monitor neighbourhood health opportunities, summarised in Table 4.7. These indicators can help provide a broader view on the characteristics of neighbourhoods in which different forms of housing (and populations) are located, and how this promotes or hinders the delivery of a healthy environment. In some cases (e.g. proximity to toxic waste release sites and the volume of nearby toxic release), the indicators can provide relevant information to complement the analysis of SDG targets and indicators (e.g. the mortality rate attributed to unsafe water, unsafe sanitation and lack of hygiene – SDG Target 3.9). It can also help track the distribution of impacts across the population. For instance, one of the SDG indicators chosen for SDG Target 6.3 measures the proportion of bodies of water with good ambient water quality. However, this does not allow tracking the impacts on different population groups or the percentage of the population exposed to poor-quality bodies of water. The retail healthy food environment indicator (proposed by the COI) considers the link between access to food quality and housing location – which is relevant to health, but not always acknowledged when discussing "good housing" or quality neighbourhoods (see the agriculture policy discussions in the second part of the report). As highlighted in a number of indicators to track SDG 2 measure undernourishment and obesity. , the retail healthy food environment indicator can help monitor the role played by access or lack of access to healthy food, depending on housing location.

Table 4.7. Indicators for measuring health opportunity in the Child Opportunity Index methodology

Domain	What is measured	Precise indicator
Health opportunity	Retail healthy food environment indicator.	Percentage of healthy food retailers located in the census tract or within a reasonable walking distance (1/2 mile) of the census tract's perimeter.
	Proximity to toxic waste release sites.	Distance (in metres) to the nearest toxic waste and release site from the census tract centroid (geographic centre).
	Volume of nearby toxic release.	Aggregated toxic release volume (in pounds), based on the proportion of the census tract area that overlays a two-mile buffer around any toxic release sites nearby.
	Proximity to health care facilities.	Number of health care facilities in the census tract or within two miles of the tract's perimeter.

Source: (Acevedo-Garcia et al., 2016[53]) .

Table 4.8. Summary table: Indicators for monitoring healthy and safe living environments and links to the SDGs and OECD well-being framework

Policy priority	Proposed indicators	SDG goal and target	SDG indicators	OECD well-being domain/dimension	OECD well-being indicators
Ensure a healthy and safe living environment	Basic facilities: • Overcrowding. • Property crime. • Indoor air pollution. • Outdoor air pollution (as part of neighbourhood quality). • COI (health opportunities).	1.4.	Proportion of population living in households with access to basic services.	Current well-being: material conditions. Housing.	• Rooms per person. • Basic sanitation.
		2.	• A number of indicators measure undernourishment and obesity.	Current well-being: quality of life. Health status.	• Life expectancy.
		3.4.	• Mortality rate attributed to cardiovascular disease, cancer, diabetes or chronic respiratory disease.		
		3.9.	• Mortality rate attributed to household and ambient air pollution. • Mortality rate attributed to unsafe water, unsafe sanitation and lack of hygiene. • Mortality rate attributed to unintentional poisoning.	Current well-being: quality of life. Personal security.	• Homicides. • Feeling safe at night.
		6.1. - 6.3.	• Proportion of population using safely managed drinking water services. • Proportion of population using safely managed sanitation services. • Proportion of wastewater safely treated. • Proportion of bodies of water with good ambient water quality.	Future well-being: resources-Social capital.	• Trust in others.
		16.1.	• Number of victims of intentional homicide per 100,000 population, by sex and age. • Conflict-related deaths per 100,000 population, by sex, age and cause. • Proportion of population that feel safe walking alone around the area they live.		

4.3.4. Promoting the efficient use and conservation of natural resources and ecosystems

Measuring resource efficiency in the dwelling is an important aspect of tracking progress towards this policy priority, based on relatively straightforward indicators, e.g. measuring the consumption of energy (energy use per square metre) and water (water use per usage type – e.g. flushing the toilet). SDG Target 6.4, for instance, includes an indicator on water-use efficiency. Indicators that measure the efficiency and emission performance of buildings are also widely used. Measuring the overall impact on water and air quality is also important. These indicators are used by the OECD well-being framework at the aggregate level, but also need more disaggregate monitoring. In the case of waste, SDG Target 11.3 uses the proportion of urban solid waste collected and adequately treated, and SDG Target 12.5 uses the national recycling rate. Again, disaggregated data and analysis for different sites and areas would be useful.

Moreover, as emphasised by (Birkeland, 2012[59]), sustainable development needs to be looked at as "development that makes everyone better off and expands future options", i.e. development that not only does not reduce the ecological base, but helps expand it. Thinking of urban development as "positive development" will promote design that supports ecosystems, eco-services and NBS. Shifting measurement tools to eco-positive thinking is key to implementing this change. Concretely, this means shifting from systems that measure impacts from "bad" to "no harm" or to "less bad", to using scales that allow measuring contribution to ecosystems and ecosystem services. The criteria according to which a project contributes to natural capital can be customised (Birkeland, 2012[59]).

Indicators and certification schemes based on energy efficiency and emission performance, for example, could shift scales to account for the possibility of energy-positive and negative-emission buildings and developments (see Table 4.9). Building design with passive solutions (e.g. orientation, ventilation) can significantly reduce energy needs (through natural daylight, heat loss reductions, etc.), while also improving thermal comfort and health (IEA, 2019[4]). Renger et al (2014[60]) argue that buildings could go beyond and become carbon sinks, even accounting for their entire life-cycle emissions, while bringing wider well-being and environmental benefits. However, they also argue that measurement tools and instruments are needed to incentivise net-positive carbon performance.

Indicators that are linked to the wider environmental characteristics and impacts of housing at the larger neighbourhood and community scales are also important, e.g. tracking residential development on brownfield land.[13] This is generally measured as the percentage change in brownfield land for residential development, providing a proxy measure for the extent to which former urban land is being re-used in the delivery of additional residential space. The indicator aims to ascertain efficient land use, as well as indicate the potential for avoiding additional carbon emissions associated with residential development as a consequence of land-use change (see residential policy chapter in the second part of the report for a discussion of incentives for brownfield development). This indicator can also add relevant information to current indicators tracking SDG Target 11.3, which uses the ratio of land consumption rate to population growth rate.

Brownfield development should proceed with green space development in mind, which requires tracking brownfield land development in tandem with the evolution of green and blue space. Most brownfield sites have some form of "greenish space" in the form of derelict, empty or vacant land, which is taken over by natural space. These green areas are often suppressed, because bringing nature back to contaminated sites is believed to be relatively expensive. Nonetheless, green space is a valuable asset that brings environmental and social benefits.

The Stockholm Royal Seaport site, for instance, was an extremely contaminated site (e.g. with coal tar and oil) that was decontaminated at the expense of the municipality (which owned the land and banked on future returns from property development). To promote the development of green areas as part of redevelopment, the Green Space Factor was used to set standards for developers (Box 4.3) for details on the Green Space Factor. In addition, where green spaces were to be located, the whole site was excavated to a depth of two metres and sealed to ensure that on-site water drainage from a previously contaminated site does not filter down into the aquifer and contaminate groundwater. Another urban infill redevelopment project, the Chatham Square in Alexandria, Virginia (United States), replaced old and deteriorated public housing units built during the 1940s that had very little natural space with higher-density buildings comprising 100 market-rate townhouses, as well as 52 affordable public-housing rental units (The Financing Sustainable Cities Initiative, 2019[61]). Chatham Square is built around green spaces and play areas; it offers pedestrian-friendly infrastructures, and short distances between transit stations, parks and commercial activities (The Financing Sustainable Cities Initiative, 2019[61]).

As previously mentioned, it is important to track changes in green and blue[14] space in cities over time. The SDG framework considers the land consumption rate relative to population growth (Target 11.3). SDG Target 15.1 also uses the proportion of forest area compared to total land area, while the OECD well-being framework includes total forest area. In terms of water sources, both frameworks use freshwater abstractions (which the OECD well-being framework measures as the proportion of total freshwater). The OECD well-being framework also includes an indicator for tracking renewable freshwater sources. Nonetheless, none of the indicators in these frameworks focus on monitoring changes in non-forest green space, nor do they explicitly track green and blue space in cities; hence, the indicators addressed in this section can make important contributions. In addition, both frameworks have indicators related to biodiversity and threatened species (including through the Red List Index, under SDG Target 11.3).

Change in the areas of parks and green space is often measured as the "change in the areas (hectares) of urban parks and open spaces per 1 000 population over the previous five years".[15] Beyond this more generic indicator, Green Space Factors are a way forward for acknowledging and rewarding the relative functionality of different types of green space areas. They are calculated by assigning different factors to diverse green-surface types, then calculating a weighted average. They can contribute, for instance, to monitoring and analysing the contribution of cities to global biodiversity targets. In many cases (e.g. Berlin, Malmo, Seattle, Stockholm, North West England and Southampton), cities have included the Green Space Factor in their planning system to establish both compulsory and voluntary standards for green space in different areas of the city or region, bringing a number of benefits.

As a way to further achieve specific goals (e.g. increasing biodiversity), the city of Malmö in Sweden designed a point system requiring developers to choose at least ten points from a list of elements involving more specific design guidelines and linked to desired outcomes (Box 4.3). This type of tool can be used to monitor and analyse the contribution of cities to global biodiversity targets.

While Malmö developed the Green Space Factor to focus on climate change adaptation and biodiversity, some of the elements in the Green Points System could be key to estimating potential carbon sequestration from trees (e.g. tree diversity – Point 10) (Hutchings, Lawrence and Brunt, 2012[37]); (Rogers, Jaluzot and Neilan, 2012[34]) or reducing energy use in buildings (e.g. wall coverage with climbing plants – Point 7). In the case of tree diversity, some studies of carbon sequestration and storage in urban green spaces suggest more specific parameters, e.g.: "no species should represent more than 10%, no genus more than 20%, and no family more than 30%" (Hutchings, Lawrence and Brunt, 2012[37]). Other parameters on the structure and composition of urban forests, which have been found to increase the potential for carbon capture, could also be included in the Green Space Factor and Green Points System, which could in turn also be used to design larger green areas. Other important parameters for estimating carbon storage potential are: size class distribution (to ensure there are enough young trees to replace old ones); tree cover area (surface made up by leaves, branches and stems of trees, viewed from above); and the leaf area index (which calculates the leaf area at all levels of the forest). Carbon capture capacity is linked closely to this index (Hutchings, Lawrence and Brunt, 2012[37]).

Finally, the previously described COI methodology also uses proximity to parks and open spaces as a component of the indicators included in the health and environmental opportunities dimension. This is measured as the distance in metres to the nearest park or open space. The relation of the COI to healthy development is based on evidence that children with better access to parks and open spaces have a greater tendency to perform safe physical activity and is therefore also linked to health priorities (Acevedo-Garcia et al., 2016[53]) .

Table 4.9. Summary table: Indicators monitoring the efficient use and conservation of natural resources and ecosystems and links to the SDGs and OECD well-being framework

Policy priority	Proposed indicators	SDG goal and target	SDG indicators	OECD well-being domain/dimension	OECD well-being indicators
Promoting the efficient use and conservation of natural resources and the ecosystem	• Resource efficiency (e.g. energy, water). • Percentage change in brownfield land for residential development. • Green Space Factor. • Plot and tree information. • * A shift to eco-positive type of tools (i.e. with scales that measure positive impacts to the environment) is important.	6.4.	• Change in water-use efficiency over time. • Level of water stress: freshwater withdrawal as a proportion of available freshwater resources.	Current well-being: quality of life. Environmental quality.	• Water quality. • Air quality.
		11.3. and 11.6.	• Ratio of land consumption rate to population growth rate. • Proportion of urban solid waste regularly collected and with adequate final discharge out of total urban solid waste generated, by cities.		
		12.5.	• National recycling rate, tonnes of material recycled.	Resources for future well-being: natural capital. Resources.	• Forest area. • Renewable freshwater resources. • Freshwater abstractions. • Threatened species.
		15.1. 15.3. 15.5.	• Forest area as a proportion of total land area. • Proportion of important sites for terrestrial and freshwater biodiversity that are covered by protected areas, by ecosystem type. • Red List Index.		

Box 4.3. The Green Space Factor and the Green Point System developed by Malmö

The Green Space Factor uses a weighted average, which is calculated using the area dedicated to each green and blue surface types, multiplied by the factor assigned to each of these (see Table 4.10). The sum of all area factor products is then divided by the total court area in a given zone. The highest factors are assigned to trees. Other factors range between 0 and 1, with higher factors assigned to vegetation that is in contact with ground water and open water surface, followed by green roofs and facade areas covered with vegetation. In 2009, factors where revised downwards to increase ambition, and the minimum overall score required was raised from 0.5 (used in the B001 eco-district) to 0.6 (Table 4.10).The point system requires developers to choose at least ten of the points (Table 4.11).

Table 4.10. Green Space Factor

Surface type	Factor
Vegetation on ground.	1
Vegetation trellis or façade.	0.7
Green roofs.	0.6
Vegetation on beams, soil depth between 200 millimetres and 800 millimetres.	0.9
Water surfaces.	1
Collection and retention of storm water.	0.2
Draining of sealed surfaces to surrounding vegetation.	0.2
Sealed areas.	0
Paved areas with joints.	0.2
Areas covered with gravel or sand.	0.4
Tree, stem girth 16-20 centimetres (20 square metres for each tree).	20
Tree, stem girth 20-30 centimetres (15 square metres for each tree).	15
Tree, stem girth more than 30 centimetres (10 square metres for each tree).	10
Solitary bush higher than 3 metres (2 square metres for each bus).	2

Table 4.11. Green Points

	Elements included
1	A bird box for every apartment.
2	A biotope for specified insects in the courtyard (water striders and other aquatic insects in the pond).
4	Bat boxes in the courtyard.
5	No surfaces in the courtyard are sealed, and all surfaces are permeable to water.
6	All non-paved surfaces within the courtyard have sufficient soil depth and quality of growing vegetables.
7	The courtyard includes a rustic garden with different sections.
8	All walls, where possible, are covered with climbing plants.
9	There is 1 square metre of pond area for every 5 square metres of hard surface in the courtyard.
10	The vegetation in the courtyard is selected to be nectar rich and provide a variety of food for butterflies.
11	No more than 5 trees or shrubs of the species.
12	The biotopes within the courtyard are all designed to be moist.
13	The biotopes within the courtyard are all designed to be dry.
14	The biotopes within the courtyard are all designed to be semi-natural.
15	All storm water flows for at least 10 metres on the surface of the ground before it is diverted into pipes.
16	The courtyard is green but there are no mowed lawns.
17	All rainwater from buildings and hard surfaces in the courtyard is collected and used for irrigation..
18	All plants have some household use.
19	There are frog habitats within the courtyard, as well as space for frogs to hibernate.

20	In the courtyard, there is at least five square metres of conservatory or greenhouse for each apartment.
21	There is food for birds throughout the year within the courtyard.
22	There are least two different old-crop varieties of fruits and barriers for every 100 square metres of courtyard.
23	The facades of the buildings have swallow nesting facilities.
24	The whole courtyard is used for cultivation of vegetables, fruit and berries.
25	The developers liaise with ecological experts.
26	Greywater is treated in the courtyard and re-used.
27	All biodegradable household waste is composted.
28	Only recycled construction materials are used in the courtyard.
29	Each apartment has at least 2 square metres of build-in growing plots or flower boxes on the balcony.
30	At least have the courtyard area consists of water.
31	The courtyard has a certain colour (and texture) as the theme.
32	All the trees and bushes in the courtyard bear fruit and berries.
33	A selection of the courtyard is left for natural succession (i.e. to grow and regenerate naturally).
34	There should be at least 50 flowering Swedish wild herbs within the courtyard.
35	All the buildings have green roofs.

Source: Authors, based on (Kruuse, 2011[62]).

4.4. Conclusion

This chapter argued for a broader view of "good housing" that can systematically guide policies in the residential sector towards considering multiple well-being priorities (including climate change mitigation) and the implications for different spatial scales. It showed how this approach could help policy makers create a two-way alignment between climate and wider well-being goals, proposing indicators to support its adoption.

References

Acevedo-Garcia, D. et al. (2016), *diversitydatakids.org The Child Opportunity Index Measuring and mapping neighborhood-based opportunities for U.S. children Contents*, http://www.diversitydatakids.org/files/Library/Child%20Opportunity/COI%20Report%20Final%207_29_16.pdf (accessed on 4 June 2019). [53]

Acevedo-Garcia, D. et al. (2016), "Housing Policy Debate Neighborhood Opportunity and Location Affordability for Low-Income Renter Families", http://dx.doi.org/10.1080/10511482.2016.1198410. [13]

Aguilar Jaber, A. and D. Glocker (2015), "Shifting towards Low Carbon Mobility Systems", http://www.internationaltransportforum.org/jtrc/DiscussionPapers/jtrcpapers.html (accessed on 30 June 2019). [30]

Ameli, N. and N. Brandt (2014), "Determinants of Households' Investment in Energy Efficiency and Renewables: Evidence from the OECD Survey on Household Environmental Behaviour and Attitudes", *OECD Economics Department Working Papers*, No. 1165, OECD Publishing, Paris, https://dx.doi.org/10.1787/5jxwtlchggzn-en. [67]

Berge, T. (2006), *Staff Memo Financial Stability Measuring and predicting household housing wealth*, http://www.norges-bank.no, (accessed on 20 March 2019). [49]

Birkeland, J. (2012), "Design Blindness in Sustainable Development: from Closed to Open Systems Design Thinking", *Journal of Urban Design*, Vol. 17/2, pp. 163-187, http://dx.doi.org/10.1080/13574809.2012.666209. [59]

Brandon, P. and P. Lombardi (2005), *Evaluating sustainable development in the built environment*, http://usir.salford.ac.uk/id/eprint/586/. [27]

Chapman, R., N. Preval and P. Howden-Chapman (2017), "How Economic Analysis Can Contribute to Understanding the Links between Housing and Health.", *International journal of environmental research and public health*, Vol. 14/9, http://dx.doi.org/10.3390/ijerph14090996. [22]

Cohen-Shacham, E. et al. (2016), *Nature-based Solutions to address global societal challenges*, http://dx.doi.org/10.2305/IUCN.CH.2016.13.en. [17]

Diversitydatakids and Kirwan Institute for the Study of Race and Ethnicity (2016), *diversitydatakids.org The Child Opportunity Index Measuring and mapping neighborhood-based opportunities for U.S. children Contents*, http://www.diversitydatakids.org/files/Library/Child%20Opportunity/COI%20Report%20Final%207_29_16.pdf (accessed on 20 March 2019). [54]

Foley, R. and T. Kistemann (2015), "Blue space geographies: Enabling health in place", *Health & Place*, Vol. 35, pp. 157-165, http://dx.doi.org/10.1016/j.healthplace.2015.07.003. [65]

Forrest, R. (2013), *Housing and Family Wealth*, https://books.google.fr/books/about/Housing_and_Family_Wealth.html?id=fXAnAAAAQBAJ&redir_esc=y (accessed on 17 December 2020). [47]

Gan, X. (2017), "How affordable housing becomes more sustainable? A stakeholder study", *Journal of Cleaner Production*, Vol. 162, pp. 427-437, http://dx.doi.org/10.1016/J.JCLEPRO.2017.06.048. [14]

Global Buildings Performance Network (2013), *Defining Positive Energy – A Spectrum Approach | Global Buildings Performance Network*, http://www.gbpn.org/positive-energy-buildings/defining-positive-energy-%E2%80%93-spectrum-approach (accessed on 5 August 2019). [29]

Guerra, E. and M. Kirschen (2016), "Housing plus Transportation Affordability Indices: Uses, Opportunities, and Challenges", http://www.itf-oecd.org (accessed on 2 July 2019). [45]

Guerreiro, C. et al. (2016), "Benzo(a)pyrene in Europe: Ambient air concentrations, population exposure and health effects", *Environmental Pollution*, Vol. 214, pp. 657-667, http://dx.doi.org/10.1016/j.envpol.2016.04.081. [57]

Hamnett, C. (1991), "A Nation of Inheritors? Housing Inheritance, Wealth and Inequality in Britain", *Journal of Social Policy*, Vol. 20/4, pp. 509-536, http://dx.doi.org/10.1017/s0047279400019784. [48]

Hargreaves, K. et al. (2013), *THE DISTRIBUTION OF HOUSEHOLD CO 2 EMISSIONS IN GREAT BRITAIN*, https://www.cse.org.uk/downloads/file/project_paper_1_household-emissions-distribution.pdf (accessed on 4 June 2019). [43]

HE, C. (2004), "Contribution from indoor sources to particle number and mass concentrations in residential houses", *Atmospheric Environment*, Vol. 38/21, pp. 3405-3415, http://dx.doi.org/10.1016/j.atmosenv.2004.03.027. [55]

Hutchings, T., V. Lawrence and A. Brunt (2012), *Estimating the Ecosystem Services Value of Edinburgh's Trees*, https://www.itreetools.org/resources/reports/Edinburgh_iTree_Report.pdf (accessed on 21 May 2019). [37]

IEA (2019), *Perspectives for the Clean Energy Transition*, https://www.iea.org/publications/reports/PerspectivesfortheCleanEnergyTransition/ (accessed on 3 July 2019). [4]

IEA (2018), *The Future of Cooling Opportunities for energy-efficient air conditioning Together Secure Sustainable*, http://www.iea.org/t&c/ (accessed on 3 July 2019). [3]

International Energy Agency (2019), *Material efficiency in clean energy transitions*, https://webstore.iea.org/download/direct/2454?fileName=Material_efficiency_in_clean_energy_transitions.pdf (accessed on 1 July 2019). [20]

International Energy Agency (2018), *The Future of Cooling*, http://www.iea.org/t&c/. [19]

Isaxon, C. et al. (2015), "Contribution of indoor-generated particles to residential exposure", *Atmospheric Environment*, Vol. 106, pp. 458-466, http://dx.doi.org/10.1016/J.ATMOSENV.2014.07.053. [56]

ITF (2017), *Corporate Partnership Board CPB Policy Directions for Establishing a Metropolitan Transport Authority for Korea's Capital Region Case-Specific Policy Analysis*, http://www.itf-oecd.org (accessed on 20 March 2019). [15]

ITF-OECD (2017), *Income Inequality, Social Inclusion and Mobility Roundtable Report 2017 Income Inequality, Social Inclusion and Mobility*, https://www.itf-oecd.org/sites/default/files/docs/income-inequality-social-inclusion-mobility.pdf (accessed on 4 June 2019). [42]

Jewkes, M. and L. Delgadillo (2009), *Analysis of housing affordability indices used by practitionners*, http://ssrn.com/abstract=2222052. [52]

King, R. et al. (2017), "Confronting the Urban Housing Crisis in the Global South: Adequate, Secure, and Affordable Housing Confronting the Urban Housing Crisis in the Global South", World Resources Institute, http://www.citiesforall.org. (accessed on 25 June 2019). [23]

Krieger, J. and D. Higgins (2002), "Housing and health: time again for public health action.", *American journal of public health*, Vol. 92/5, pp. 758-68, http://dx.doi.org/10.2105/ajph.92.5.758. [31]

Krieger, J. and D. Higgins (2002), "Housing and health: time again for public health action.", *American journal of public health*, Vol. 92/5, pp. 758-68, http://dx.doi.org/10.2105/ajph.92.5.758. [7]

Kruuse, A. (2011), *The green space factor and the green points system*, http://www.grabs-eu.org (accessed on 25 March 2019). [62]

Lucon, O. et al. (2014), *9 Buildings Coordinating Lead Authors: Lead Authors: Contributing Authors: Review Editors: Chapter Science Assistants: tion of Climate Change. Contribution of Working Group III to the Fifth Assessment Report of the Intergovernmental Panel on Climate Change [Edenhofer Contents*, https://www.ipcc.ch/site/assets/uploads/2018/02/ipcc_wg3_ar5_chapter9.pdf (accessed on 31 May 2019). [9]

Nero, B. et al. (2017), "Urban Green Spaces Enhance Climate Change Mitigation in Cities of the Global South: The Case of Kumasi, Ghana", *Procedia Engineering*, Vol. 198, pp. 69-83, http://dx.doi.org/10.1016/J.PROENG.2017.07.074. [38]

Nesshöver, C. et al. (2016), "The science, policy and practice of nature-based solutions: An interdisciplinary perspective", *Science of the Total Environment*, Vol. 579, pp. 1215-1227, http://dx.doi.org/10.1016/j.scitotenv.2016.11.1060048-9697/ (accessed on 2 July 2019). [16]

NICOLE Brownfield Working Group (2011), *Environmental Liability Transfer in Europe: Divestment of Contaminated Land for Brownfield Regeneration Report Environmental Liability Transfer for Brownfield Divestment in Europe*, http://www.nicole.org/uploadedfiles/2011-wg-brownfields-finalreport.pdf (accessed on 20 March 2019). [63]

OECD (2019), *Affordable Housing Database - OECD*, http://www.oecd.org/social/affordable-housing-database.htm (accessed on 20 March 2019). [51]

OECD (2019), *Affordable Housing Database - OECD*, https://www.oecd.org/social/affordable-housing-database.htm (accessed on 2 July 2019). [46]

OECD (2018), *Rethinking Urban Sprawl: Moving Towards Sustainable Cities*, OECD Publishing, Paris, https://dx.doi.org/10.1787/9789264189881-en. [21]

OECD (2017), *National Urban Policy in OECD Countries*, OECD Publishing, Paris, https://dx.doi.org/10.1787/9789264271906-en. [35]

Power, A. et al. (2009), *Strategic Review of Health Inequalities in England post-2010 Task Group 4: The Built Environment and Health Inequalities*, http://www.instituteofhealthequity.org/resources-reports/built-environment-task-group-report/task-group-4-the-built-environment-and-health-inequalities.pdf (accessed on 2 July 2019). [33]

Ravetz, J. (2015), *The future of the urban environment and ecosystem services in the UK*, https://assets.publishing.service.gov.uk/government/uploads/system/uploads/attachment_data/file/469798/gs-15-34-future-cities-ecosystems.pdf (accessed on 3 June 2019). [18]

Renger, C. et al. (2014), "Building Research & Information Net-positive building carbon sequestration Net-positive building carbon sequestration", http://dx.doi.org/10.1080/09613218.2015.961001. [60]

Robinson, E. and R. Adams (2008), *Housing stress and the mental health and wellbeing of families*, http://www.ag.gov.au/cca (accessed on 3 July 2019). [5]

Rogers, K., A. Jaluzot and C. Neilan (2012), *Green benefits in Victoria Business Improvement District*. [34]

Salvi Del Pero, A., W. Adema and V. Ferraro (2014), "POLICIES TO PROMOTE ACCESS TO GOOD-QUALITY AFFORDABLE HOUSING". [10]

Scottish Government (2019), "Scottish Crime and Justice Survey 2017/18: Main Findings", https://www.gov.scot/publications/scottish-crime-justice-survey-2017-18-main-findings/ (accessed on 25 June 2019). [58]

Srinivasan, S., L. O'Fallon and A. Dearry (2003), "Creating healthy communities, healthy homes, healthy people: initiating a research agenda on the built environment and public health.", *American journal of public health*, Vol. 93/9, pp. 1446-50, http://dx.doi.org/10.2105/ajph.93.9.1446. [1]

Strohbach, M., E. Arnold and D. Haase (2012), "The carbon footprint of urban green space-A life cycle approach", *Landscape and Urban Planning*, Vol. 104, pp. 220-229, http://dx.doi.org/10.1016/j.landurbplan.2011.10.013. [36]

The balance small business (2018), *How to Calculate the Fair Market Rent for Your Unit*, https://www.thebalancesmb.com/fair-market-rent-definition-2124953 (accessed on 20 March 2019). [66]

The Financing Sustainable Cities Initiative (2019), *Solution detail | Sustainable Cities*, http://financingsustainablecities.org/solutions/162 (accessed on 28 June 2019). [61]

Turcu, C. (2012), "Local experiences of urban sustainability: Researching Housing Market Renewal interventions in three English neighbourhoods", *Progress in Planning*, Vol. 78/3, pp. 101-150, http://dx.doi.org/10.1016/J.PROGRESS.2012.04.002. [26]

Turcu, L. (2010), *Examining the impact of housing refurbishment-led regeneration on community sustainability: A study of three Housing Market Renewal areas in England*, http://etheses.lse.ac.uk/635/1/%40Catalina%20TURCU%20-%20PhD%20Thesis%20Sept%202010.pdf (accessed on 25 July 2019). [25]

UN Habitat (2015), *Tracking Improvement in the Lives of Slum Dwellers*. [12]

UNEP (2018), *2018 Global Status Report Towards a zero-emission, efficient and resilient buildings and construction sector*, http://www.iea.org (accessed on 3 July 2019). [11]

UN-Habitat (2016), *Urbanization and development: emerging FUtUres*, http://www.unhabitat.org (accessed on 1 July 2019). [2]

United Nations (2017), "New Urban Agenda", http://habitat3.org/wp-content/uploads/NUA-English.pdf (accessed on 25 June 2019). [24]

Urge-Vosatz, D. et al. (2013), "Energy use in buildings in a long-term perspective", *Current Opinion in Environmental Sustainability*, Vol. 5/2, pp. 141-151, http://dx.doi.org/10.1016/J.COSUST.2013.05.004. [28]

Usaid (2017), *Clean and Efficient Cooking Technologies and Fuels: Section 3 - Climate Impacts of Traditional Stoves and Fuels*, https://www.usaid.gov/sites/default/files/documents/1865/cookstoves-toolkit-2017-mod3-climate-impacts.pdf (accessed on 4 June 2019). [44]

Victoria Business Improvement District (2015), *Green Benefits in Victoria Business improVement District*, https://www.victoriabid.co.uk/wp-content/uploads/2015/02/VBID_i-Tree_Report_2012.pdf (accessed on 3 June 2019). [39]

Wentworth, J. and C. Clarke (2016), *Green Space and Health*, https://researchbriefings.parliament.uk/ResearchBriefing/Summary/POST-PN-0538 (accessed on 2 July 2019). [32]

WHO (2018), *WHO HOUSING AND HEALTH GUIDELINES*, http://apps.who.int/bookorders. (accessed on 1 July 2019). [6]

WHO (2007), *Housing, Energy and Thermal Comfort Housing, Energy and Thermal Comfort A review of 10 countries within the WHO European Region The WHO Regional Office for Europe*, http://www.euro.who.int/pubrequest. (accessed on 1 July 2019). [8]

Williams, K. (2014), *Urban form and infrastructure: a morphological review*, https://assets.publishing.service.gov.uk/government/uploads/system/uploads/attachment_data/file/324161/14-808-urban-form-and-infrastructure-1.pdf (accessed on 31 May 2019). [64]

Winston, N. and M. Eastaway (2008), *Sustainable Housing in the Urban Context: International Sustainable Development Indicator Sets and Housing*, Springer, http://dx.doi.org/10.2307/27734657. [41]

World Health Organization (2011), *Health co-benefits of climate change mitigation-Housing sector green economy in the*, http://www.who.int/about/ (accessed on 28 June 2019). [40]

Yates, J. and V. Milligan (2007), "Housing affordability: a 21st century problem National Research Venture 3: Housing affordability for lower income Australians authored by", https://www.ahuri.edu.au/__data/assets/pdf_file/0018/2178/AHURI_Final_Report_No105_Housing_affordability_a_21st_century_problem.pdf (accessed on 20 March 2019). [50]

Notes

[1] The terms "residential sector" and "housing sector" are used interchangeably in the literature, with a preference for "residential" in policy-making circles and "housing" in academic debates. It is mainly understood as comprising material objects, i.e. goods that can be manufactured, demolished, produced, consumed and bought. However, it can also reflect a wider understanding, where it can be defined as a "commodity" in the economic literature, but also as "one of the pillars" of the welfare state in policy studies.

[2] Of which 9% were direct emissions and 19.5% indirect emissions from electricity use (IEA, 2019[4]).

[3] Urban form is defined as "the physical characteristics that make up built-up areas, including the shape, size, density and configuration of settlements" (Williams, 2014[64]).

[4] Total floor area in buildings increased by more than 15% between 2010 and 2017, while global population increased in less than 10%.

[5] Defined as "a contiguous settlement that lacks one or more of the following five conditions: access to clean water, access to improved sanitation, sufficient living area that is not overcrowded, durable housing and secure tenure" (UN Habitat, 2015[12]).

[6] Although neighbourhoods are already communities, the term "community" here refers to the wider community making up the city in which a neighbourhood and dwelling are embedded.

[7] "[N]atural or semi-natural areas partially or completely covered by vegetation that occur in or near urban areas" (Wentworth and Clarke, 2016[32]).

[8] GHG emissions from domestic production and CO2 emissions from domestic consumption.

[9] For instance, the Norwegian Bank (Norges Bank) uses two different methods to calculate housing wealth, discussed in: (Berge, 2006[49]).

[10] HUD publishes the FMR for more than 2 500 metropolitan and non-metropolitan counties every year (The balance small business, 2018[66]). It derives the FMR for each area based on census data and through renter surveys (The balance small business, 2018[66]).

[11] The index was developed by the Partnership for Sustainable Communities in the United States, comprising HUD, the U.S. Department of Transportation and the U.S. Environmental Protection Agency.

[12] In 2014, the incidence of overcrowding in the bottom quintile reached shares as high as 47% in Poland, 45% in Mexico, 44% in Hungary and 43% in Romania. Also in 2014, the share of poor households (i.e. below 50% of equalised disposable income) that did not have an indoor flushing toilet was as high as 73% in Romania, 60% in Mexico, 42% in Bulgaria and 32% in Lithuania (Salvi Del Pero, Adema and Ferraro, 2014[10]). In addition, among OECD countries for which data are available, Bulgaria, Greece, Portugal and Cyprus present the highest percentage of population in the lowest quintile that cannot afford to keep the dwelling warm (Ameli and Brandt, 2014[67]).

[13] "Brownfield" is not easy to define, and is also known as "previously developed", contaminated, derelict, vacant, underused land, etc. It generally comprises land subject to legal sanction and the opposite of greenfield. Definitions vary across countries. For example, brownfield can be synonymous with contaminated land (e.g. in Italy and Spain); previously developed land (e.g. in the United Kingdom and Germany); derelict, underused or vacant land (e.g. in Scotland, Ireland and the Netherlands); and land where intervention is needed (e.g. in France) (NICOLE Brownfield Working Group, 2011[63])

[14] Defined as "[h]ealth-enabling places and spaces, where water is at the centre of a range of environments with identifiable potential for the promotion of human wellbeing" (Foley and Kistemann, 2015[65]).

[15] Open space can refer to freely accessible public parks, formal gardens, nature reserves, local nature reserves, cemetery and crematoria, water parks, open spaces, sites of special scientific interest, woodlands, playgrounds, and so on.

5 Delivering accessible and sustainable mobility

This chapter is dedicated to the transport sector, with a focus on surface transport. It discusses policy priorities that are central for the sector to contribute to current and future well-being objectives. The chapter proposes a number of indicators that can be used to translate the discussed policy priorities into measurable outcomes, and can support policy makers in attaining a two-way alignment between climate and other policy goals. The chapter also examines the relation between the indicators proposed, and indicators used by the Sustainable Development Goals and the OECD Framework for Measuring Well-being and Progress.

The statistical data for Israel are supplied by and under the responsibility of the relevant Israeli authorities. The use of such data by the OECD is without prejudice to the status of the Golan Heights, East Jerusalem and Israeli settlements in the West Bank under the terms of international law.

In Brief

Delivering accessible and sustainable mobility

Mobility systems connect people and places, increasing quality of life as well as adding social and economic value to communities. The transport sector underpins peoples' well-being by enabling them to travel between their home and work, delivering food to our grocery stores, and transporting products around the world and within countries, regions and cities to meet our daily needs.

However, emissions from transport have grown faster than any other sector over the last 50 years, accounting for approximately 23% of global CO_2 emissions. This largely stems from the fact that mobility systems over the last century have aimed to increase physical movement, are heavily reliant on fossil fuels, and are centred on private ownership, which has in turn led to cities planned around cars. Today's mobility systems also lower our air quality, entrench social inequalities, exclude vulnerable groups, deteriorate natural habitats and exacerbate climate change. If our mobility systems do not change, then transport CO_2 emissions could increase by 60% globally by 2050.

The solution is to re-design mobility systems around accessibility - ensuring that people are able to easily reach jobs, opportunities, goods, services and amenities – instead of physical movement. This would mean giving priority to sustainable transport modes, such as walking, cycling, public transport and other forms of shared mobility, and even new modes (e.g. electric scooters known as micro-mobility), which can bring relevant value to society, particularly in cities. It would also entail giving priority to creating proximity between people and places. Such an approach will lead to a redistribution of budgets and public space in a way that can improve life quality by contributing to equity, health, the economy, climate and other environmental goals.

An important next step is developing and using the right indicators to make the focus on accessibility a reality. The use of physical accessibility indicators for planning transport networks and city development has allowed some cities to reach important modal shift targets- i.e. incentivising people to bike, walk, and use public transport instead of the car. Indicators incorporating transport affordability as criteria for supporting social and affordable housing development have also allowed cities to improve both housing and transport affordability for poorer households while achieving climate change mitigation goals. Governments will also need to set criteria according to safety and security, air quality, noise reduction, and impacts on natural habitats, in order to transform mobility systems.

Policies for improving technologies, but also for avoiding unnecessary trips and shifting trips from cars to bikes, public transport, and walking, will be necessary for decarbonising the sector while bringing multiple other benefits. But the transport sector needs to co-ordinate closely with land-use and housing sectors to ensure access through sustainable modes of transport that provide a high-quality alternative to cars. This involves investment on sustainable transport modes but also policies that can make explicit links between land-use and transport (e.g. transport-inclusive development standards). Overall, policy design that takes multiple priorities into account can lead to more acceptable, feasible and effective mitigation action.

Infographic 5.1. Delivering accessible and sustainable mobility

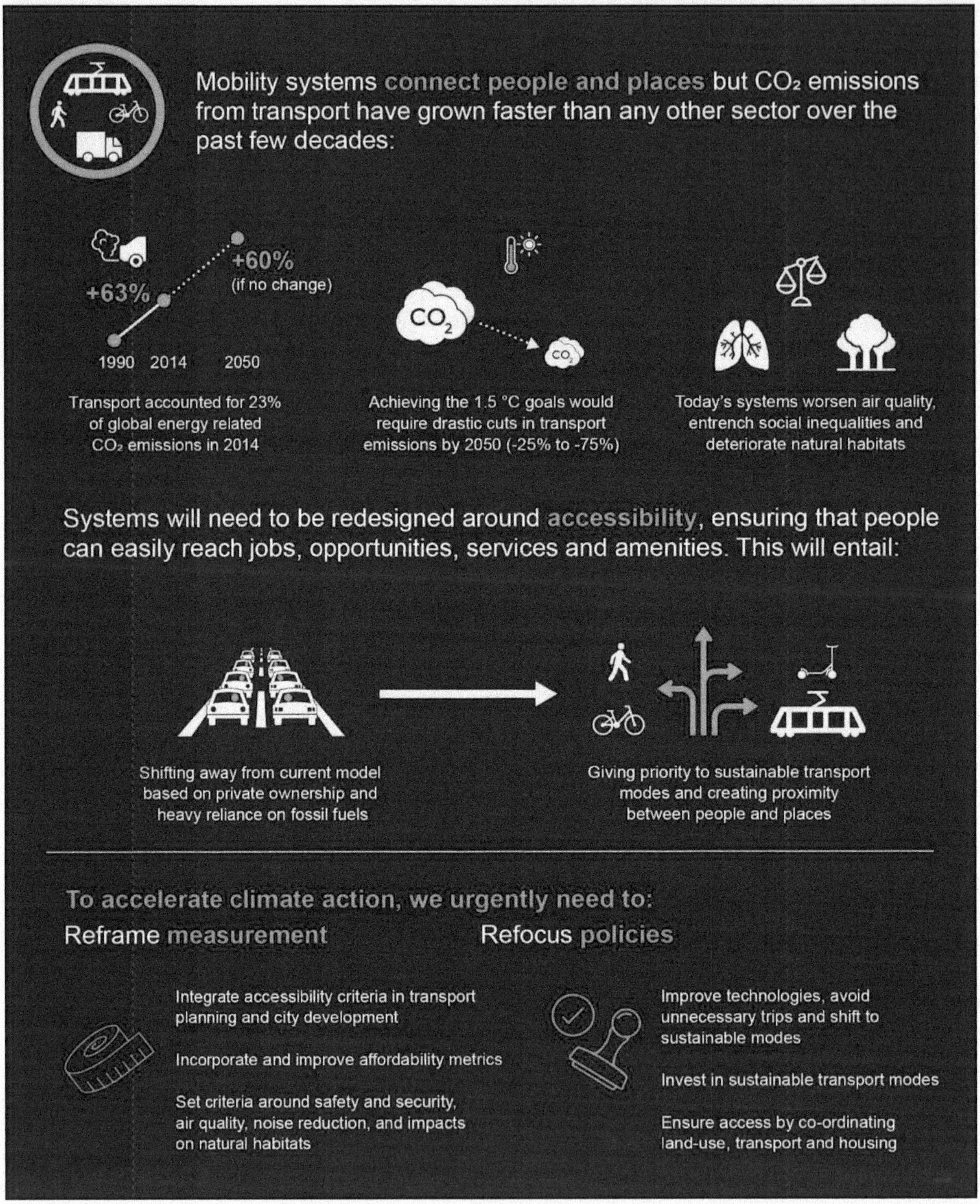

5.1. Introduction

Chapter 1 of this report argues for applying a **well-being lens** to policy making, explaining why this is key to ensuring a **two-way alignment** between climate and broader well-being goals. Adopting a well-being lens implies that societal goals are defined in terms of well-being outcomes (climate change risks and impacts included), and are systematically reflected in decision-making across the economy. It also entails that decisions are taken keeping multiple well-being objectives in mind, rather than focusing on a single (or very narrow range of) objective(s). Finally, the interrelations between the different economic sectors and systems in which a policy intervenes should be sufficiently well understood. This chapter applies the well-being lens to the transport sector.

The transport sector is a key enabler of human activity, hence well-being heavily depends on its performance and characteristics. Mobility systems connect people and places, bringing important economic and social added value, and increasing life quality. Nonetheless, mobility systems can also generate a series of negative impacts on well-being, by polluting the air; threatening user's lives and physical integrity (e.g. through high risks of accidents); increasing economic and social inequalities, and the social exclusion of vulnerable groups; and even causing habitat loss and degradation. Mobility systems are also important emitters of global greenhouse gases (GHG), significantly contributing to climate change.

Global carbon dioxide (CO_2) emissions from transport increased by 63% between 1990 and 2014 (OECD/IEA, 2019[1]). Over the past 50 years, emissions from the transport sector have grown faster than in any other sector, with CO_2 transport emissions accounting for 23% of global energy-related CO_2 emissions in 2014 (IPCC, 2018[2]). In terms of composition, emissions from surface passenger transport accounted for almost 50% of total global CO_2 emissions from transport in 2015 (ITF, 2017[3]), largely as a result of growth in private-vehicle ownership and use (ITF, 2017[3]), even in urban areas where density of demand provides a potentially larger scope for non-motorised and public transport (Aguilar Jaber and Glocker, 2015[4]). International and domestic aviation accounted for 10% of transport CO_2 emissions in 2015, surface freight (road and rail) 28%, and sea and air freight 12% (ITF, 2017[3]).

If current conditions persist, there is no prospect of reversing this upward trend in transport emissions anytime soon. Improvements in vehicle technology, particularly fuel efficiency, are likely to continue. However, the sector is still heavily reliant on fossil fuels, and significant growth in global transport volumes is expected in the coming decades. Under the current trends, total passenger and tonne-kilometres are expected to grow by a factor of three between 2015 and 2050 (ITF, 2019[5]). Even in a scenario where current and announced policies are implemented, transport CO_2 emissions will still increase by 60% by 2050 (ITF, 2019[5]) – far from projections of where the sector would need to go to be consistent with well-below 2 degrees Celsius (°C) and 1.5°C scenarios. While integrated assessment models project the necessary CO_2 emission reductions in the transport sector to be far smaller than reductions in sectors like electricity (and other demand-side sectors), in scenarios with a greater than 67% chance of staying below a 2ºC goal (Luderer et al., 2018[6]), they still need to fall modestly by 2050, relative to 2010 levels (ranging from non-growth to - 25% according to the different 2ºC pathways). Achieving a 1.5°C goal would require much deeper cuts in transport emissions by 2050 (ranging from -25% to -75%, according to different 1.5ºC pathways) (Luderer et al., 2018[6]).

How the transport sector evolves – e.g. whether systems based on private ownership and low vehicle-occupancy rates persist, or more sustainable modes (e.g. walking, cycling, and public and other shared mobility modes) gain a prominent role – will be key to the sector's contribution to climate change mitigation and multiple other well-being goals. As in other sectors, the development of new technologies is an important driver for change. Three "revolutions" have been particularly identified as "game changers" (Fulton et al., 2017[7]): 1) the increasing availability and decreasing cost of low- and zero-emission vehicle technologies; 2) the development of automated vehicles; and 3) the development of new business models made possible by digitalisation, such as ride-hailing and "on-demand" shared mobility services (Fulton et al., 2017[7]). In addition, technology has also increasingly allowed the emergence and growing role of new transport modes (e.g. electric vehicles and scooters, often called micro-mobility). Several governments are also looking into mobility as a service (MaaS) as the desired model for using technologies to improve transport services. The Finnish government, for instance, passed the new Act on Transport Services in 2018, with the aim of promoting MaaS, which it defines as providing the following advantages: "[T]hrough technology information and innovations, transport services become a customer-oriented service, in which the boundaries between transport modes disappear and transport chains will be smooth" (ITF, 2018[8]). The policy framework in which these technologies, stakeholders and models evolve will determine their role, as well as their ultimate impact on shaping mobility systems and delivering climate change mitigation and other societal goals.

Section 5.2 argues that applying a well-being lens to the transport sector requires rethinking mobility policies, investment priorities and planning. The focus needs to shift from generating physical movement to delivering access to economic, social and environmental opportunities, by improving physical accessibility, affordability and road safety (particularly through sustainable modes). Discussions emphasise potential synergies and identify potential trade-offs needing to be managed when undertaking climate action in the sector. They examine how the proposed change in perspective can enhance synergies and minimise/mitigate trade-offs. Section 5.3 proposes several indicators that could be used to better track and evaluate the transport sector's contribution to wider well-being and the Sustainable Development Goals (SDGs). Based on examples from different countries and cities, it discusses how using such metrics allows tracking progress in terms of different policy priorities and gaining a better understanding of how mitigation actions can impact on other dimensions of well-being and vice versa, facilitating the two-way alignment discussed in Chapter 1. This chapter has a stronger focus on passenger surface (i.e. road and rail) transport, although a shift to accessibility-based systems will directly impact on the efficiency of surface freight modes (including by giving the transport of goods priority over private cars), with implications for their regulation. Also, many of the indicators discussed throughout the chapter, as well as the impacts covered are as important to monitor the performance of passenger as freight transport modes.

5.2. A shift in focus from physical movement to accessibility

It is important to be clear about the desired outcomes from transport policies. More physical movement does not necessarily result in better outcomes in terms of well-being and sustainability. Congestion and other negative externalities, as well as the excessive time and money spent by certain groups on travel, can all significantly reduce disposable incomes, exacerbate inequalities, and damage health and the environment. Evidence exists that car-centred planning, based on a "predict-and-provide" approach (i.e. predicting traffic and providing road infrastructure accordingly) leads to additional car traffic (induced demand). It does not ease congestion or reduce environmental externalities (including a range of other pollutants co-emitted with CO_2 emissions), nor does it contribute to widespread access to opportunities for the population.

Evidence of induced demand was generated in the early 1990s in Europe, and growing evidence both in Europe and elsewhere has since contributed to a progressive revision of the rationale behind mobility policy and investment in transport infrastructure (OECD, 2016[9]).[1] Shifting the focus behind policy decisions and investment from following mobility demand (passenger and tonne-kilometres) and increasing speed to improving accessibility, i.e. the ease of reaching destinations for goods, services, jobs and other activities (Litman, 2008[10]), has increasingly been recognised as a more adequate means of delivering sustainability goals. Nonetheless, important challenges remain in expanding accessibility-based planning and policy, as analysed by (Silva and Larson, 2018[11]). One of the most important issues is the common confusion between mobility and accessibility, leading to the general assumption that mobility is equal to or at least a good proxy for accessibility. Consequently, policies and planning often still focus strongly on increasing mobility, even when the word "accessibility" is used (Silva and Larson, 2018[11]).

These issues are reinforced by the correlation of transport volume measures (e.g. passenger and tonne-kilometres) with gross domestic product (GDP) and GDP per capita. The effect has often been interpreted as mutually reinforcing: as the economy grows and incomes rise, more transport activity is generated. At the same time, more transport activity contributes to more connections and economic activity, leading to economic development.

The correspondence between physical movement and speed, and effective access to activities and opportunities – let alone other dimensions of well-being, such as air pollution – is, however, imperfect (ITF-OECD, 2019[12]). In many cases, overall transport volumes can be high precisely because accessibility is limited, causing people and/or freight services to travel longer distances and incur higher expenditure on travel, while generating greater CO_2 emissions and air pollution (which costs are not reflected or positively accounted for in GDP). One example is when limited accessibility by public transport generates higher car travel. Other examples are when destinations are located far away from trip origins, increasing travel distances, and/or accessibility by walking and cycling is difficult or unsafe, generating more travel on motorised modes in both situations. Thus, while keeping track of transport volumes will still be key to understanding emission drivers and demand trends, their inadequate use as measure of ultimate performance for the sector needs to be acknowledged (this is further discussed in Section 5.3).

Important opportunities exist for generating two-way alignment between climate change mitigation action, and broader well-being and sustainable development objectives in the transport sector, by focusing on accessibility instead of mobility. Such a shift in perspective can better align decisions in the sector with well-being and the SDGs. Firstly, because it is improved access to opportunities and activities, rather than higher physical movement that is directly linked to generating well-being. Second, focusing on improving accessibility recognises the role and value of sustainable modes of transport. This includes potential opportunities for new transport modes (e.g. micro-mobility), which under a reconfiguration of road space allocation that would prioritise low-carbon and space efficient modes, could bring relevant benefits and avoid potential trade-offs (e.g. accidents). Third, an accessibility-based approach emphasises the importance of designing cities in a way that enhances proximity – which, although not in the hands of policy makers in the sector, is a key enabler for moving towards sustainable transport systems. All of this would support governments in delivering climate change mitigation and other policy priorities that are central to generating well-being, such as: enhancing physical accessibility, ensuring affordability of services, improving road safety. Indeed, analysing climate change mitigation policies through the lens of their impacts on other policy goals linked to the different dimensions of accessibility, as well as pollution, noise, related health impacts and other environmental damages, can increase their effectiveness and help avoid important trade-offs. These relations are summarised in Table 5.1 and further discussed in Section 5.3.

Focusing on accessibility instead of mobility is at the heart of the two-way alignment. It recognises the role and value of sustainable modes of transport and the importance of designing cities in a way that enhances proximity. Both conditions are central to the sector reversing increasing GHG emissions trends and delivering a wide number of other well-being objectives.

Table 5.1. Potential two-way alignment benefits from applying the well-being lens to the transport sector

Other policy priority	Contributing to limiting climate change	
	Generating synergies	Avoiding / reducing trade-offs
Enhancing physical accessibility	An accessibility-based approach can improve linkages across the transport system, especially easing travel, and increasing the competitiveness of non-motorised modes and public transport. This makes it easier to incentivise a modal shift to more sustainable modes (which is the focus of a number of climate change mitigation policies). Adopting an accessibility focus for expansions and upgrades to public transport and facilities for non-motorised modes is also relevant to effectively attract users to sustainable modes. The focus on accessibility also allows recognising land-use solutions and better co-ordinating transport and land-use planning. The creation of better alignment between these policies is at the heart of climate change mitigation policies aiming to avoid unnecessary travel and create a shift towards sustainable modes.	Being aware of changes in accessibility is also key to reducing risks of negative social impacts (e.g. affordability, social exclusion). This is particularly relevant when implementing transport demand management (TDM) policies (e.g. carbon and congestion pricing). A number of these policies are used to correct the pricing of different transport modes to reflect negative externalities (including GHG emissions), and hence aim to incentivise the use of less carbon-intensive modes. However, without ensuring accessibility through alternative modes, these policies could result in imposing important burden on users, while not being significant in delivering climate change mitigation.
Ensuring affordability of services	Taking into account households' transport expenditures when deciding on the location of housing developments can result in promoting construction in locations that are better connected to final destinations (e.g. jobs, education services) through sustainable modes. It can also avoid generating disproportionate transport expenditures for households and importantly contribute to higher use of sustainable modes.	Consider households' transport expenditures when deciding on the location of affordable and social housing schemes can avoid disconnecting the most vulnerable population from areas where transit-oriented development (TOD) has been created. Analysing household's vulnerability (according to income and location) when implementing TDM policies can provide important insights for mitigating the risks of imposing a high burden on vulnerable groups and increasing the scope for modal shift.
Ensuring safety and security	Safer streets (both in terms of road safety and public security) increase confidence to walk, cycle and use public transport (which generally implies increasing walking segments of trips). This supports climate change mitigation and promotes a shift towards more sustainable modes of transport.	Designing walking, cycling and public transport infrastructure for attracting users, in line with best practices for reducing risk of accidents, is key to avoid generating safety issues from higher use of non-motorised and public modes. Monitoring and increasing public security along public transport corridors, and preferred walking and cycling pathways, can also reduce risks for pedestrian and cyclists.
Reducing local pollution, reducing health risks and habitat damage	Policies that promote the renewal of the vehicle fleet (e.g. energy efficiency and electrification) with the aim of reducing pollution and/or noise can also contribute to GHG mitigation, and vice versa. Monitoring and taking measures to avoid habitat damage by construction of transport projects (e.g. through air pollution) can also help mitigate GHG emissions. Also, looking into potential biodiversity loss due to projects could mean opting for options that reduce land conversion, potentially also avoiding GHG emissions.	Accurate data on local air pollution emissions are an important input for ensuring that vehicle standards and policies that promote the renewal of the vehicle fleet can contribute to both GHG mitigation and pollution reduction, avoiding potential trade-offs.

Note: This table builds on work cited throughout the chapter.

5.3. Indicators for monitoring transport's contribution to well-being

As argued in Chapter 1, a measurement system that supports governments in monitoring and assessing policies in terms of their multiple impacts on well-being is necessary. This section proposes and discusses a range of indicators that are not widespread, but can improve policy makers' ability to monitor progress towards climate and other well-being policy goals. The section provides a way to better capture the potential synergies and trade-offs created by different decisions and policies, by drawing on examples of how this type of assessment and tracking is being initiated in some countries and cities.

Table 5.2. Policy priorities for the transport sector and their link to the SDGs and the OECD well - being framework

Policy priority	SDG goal and target	OECD Well-being domain	OECD Well-being dimension
Limiting climate change	13. Climate action. 11.2. By 2030, provide access to safe, affordable, accessible and sustainable transport systems for all. 11.6. By 2030, reduce the adverse per capita environmental impact of cities.	Future well-being: resources.	Natural capital.
Enhancing physical accessibility	1.1. By 2030, eradicate extreme poverty for all people everywhere. 1.2. By 2030, reduce at least by half the proportion of men, women and children of all ages living in poverty.	Current well-being: material conditions.	Job and earnings. Income and wealth. Housing. Education skills. Work and life balance. Social connections. Health status.
	8.5. By 2030, achieve full and productive employment and decent work for all. 3.8. Achieve universal health coverage. 8.5. By 2030, achieve full and productive employment and decent work for all 9.1. Develop quality, reliable, sustainable and resilient infrastructure, 11.1. By 2030, ensure access for all to adequate, safe and affordable housing and basic services and upgrade slums 11.2. By 2030, provide access to safe, affordable, accessible and sustainable transport systems for all	Current well-being: quality of life.	
Ensuring affordability of services	1.1. By 2030, eradicate extreme poverty for all people everywhere. 1.2. By 2030, reduce at least by half the proportion of men, women and children of all ages living in poverty. 11.2. By 2030, provide access to safe, affordable, accessible and sustainable transport systems for all.	Current well-being: material conditions.	Income and wealth. Jobs and earnings. Housing.
Ensuring safety and security	3.6. By 2020, halve the number of global deaths and injuries from road traffic accidents. 11.2. By 2030, provide access to safe, affordable, accessible and sustainable transport systems for all.	Current well-being: material conditions.	Personal security.
Reducing local pollution and noise, associated health risks and habitat damage	3.9. By 2030, substantially reduce the number of deaths and illnesses from hazardous chemicals and air, water and soil pollution and contamination. 11.6. By 2030, reduce the adverse per capita environmental impact of cities.	Current well-being: quality of life. Future well-being: resources.	Health status. Environmental quality. Natural resources.

Discussion on different indicators is structured according to the five policy priorities identified in Section 5.2 as being key for the sector to achieve wider well-being and sustainability goals: limiting climate change; enhancing physical accessibility; ensuring affordability of services; improving road safety and security; and reducing local pollution and noise, associated health risks and habitat damage. Table 5.2 summarises the links between these policy priorities and SDG goals and targets, as well as with different dimensions and domains of the OECD Framework for Measuring Well-being and Progress (henceforth the OECD well-being framework).

Summary tables in each subsection show indicators that could be used as tools to translate the different policy goals into measurable outcomes. They also show the link between the indicators proposed and those used for the specific SDG targets, and the well-being domains and dimensions set out by the OECD well-being framework. As discussed throughout the section, the indicators proposed complement those already used in the SDG and OECD well-being frameworks by: a) contributing sector-specific disaggregated data to understand performance towards the SDG target and/or well-being; or b) improving understanding of the transport-related enabling conditions needed to achieve the SDG targets and/or well-being goals.

The indicators discussed throughout this section are not exhaustive. Rather, the analysis here is suggestive and intended to open discussion by highlighting data limitations and potential data enhancements, as well as illustrating good practice where improved indicators are already proving valuable.

5.3.1. Limiting climate change

Monitoring GHGs from transport is a way of directly quantifying the sector's contribution to climate change mitigation goals. As stated before, CO_2 emissions from transport account for around 23% of world energy-related emissions and have grown continuously over the last decades.

Data on CO_2, and in some cases GHG emissions from the transport sector, are more or less available at the national level. A growing number of countries have developed emission inventories, which include specific GHG emissions from the transport sector. However, inventories for the transport sector are often estimated by using national data on fuel consumption, making it difficult to track emissions at a subnational level. Contributing to bridging this information gap, some cities that are actively committed to climate change mitigation have developed their own inventories, often linked to support from international institutions. Contributing to bridging this information gap, some cities that are actively committed to climate change mitigation have developed their own inventories, often linked to support from international institutions. For example, the Global Protocol for Community-scale Greenhouse Gas Emission Inventories (GPC) is a framework created by the C40 Cities Climate Leadership Group, the World Resources Institute and ICLEI-Local Governments for Sustainability to support cities in accounting and reporting city-level GHG emissions (including for the transport sector) (C40, 2019[13]). As a general rule, participating cities are often larger cities that have more resources; many other cities do not have such tools.

Overall, improving the granularity of transport-related data on GHG emissions is necessary: detailed data on emissions by mode and type of vehicles, as well as information regarding the contribution of different territories across countries, would better inform decisions and improve certainty on reaching targets. Systematically conducting ex-post analysis on GHG emission reduction from policy interventions and investment decisions would also improve estimations for incorporating climate change mitigation into appraisal methodologies.

An important challenge is measuring different GHG emissions from transport. The most recent version of the *Handbook on the external costs of transport,* published by the European Commission, (van Essen et al., 2019[14]), estimates climate change mitigation costs as part of a number of other external costs from transport. The report includes road, rail, maritime and inland waterway transport, accounting for costs related to carbon dioxide (CO_2', nitrous oxide (N_2O) and methane (CH_4) emissions. It provides guidance on state-of-the-art methodologies for estimating climate change and other external costs from transport, including : a) best-practice recommendations for cases where disaggregated and detailed case-specific data exist; b) typical input values that can be used by EU Member States when calculating their own total costs of transport externalities; and c) average and marginal costs for different externalities, for cases where data for calculating these based on more disaggregated and case-specific data are not available (van Essen et al., 2019[14]). Figure 5.1 shows the share of total transport external costs of climate change (estimated at EUR 987 billion [euros]), as well as for other costs (linked to other priorities discussed in this chapter): congestion, accidents, air pollution, noise and habitat damages estimated for the European Union (EU28) for 2016. In the case of both pollution and GHG emissions, separate estimations are made for well-to tank emissions (i.e. emissions from energy production). The different costs included (in addition to those stemming from climate change) will be discussed in the corresponding subsections.

The document estimates the total climate change cost of transport for the EU28 by using central values for damage costs of GHG emissions (EUR 100 per tonne of CO_2eq), based on a literature review.[2] The total estimated cost for the EU28 in 2016 is EUR 83.14 billion, of which total passenger transport (passenger cars, motorcycles, buses and coaches) accounts for 70% (van Essen et al., 2019[14]). The

Handbook also estimates and presents average costs per passenger and vehicle kilometre for different types of vehicles with different technologies (van Essen et al., 2019[14]).

Figure 5.1. EUR 987 billion in external costs for transport in the EU28 in 2016

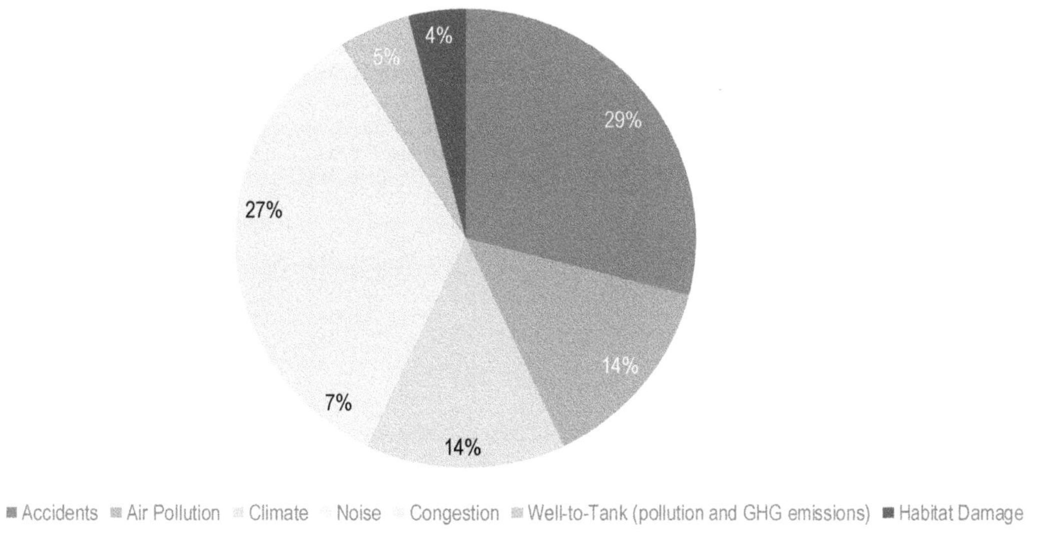

Note: Estimations include road, rail, aviation and maritime transport, except for congestion, which only includes road modes.
Source: (van Essen et al., 2019[14]).

StatLink https://doi.org/10.1787/888933993085

As reflected in Figure 5.1 accounting for well-to-tank emissions generated by the sector is also relevant. The *Handbook* estimates the total cost of GHG and pollution of well-to-tank transport emissions for the EU28 at EUR 31.2 billion in 2016, including 60% from climate change emissions (van Essen et al., 2019[14]).

Having accurate and disaggregated data on drivers of transport GHG emissions, such as transport volumes, share of electric vehicles, fuel efficiency and carbon intensity by type of vehicle, and car ownership, is key. Discussing these data requirements and indicators is beyond the scope of this report, which focused on indicators that can show ultimate outcomes and progress towards different goals. Institutions such as the International Energy Agency (IEA), the International Transport Forum at the OECD (ITF) and the International Council for Clean Transportation have focused on collecting data and supporting countries in improving this type of indicators. For instance, the IEA report *Tracking Clean Energy Progress 2018* provides a number of indicators for transport and other sectors, reflecting short-term actions that are necessary to drive the transition towards clean energy (IEA, 2018[15]). The report indicates the necessary evolution of the selected drivers of emissions in the different sectors (at the global level) from now to 2030 in order to be consistent with the IEA Sustainable Development Scenario (IEA, 2018[15]).

Table 5.3. Summary table: Indicators for monitoring progress in limiting climate change and links to SDGs and OECD well-being framework

Policy priority	Proposed indicators	SDG goal and target	SDG indicators	OECD well-being domain/dimension	OECD well-being indicators
Limiting climate change	• Transport-related CO2 and other relevant GHG emissions such as N_2O and CH4. • Total and disaggregated data by transport mode, vehicle type and type of user, and for different territories is needed. • Both well-to-tank and tank-to-wheel data are necessary.	13. 11.6.	• The framework does not collect specific data. • City-specific transport emissions would also be relevant to the target, which calls for reducing the adverse per capita environmental impact of cities.	Future well-being: resources. Natural capital	• GHG emissions from domestic production. • CO2 emissions from domestic consumption.

5.3.2. Enhancing physical accessibility

As shown in Table 5.2, enhancing transport accessibility is linked to a number of SDG goals, and OECD well-being dimensions and domains. However, despite growing recognition of these links, there exists a need for "indicators that can be used to compare the quality of access delivered by different transport modes, at different territorial scales, and for distinct populations" (ITF-OECD, 2019[12]). These indicators will be key to tracking progress in the delivery of accessibility goals, as well as to developing accessibility-based decision-making frameworks, "i.e. policy, planning, and investment frameworks in which accessibility considerations are central criteria systematically guiding decisions" (ITF-OECD, 2019[12]).

The development of accessibility indicators is not new, but the number of indicators of this type has been growing. The increasing availability of spatial data has greatly contributed to this phenomenon (Geurs, 2018[16]). This subsection first explores how accessibility indicators could be used to monitor progress in the sector and its contribution to SDG targets and OECD well-being dimensions (summarised in Table 5.1). It then discusses in detail different types of accessibility indicators, and how these have been used in planning and appraisal in selected cities and countries.

SDG Target 11.2 calls explicitly for providing access to safe, affordable, accessible and sustainable transport systems. While useful, the indicator (proportion of population that has convenient access to public transport) selected by the SDG framework could be enhanced by accounting for frequency of service. In addition, tracking not only access to transport, but also access by public transport and other modes, and for different population groups to final destinations (e.g. jobs, education and health centres, etc.) is also key to understanding the sector's contribution to a number of other SDGs and well-being objectives. Transport authorities (e.g. Transport for London [TfL]) and international organisations, such as the European Commission and the ITF, have done important work on this, by developing methodologies for computing indicators that go in this direction (see Table 5.5 and Box 5.4 in this section). Other indicators, such as a new approach developed by WhereIsMyTransport and applied to the City of Cape Town in South Africa, incorporate affordability and public security elements alongside physical accessibility to a range of relevant destinations (see Box 5.5). WhereIsMyTransport is a data platform for sustainable mobility in emerging markets that maps formal and informal public transport networks. All of these methodologies and indicators could be replicated in a number of cities, and thus could gradually become part of the indicators used for monitoring this target.

Access to employment is particularly central to delivering SDGs linked to employment and productivity. For instance, an evaluation of a subsidy scheme for lower-income households in Bogotá showed an increase in productivity as a result of increased public transport accessibility to economic activities (Peralta-Quiros and Rodríguez Hernández, 2016[17]). As such, indicators measuring changes in accessibility to employment are linked to SDG Target 8.5 (full and productive employment) and changes in the employment rate (an indicator used by the OECD well-being framework). In the same way, indicators measuring the levels and quality of physical accessibility to health and education centres will add valuable information on how the sector is contributing to SDG Target 3.8 (universal health coverage), as well as educational attainment (part of the "quality of life" domain and "education skills" dimension in the OECD well-being framework).

Together, indicators measuring transport access to health, education, employment and recreational centres can also add relevant information for understanding the sector's contribution to social connections, a dimension recognised by the OECD well-being framework. While directly related to different dimensions of social, human and economic capital, good transport accessibility to different activities and points of interests are ultimately necessary to prevent social exclusion and eradicate poverty (SDG Target 1.1). "Broad evidence [...] suggests that lack of, or poor access to transport options is central to limitations on access to jobs, educational institutions, health facilities, social networks, etc., which in turn generates a "poverty trap" (Lucas, 2018[18]).

The inclusion of transport accessibility to employment and other activities, especially through public transport, has also been increasingly recognised as a necessary element of housing quality (ITF-OECD, 2017[19]). Therefore, the level of accessibility from housing to different points of interest could also be included as part of indicators tracking the delivery of "good housing". Housing is recognised as part of the "materials condition" dimension of the OECD well-being framework and by SDG Target 11.1, which calls for ensuring access for all people to adequate, safe and affordable housing. Chapter 4 on the residential sector develops this discussion in more detail.

Finally, accessibility indicators could also bring valuable information for keeping track of SDG Target 9.1, "develop quality, reliable, sustainable and resilient infrastructure ... to support economic development and human well-being". Indicators focused on access to frequent public transport services are important for identifying transport infrastructure gaps as well as the need for infrastructure upgrades across the transport system. In addition, developing indicators that allow comparing the levels of access provided to reach activities by different transport modes and population groups are key to identify particular gaps across territories, particularly in terms of sustainable transport infrastructure and vulnerable users.

Indicators on modal split, and the quantity and quality of infrastructure (e.g. data on allocation of road space and quality of infrastructure for different transport modes, such as median block size, share of roads with a low speed limit, bus rapid transit (BRT) lanes, bicycle lanes and facilities for freight transport would also be required to better track SDG Goal 9.1. As explained in Section 5.2, current indicators for this target (i.e. passenger and freight volumes) are not an adequate proxy for progress on delivering sustainable transport infrastructure. Rather, they tend to bias thinking towards a "predict-and-provide approach", which has proved detrimental for prioritising sustainable transport options. The limitation of the current SDG Goal 9.1 indicators and the need for considering modal split, and particularly shares of more sustainable modes, has been raised by other organisations as well. For instance, the UN Economic Commission for Europe (UNECE) points out that a lack of compilation and interpretation guidance for the current indicators makes it difficult to determine progress on SDG Target 9.1. Some countries are reporting lower passenger and goods volumes as a negative, although it may simply indicate higher shares of active modes, lower commuting distances or efficient supply chains. The indicator and its metadata does not currently indicate how to assess progress (Blackburn, 2019[20]), but international work is now starting on this objective.

As discussed in Section 5.2, beyond the immediate links with sustainability and well-being goals explained above and reflected in Table 5.4. , the focus on enhancing accessibility is linked to climate change mitigation and other environmental and health benefits. First, an accessibility-based approach can recognise the value of and promote a central role for more sustainable transport modes (walking, cycling, public transport and other shared-trip services, including intercity rail). In addition, it allows increasing co-ordination between transport and land-use policy and planning, which is key to creating location-efficient and TOD patterns (see definitions in Box 5.1).The relevant role of these transport modes and the characteristics of the development patterns mentioned can generate widespread access, while significantly reducing overall distance, space consumption and travel, leading to lower GHG emissions and other negative externalities.

Research and analysis using accessibility indicators has multiplied as the relevance of generating not only social and economic benefits, but also environmental benefits, has become more evident. The use of accessibility indicators, particularly in the context of accessibility-based planning, is increasingly acknowledged as a way to "invert the growing unsustainability of urban settlement and mobility patterns" (Silva and Larson, 2018[11]). (ITF-OECD, 2019[12]), however, highlights that certain principles are necessary to ensure that accessibility-based frameworks effectively promote policies supporting sustainable development. Among these are using accessibility indicators that can: a) track accessibility needs for different transport users; b) reflect multiple modes of transport and their relative performance (specifically including sustainable modes like cycling, walking and public transport); and c) account for territorial differences (e.g. urban vs. non-urban territories), particularly acknowledging the neighbourhood scale.

Box 5.1. Transit-oriented development and location efficiency

TOD is commonly defined as a type of mixed-use urban development within close proximity (walking distance) to mass transit facilities. TOD principles are based on organising new development and redevelopment along mass transit corridors that serve as main transport axes, building high-density development along these corridors and fostering mixed land use and jobs.

Location efficiency refers to an urban development pattern where new housing developments are steered to locations that are affordable and can offer easy access through well connected sustainable transport modes.

Source: (ITF-OECD, 2017[19]).

Table 5.4. Summary table: Indicators for monitoring progress in enhancing physical accessibility and links to SDGs and OECD well-being framework

Policy priority	Proposed indicators	SDG goal and target	SDG indicators	OECD well-being domain/dimension	OECD well-being indicators
Enhancing physical accessibility	• Accessibility to frequent public transport services. • Share of population without easy walking access to public transport. • Absolute accessibility; i.e. # of points of interest available by different modes of transport within different time thresholds. • Transport performance. • Proximity. • % of population with access to a minimum number of points of interest by different transport modes and within different time thresholds.	1.1. 2.3. 3.8. 8.5. 9.1. 11.1. 11.2.	• % of population and employed population below the poverty line. • Would allow measuring access to markets (mentioned in target but no indicator). • Coverage of essential health services. • Average hourly earnings of employees, by occupation. • Unemployment rate. • Indicator currently used are not useful to track 9.1.2. • Proportion of the rural population who live within 2 km of an all-season road (does not account for urban transport and only considers access to roads). • Passenger and freight volumes (promotes "predict-and-provide" approach and says nothing about delivery of sustainable infrastructure). • Proportion of urban population living in slums, informal settlements or inadequate housing. • Proportion of population that has convenient. • Access to public transport, by sex, age and persons with disabilities.	Current well-being: material conditions. Jobs and earnings Current well-being: material conditions. Housing Current well-being: quality of life. Education skills Current well-being: quality of life. Health status Current well-being: quality of life. Social connections.	• Employment rate. • Rooms per person. • Sanitation (could provide information on connections between housing and points of interest) • Education attainment. • Perceived health. • Indicators could add relevant information on how people are connected to other people and activities, allowing participating in social and economic life.

Measuring accessibility requires having information reflecting its many determinants: land use (spatial distribution of activities), transport, temporal constraints and individual characteristics (e.g. income, gender). Different types of accessibility indicators can provide information on these different dimensions; within each type, simple and more complex indicators can also be developed. (Geurs, 2018[16]) divides accessibility indicators into four categories and analyses the characteristics, strengths and weaknesses of each type (Box 5.2). Within the different types of indicators, infrastructure-based and location-based measures are easier to operationalise, since they are less data-demanding, and are easier to interpret and communicate (Geurs, 2018[16]). Thus, these types of indicator have been more widely used by policy makers and planners. Examples in this section also focus on indicators from these categories.

Box 5.2 Types of accessibility indicators

a) Infrastructure-based measures focus on the transport component and provide insight on the relative quality of infrastructure throughout the transport network. Travel speed and congestion indices are examples of very simple measures of this type. More sophisticated examples can measure the average travel time needed to get to every location in an area from a specific location. The Public Transport Accessibility Level (PTAL) indicator used by TfL is another example (see more in Table 5.5).

b) Location-based indicators incorporate both the transport and land-use components. Contour-based or cumulative opportunity indicators are the simplest forms. These tools measure the number of opportunities (e.g. services, jobs) that can be reached within a certain time threshold, or the average time or cost needed to access a certain number of opportunities from a selected origin. Potential accessibility indicators are more sophisticated versions, which add an impedance function to calculations, i.e. a function that simulates the reduction in desirability of an opportunity in relation to the cost of travel (e.g. monetary, travel time). In some cases, indicators can also add competition effects i.e. the fact that opportunities are limited, which could also restrict access.

c) Utility-based indices estimate the welfare benefits that come with different levels of access to spatially distributed activities. They are based on modal-choice modelling tools and are thus a necessary input to calculating the indicators. Utility-based measures are highly complex, and thus more challenging to interpret, communicate and operationalise.

d) Person-based indicators quantify an individual's ability to reach a certain location given spatio-temporal constraints, and according to the activities the individual needs to realise. The indicator in this case is calculated as the volume of a space-time prism, and represents the feasibility of opportunities according to space and time constraints. Person-based indicators are complex and data-demanding. As for utility-based measures, although rich in detail, they are relatively challenging in terms of communication, interpretation and operationalisation.

Person-based indicators are intrinsically linked to the temporal and individual components of accessibility. For the other type of indicators, using variants, differentiating between peak hours, population groups, transport modes and/or taking into account infrastructure quality can incorporate the temporal and individual elements. This allows linking accessibility to other policy goals (e.g. accessibility of lower-income groups and equity related issues, and sustainability and climate change mitigation).

Source: based on (Geurs, 2018[16]).

Accessibility indicators can improve transport planning if they are incorporated into the decision-making frameworks used by countries and cities. TfL, for instance, has developed a number of accessibility-based indicators (Table 5.5) that it uses to plan both the transport network, and commercial and residential development. Accessibility analysis based on these indicators has been at the centre of a number of policies, initiatives and infrastructure upgrades, which have allowed the City of London to double public transport's modal share (from 25% to 50%) between 1995 and 2012. "This type of analysis [...] enables TfL to understand where and to what extent sustainable transport options are available throughout London in accessing jobs and other amenities. This is important as the availability of public transport alternatives is obviously a clear driver of public transport mode share. Increased public transport use also correlates to higher use of active modes (walking and cycling) as these are often used as access and egress modes" (Inayathusein and Cooper, 2018[21]). It is estimated that if all Londoners walked or cycled for 20 minutes a day, the National Health System could save 1.7 billion GBP (British pounds) in the next 25 years (GLA,

2017[22]) and account for at least 60 000 years of healthy life (thanks to prevented illness and early death) each year for the next 20 years (GLA, 2018[23]).

Analysis based on accessibility indicators has been at the centre of a number of policies, initiatives and infrastructure upgrades, which have allowed the City of London to double public transport's modal share (from 25% to 50%) between 1995 and 2012.

At the national level, the most recent Transport Investment Strategy published by the Department for Transport (DfT) cites the improvement of accessibility (referred to as connectivity) as one of its principal objectives. The DfT uses statistics and heat maps plotting accessibility to jobs by public transport and car across the country to identify infrastructure gaps and investment needs (ITF-OECD, 2019[12]).

Table 5.5 Accessibility indicators developed by TfL

Indicator	Existing/under development	Description of methodology
PTAL	Existing	Total access time by route is calculated by combining walk time + service wait time + a mode-based reliability factor. Total access times are converted to an "equivalent doorstop frequency (EDF)" to compare the benefits offered by routes at different distances. The sum of all EDFs with a weighting factor in favour of the most dominant route for each mode is calculated. This gives the access index (AI) score of each service. The PTAI (public transport access index) is the sum of AIs by grid point. This is converted to the final PTAL by using nine ranges : PTAL 0 is reflects a PTAI of 0, PTAL 1a reflects a physical accessibility index (PAI) between.01 and 2.5, and so on, until the highest PTAL measure (6b), which reflects a PAI above 40.
Catchment areas and London-wide catchment analysis	Existing	Analysis consists of mapping travel times from or to a selected location. TfL has not formalised an actual indicator, but rather uses a range of measures that come from this mapping exercise. The transportation model of TfL (Railplan) is used to derive travel time data. The model provides information on the likely routes and service choices of public transport users. Thus, it also provides flows, journey times and levels of crowding in and around London. London is divided into 3 288 zones, for which matrices of journey times for all combinations of origins/destinations can be derived. London-wide catchment analysis is also used for analysing changes across the city.
ATOS (access to opportunities and services)	Existing	A number of origin points are calculated by dividing London into grids and calculating a centroid (based on the distribution of population according to 2011 census data). Service and destination points are then defined, based on a definition of a "basket" of key opportunities. The basket includes a minimum number of services related to jobs, education and health, quality food shopping and open spaces. A variant of the Railplan model (CAPITAL) is used to calculate point-to point public travel times, which are combined with walking travel times for shorter trips. Scores are divided into five different ATOS levels (A through E), where A is the best or quickest level of accessibility to services, and E is the worst or lowest.
CYTAL	Under development	CYTAL extends the PTAL analysis by including cycling as an access mode to public transport. The methodology is under development and some issues need to be solved: setting maximum cycle-access distance and possibly a minimum distance under which bicycle access is not relevant; accounting for differences between inner and outer London; and accounting for availability and quality of cycling infrastructure are among the points being discussed.
New walking connectivity measures	Under development	These new tools will use a detailed walk network to calculate the shortest routes between given origins and destinations (building on ATOS analysis). The assumptions to be used (e.g. average walk speed, whether these should be differentiated by user type, maximum walking distances for individual services, and actual and perceived distance) are still under discussion.

Note: TfL uses the word connectivity to refer to accessibility as defined in this chapter. In parallel, the institution uses the word accessibility to refer to the narrower term that looks at the ease of access for population with impaired mobility.
Source: Based on (Inayathusein and Cooper, 2018[21]).

The transport appraisal methodologies of the DfT and its Transport Analysis Guidance (WebTAG), a web-based tool to support appraisal, have also progressively widened the scope of accessibility impacts included in transport appraisal. This has helped overcome some of the challenges raised by critics of cost-benefit analysis, including that conventional appraisal methodologies' heavy focus on travel-time savings tends to overlook the impacts on social inclusion/exclusion and favour motorised over non-motorised transport projects (ITF-OECD, 2019[12]). The framework developed by the DfT includes a number of monetised and non-monetised impacts. It presents decision makers with appraisal summary tables, which highlight non-monetised benefits and costs alongside the benefit-cost ratio (BCR). These tables provide more comprehensive information on whether the projects assessed are compatible with government objectives (ITF-OECD, 2019[12]) (see Box 5.3).

Box 5.3 The use of accessibility indicators for appraisal in the United Kingdom

Transport appraisal in the United Kingdom is developed under the Value for Money (VfM) framework developed by the DfT. Different elements related to accessibility (physical access, affordability and safety) are included in these different impacts:

- Established monetised impacts are the main inputs used to calculate the BCR; these impacts include journey time savings, impacts on accidents, journey quality and GHG emissions.
- Evolving monetised impacts allow adjusting the BCR according to impacts that are relevant, but for which methodologies are less robust. These include journey time reliability, labour supply (i.e. the number of people who can access the labour market as a consequence to reduced commuting costs) and static clustering (i.e. improved connections between firms and households thanks to lower generalised costs of transport and related productivity gains).
- Indicative monetised impacts and non-monetised impacts are used to inform VfM considerations, but not to estimate or adjust the BCR. Impacts in this assessment include security, severance, townscape, accessibility (in this context referring to usability by population with physical and hidden disabilities) and affordability. Methodologies under this assessment are continuously updated and improved by the DfT.

Source: (ITF-OECD, 2019[12]).

Accessibility indicators can also be used for benchmarking purposes. Indices like the TomTom Traffic index provide comparable and updated information on congestion levels in a number of cities, measured as the percentage of time added to the average trip due to congestion, compared to free-flow conditions. The social costs of congestion have been increasingly acknowledged, and congestion alleviation ranks high in the public and political agendas. As discussed earlier, congestion is estimated to account for 27% of the total external costs of transport (estimated at EUR 270 billion) in the EU28 (van Essen et al., 2019[14]).[3] Having indicators on congestion helps keep track of the magnitude of the problem and the effectiveness of policies (e.g. congestion charging, addressed in the next section). However, an important caveat of measures taking free flow as a benchmark is that free-flow conditions are neither possible nor efficient (OECD/ECMT, 2007[24]). To avoid this caveat, the Joint Research Centre of the European Commission, in collaboration with the European Commission's Directorate-General for Regional and Urban Policy (DG REGIO), has developed indicators that take as a base absolute accessibility and transport performance indicators, in this case for cars (see Box 5.4 for an explanation of these indicators), as well as other accessibility indicators, to measure the absolute and percentage changes to accessibility due to congestion during peak times. This work has been done for various cities (e.g. Seville, Brussels and Krakow), and future work is planned to cover all functional urban areas with more than 250 000 people in the European Union, plus other countries in Europe (Christodoulou, 2019[25]).

Benchmarking accessibility across territories can contribute to placing accessibility at the centre of what is considered good performance and can also be a valuable input for determining investment priorities. The

ITF has developed a database with contour-based indicators on accessibility to services of different categories and through different transport modes for European cities. This is part of a project developed jointly with the OECD Centre for Entrepreneurship, SMEs, Regions and Cities (CFE), and supported by the European Commission.

The work builds on previous work from the ITF-OECD and the European Commission that measured accessibility to transport stops and other populations. The new indicators also calculate accessibility to final points of interest, i.e. different categories of services (shops, schools, universities, hospitals and green spaces). The database builds on available standardised open and crowdsourced data sets, and uses harmonised computational methods. The data set provides indicators for multiple transport modes: walking, cycling, public transport and car. Thus, it allows assessing the relative competitiveness of different modes, which is key to addressing environmental sustainability concerns. Working alongside the Inter-American Development Bank (IDB), the ITF also applied the framework to four Latin American cities – Mexico City, Bogota, Santiago de Chile and Montevideo – calculating indicators for accessibility to other population, jobs and basic services (i.e. education and health). Box 5.4 describes indicators in the European Commission-ITF-OECD Urban Access Framework, and shows some results comparing European and Latin American cities.

Among the most relevant challenges for tracking accessibility in cities from developing countries is the presence of informally or semi-formally run public transport. To overcome this challenge, the ITF and the IDB worked in partnership with WhereIsMyTransport for this project. Analysis shows that informal services can be central to delivering accessibility in some cities in developing countries (see Box 5.4). Nonetheless, it is important to take into account the quality of services provided by these modes and the issues that are often associated to them (e.g. safety, air pollution and GHG emissions). This highlights the importance of using physical accessibility indicators in tandem with a range of other indicators discussed throughout this section.

Box 5.4 European Commission-ITF-OECD Urban Access Framework

The indicators in the Urban Access Framework consider different modes of transport (walking, cycling, public transport and private car), and a number of opportunities (services of different categories) people actually want to reach. The methodology uses the harmonised definition of a city developed by the European Union and the OECD, according to which a "functional urban area" is a city and its surrounding commuting zone. The framework acknowledges that accessibility is the product of the proximity of valued destinations (the result of land-use policies) and of the performance of the transport system (the result of transport policies and investments in infrastructure).

The first indicator is **absolute accessibility**. The indicator reflects the absolute number of opportunities (e.g. schools, hospitals, jobs or other population that can be used as a proxy for concentration of activities) that can be reached by a given transport mode within a set travel time. This indicator highlights the differences in absolute access levels across cities or different areas, and allows comparing the levels of access delivered by different transport modes. However, accessibility in absolute terms tends to increase with city size. To overcome this city-size bias, two additional indicators were developed that reveal the contributions of the two main underlying factors in driving accessibility, i.e. the performance of transport systems and the structure of land-use development.

Land-use factors are reflected in the **proximity indicator**, i.e. the number of other populations, formal jobs, education and health opportunities located in a specific radius (2, 4, 8 or 16 km). **Transport performance** reflects the capacity of a given mode (car, public transport, bike or walking) to provide access to the opportunities located in proximity in a given time. This indicator is the result of a ratio between the absolute accessibility (overall number of opportunities reachable in a defined time threshold) and proximity (number of opportunities located in a defined radius). Using proximity as a fixed area of reference overcomes the small- and big-city-bias. This approach also separates the effect of urban form on accessibility from transport-service efficiency, which is essential for identifying service gaps and investment opportunities.

The framework was applied to benchmark accessibility levels in 121 European cities. The results suggest that cars tend to provide better accessibility than public transport or cycling, especially for longer travel times. For trips of 15 minutes, however, bicycles perform better in most cities. The results also suggest that people can access more destinations in dense cities despite higher levels of congestion, because people live close to many destinations and therefore make shorter trips. Nonetheless, cities with similar density can have different absolute accessibility levels, depending on the performance of their transport system.

Comparing public transport and car, the results reveal that in European cities, an average car driver can reach twice the number of opportunities accessible by public transport. London is an exception to the rule. Here, the public transport network is more extensive than in any other European city, while the road network performs comparatively poorly (the worst among the 121 European cities analysed). To a large extent, this the result of decisions not to build expressways in central London, coupled with recent policies to prioritise road space for public and non-motorised (cycling and walking) transport.

In the case of Latin American cities, cars also tends to be the most competitive option for providing access to a wide range of opportunities. This is the case even in Mexico City, one of the most congested cities in the world. In the Mexico City Metropolitan Area (Valle de México), in the space of one hour, public transport provides access to 30% of all jobs located within the urban centre, while cars provide access to 90% of all jobs. However, only 43% of the population own private vehicles, and cars are thus used predominantly by higher-income residents.

Results on accessibility to other populations in cities from both regions also show that despite huge differences in city size, public transport systems in smaller European cities reach a much higher number of people/opportunities (see Figure 5.2). In Paris, an urban area of 9 million people, an average resident can reach 40 times more people/opportunities than an average resident of Mexico City, an urban area of 30 million people. City size differences are also off-set in cities within regions. For instance, Santiago de Chile has 4.8 million population but absolute accessibility to other population by public transport is very similar to that in Mexico City. The estimation of proximity and transport performance indicators allows to identify that while higher proximity is created in Mexico City (due to higher density), the performance of the public transport system is better in Santiago de Chile.

The differences in absolute accessibility by public transport are even more visible when excluding the informal bus and micro-bus networks in Mexico City and Bogotá from the analysis. Informal transport modes (featured in the graph below) account for 54% of public transport accessibility levels in Mexico City and 35% in Bogotá. In both cities, informal transport also accounts for around 40% of accessibility to jobs provided by public transport. These networks make the biggest difference in terms of accessibility in peripheral low-income areas, as lower-income neighbourhoods often have inefficient or almost non-existent formal public transport.

Figure 5.2. Accessibility to other population in selected cities

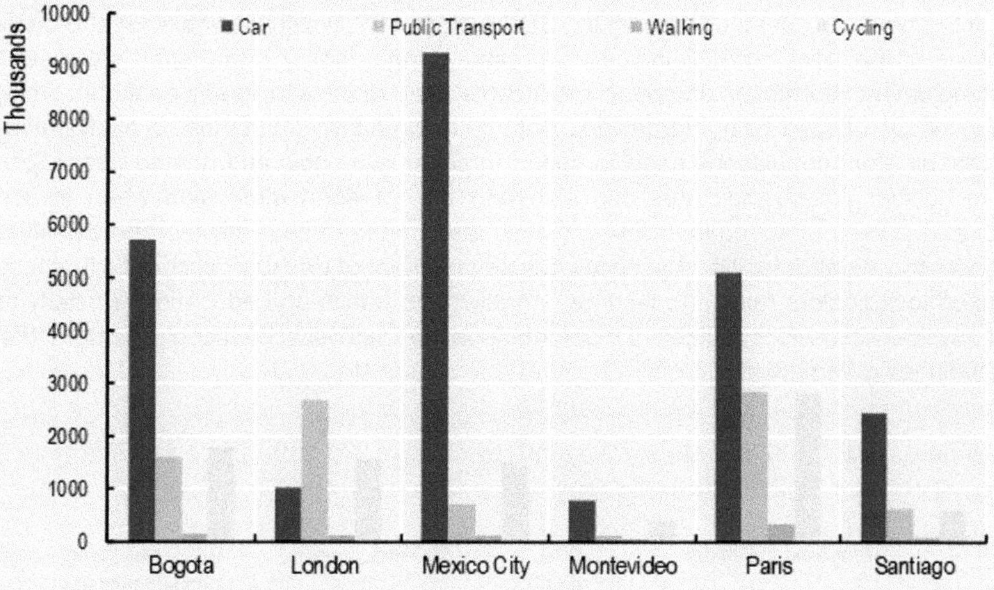

Note: In the case of the Mexico City Metropolitan Area, formal transport refers to BRT, metro, light rail and regular buses (Nochebus, RTP). Informal networks include the loosely regulated micro-bus sector operating across the metropolitan area. In the case of Bogotá, formal transport refers to all the modes included in the Sistema Integrado de Transporte Público-SITP system (BRT and regular buses). Informal transport consists of loosely regulated privately operated bus services in the Southern municipalities of the Capital District, as well as across the municipalities outside of Capital District.
Source: (ITF-OECD, 2019[26])

StatLink https://doi.org/10.1787/888933993104

5.3.3. Ensuring affordability of services and contribution to equity

Monetary costs can be incorporated into the accessibility indices described above, either reflecting both time and monetary cost in a single measure, or using separate indices to reflect each cost. As accessibility indicators become more complex (e.g. using potential rather than contour-based measures), it could be convenient to have separate indicators showing physical accessibility and financial accessibility, or monetary cost of access (ITF-OECD, 2017[19]).

Other types of indicators measuring the share of income (or disposable income) spent on transport can also be used. Moreover, combining transport with other relevant expenditures borne by households has provided better insights on the final impact of policy decisions on livelihood. The use of these combined indices can also help better integrate infrastructure planning if used by authorities in charge of the different sectors involved.

Housing plus transport affordability indicators are good examples of combined indices. Combining housing with transport expenses is particularly important because these tend to be highly correlated with location, but through the opposite relation, i.e. housing expenditures increase as housing location is more central and/or in more attractive locations, while transport expenditure increases as housing location is further away from central/attractive locations. The result is that households often need to make trade-offs between housing and transport conditions. Considering and incorporating both housing and transport expenditures into a same definition of affordability can help authorities improve households' housing and transport situation. In addition, housing and transport expenditures are often the two largest household expenses, and are therefore extremely relevant to the disposable income households can use to cover other needs (ITF-OECD, 2017[19]).

Indicators of this type can contribute to tracking SDG Target 11.2, which also calls for affordable transport; currently, none of the selected SDG indicators measures affordability of transport services. In addition, they can complement information on household income used to track progress on the income and wealth dimension in the OECD well-being framework. Data on income levels can thus be analysed in the light of the share that different populations need to spend to cover two basic and related needs (transport and housing). In addition, these indicators can also add the transport dimension when tracking housing affordability and access to adequate housing (which also needs to consider the affordability of available transport services). As affordability of services is a key element of transport accessibility, these indicators are also linked to indicators related to income, employment, health and education (similarly to indicators measuring physical accessibility). Table 5.6 summarises the links between these indicators, the SDGs and the OECD well-being framework.

Table 5.6 Summary table: Indicators for monitoring progress in ensuring affordability of services and links to SDGs and OECD well-being framework

Policy priority	Proposed indicators	SDG goal and target	SDG indicators	OECD well-being domain/dimension	OECD well-being indicators
Ensuring affordability of services	• Accessibility indicators using cost instead or in addition to time. • Share of household income spent in transport (often 30% threshold used). • Housing plus Transport (H+T) affordability indicators (often 30% threshold used for housing expenditures and 15% threshold used for transport expenditures). • Vulnerability index.	1.1. 3.8. 8.5. 11.1. 11.2.	• % of population and employed population below the poverty line. • Coverage of essential health services. • Average hourly earnings of employees, by occupation. • Unemployment rate. • Proportion of urban population living in slums, informal settlements or inadequate housing.	Current well-being: quality of life. Income and wealth Current well-being: material conditions. Housing	• Household income • Housing affordability

Income and expenditure surveys are relevant sources of data for calculating housing and housing plus transport affordability indicators. It is important to ensure that data analysis is conducted in a way that provides accurate results. For instance, accounting for income transfers and savings (e.g. for students or by the elderly) is important when breaking down population by income levels. In addition, in some cases the data groupings chosen may impede the management of data in a way that is useful (e.g. for calculating expenditures in transport and telecommunications) (ITF-OECD, 2017[19]).

The Center for Neighborhood Technology (CNT) in the United States has developed a methodology for estimating housing plus transport affordability indicators. The resulting Housing and Transport (H+T©) Affordability Index was used to develop a national framework that calculates neighbourhood affordability within and across US cities. It also generates heat maps that present the results spatially. The thresholds used by the CNT for considering affordability are below 15% of household income spent on transport expenditures and below 30% of household income on housing expenditure. Figure 5.3 presents housing plus transport expenditures for a number of cities in the United States. It shows that the relative affordability of housing across cities is different when considering both housing and transport costs, as opposed to only housing. Cities like New York or San Francisco with average housing expenditures close to what is considered unaffordable (30% of income) rank better when combined transport and housing costs are accounted for. In contrast, cities like Indianapolis, where housing is on average a lower burden for households, do not rank as well when transport expenditures are included into affordability analysis.

Spatial analysis of affordability across cities using this tool has helped improve decisions at both the national and local levels. The H+T© Affordability Index has been used for implementing policies (e.g. subsidies for affordable housing) that promote transport-oriented and location-efficient development, delivering both climate change mitigation and affordability goals.

Figure 5.4 shows the overall correlation between transport-related GHG emissions in cities and the proportion of affordable neighbourhoods found in the United States (where affordability is determined by the compound H+T© Affordability Index of the CNT).

Figure 5.3. Housing and transport affordability in the 20 most populous cities in the United States

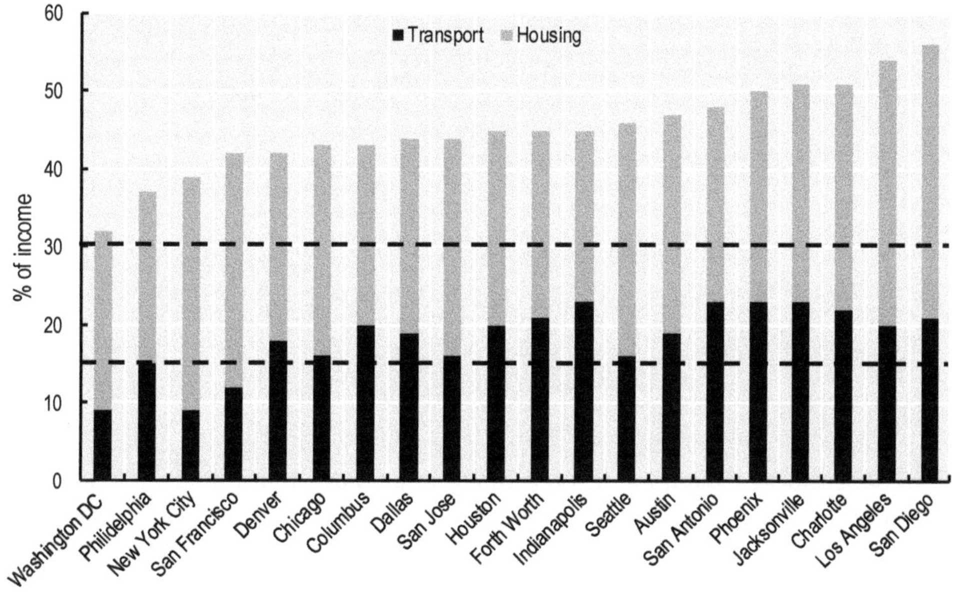

Note: The two horizontal lines show the thresholds set for housing (30%) and transport (15% in addition to housing expenditures).
Source: (CNT, 2018[27]).

StatLink https://doi.org/10.1787/888933993123

Figure 5.4. GHG emissions from car use versus location efficiency in 20 most populous cities in the United States

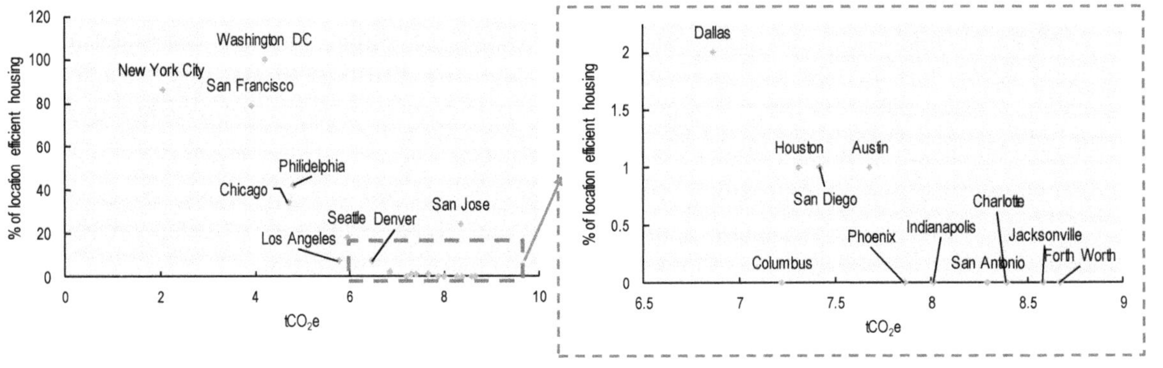

Note: The right panel magnifies the light blue box in the left panel.
Source: (CNT, 2018[27])

StatLink https://doi.org/10.1787/888933993142

Evidence from the United States shows that cities with a higher share of neighbourhoods that have housing that is affordable in terms of both housing and transport costs have lower annual household CO_{2eq} emissions from automobile use.

As in the case of accessibility indicators, using a range of provides more detailed insights. For example, (Guerra and Kirschen, 2016[28]) adapt the CNT methodology to the case of the Metropolitan Area of Valle de Mexico (Mexico City and the enlarged metropolitan area). The same thresholds used by the CNT for housing (30%) and transport (15%) expenditures were used to determine if a household is burdened or if housing is affordable. The authors use three variants of the CNT indicator: the proportion of households burdened by housing and transport costs; the average level of affordability for low-income households (defined as belonging to the 25th income percentile) across municipalities; and the percentage of housing options affordable to a household earning the 25th percentile income. All indicators are represented spatially for the metropolitan area.

Other useful indicators can be vulnerability indices: these can account for the cost burden imposed by current transport conditions or potential changes (e.g. implementation of a given policy) and incorporate spatial factors. Analysis of some policies (e.g. road pricing) have highlighted that fairness in regard to spatial distribution of people within the same income group (i.e. horizontal equity) has been as relevant as the potential impacts on different income groups (vertical equity) (ITF-OECD, 2018[29]), hence the importance of monitoring changes and climate policies with this type of indicator to avoid potential trade-offs. In (Mattioli et al., 2017[30]), the vulnerability index used to identify spatial vulnerability to increases in fuel prices across London takes into account exposure or the cost burden of travel, sensitivity and adaptive capacity. Cost burden is defined as household expenditure on fuel as a percentage of median income. Sensitivity is proxied using the median income in the region. Finally, adaptive capacity refers to accessibility through alternatives to car use, which in addition to being an important component for measuring equity, is key to understanding the potential modal shift. The accessibility indicators discussed in Section 5.2 are used to measure the accessibility to jobs and services by public transport and walking. The result showed that in London, the urban core tends to be less vulnerable to increases in fuel prices according to the vulnerability index, but pockets of the city are exposed to very high vulnerability. The findings underline the need to assess policy effects using disaggregated information, rather than focusing on average users (ITF-OECD, 2018[29]).

5.3.4. Ensuring safety and security

Injuries and deaths generated by crashes represent important social costs related to transport activity. The European Commission's recent handbook estimating the external costs of transport in Europe reveals that accidents account for one-third of total external costs in the EU28 (Schroten et al., 2019[31]). The report finds that motorcycles, for instance, have the largest average external costs, owing to high accident rates and noise levels (Schroten et al., 2019[31]).

The number of road deaths and casualties is often used as a central indicator to analyse road safety. SDG Goal 3.6 sets as an explicit target to halve the number of global deaths and injuries from road traffic accidents by 2020 relative to 2015. As shown in Table 5.7, other indicators providing additional information on severity, type of road user and population group would contribute to disaggregated data to understand performance towards the SDG target. They can also contribute to tracking SDG Target 11.2, which mentions the need to ensure safe transport, but for which the SDG framework provides no specific indicator. They could also complement the OECD well-being framework (personal security dimension).

The latest report by the International Traffic Safety Data and Analysis Group (IRTAD)[4] provides comparable indicators at the national level that reflect the current state and evolution of road safety for different user and age groups, road types and severity of injuries, as well as deaths (ITF, 2018). For instance, Figure 5.5 shows the change in road fatalities of car users and pedestrians for selected countries since 2010, using data collected by this group. It reveals that the number of pedestrian deaths is still going in many countries.

The ITF at the OECD is also running a network of road safety experts at city level called Safer City Streets. The network's primary objective is to maintain a database of road safety indicators for cities to monitor and compare their progress against performance in other cities. Pedestrians, cyclists and motorcyclists make up 80% of fatalities in dense urban areas, which is why cities are encouraged to focus on protecting vulnerable road users. Road safety indicators should support and guide such efforts, by assessing and monitoring the level of risk experienced by specific road user groups. To do so, it is essential to measure and control for the volume of travel, i.e. the trips taken and distances travelled with each mode; only then can changes in modal split across cities and over time be accounted for. Road safety experts also recommend monitoring behaviours, such as speeding and seat-belt use. Beyond monitoring casualties, risk and behaviour, there also exists a need to monitor attitudes. Regular surveys should assess how complacent people are with risky behaviours, how unsafe people feel in traffic, and whether they would let their children walk or cycle. Work developed in the context of the Safer City Streets network is in line with these recommendations.

The ITF has computed risk indicators by mode as part of a project developed in partnership with the Centre for Entrepreneurship, SMEs, Regions and Cities (CFE), and supported by the European Commission. Indicators on outcomes (road fatalities) are normalised by mode and per population, daytime population, unit of travel and vehicle-kilometres in 60 European cities, and are available in the Road Safety in European Cities report (ITF, 2019[32]).

A particular challenge is that road safety indicators should track the true number of traffic fatalities and serious injuries. This can be done using a range of sources – including, of course, police crash data, but also complementary data sources. The monitoring and benchmarking of serious injuries is particularly difficult because a high number of serious injuries are not reported to the police and because of the need to consistently record severity levels; to this aim, medical injury scales such as the Abbreviated Injury Scale and the definition of a serious injury as MAIS3+ can be used.

Figure 5.5. Change in car and pedestrian deaths in selected countries from 2010 to 2017

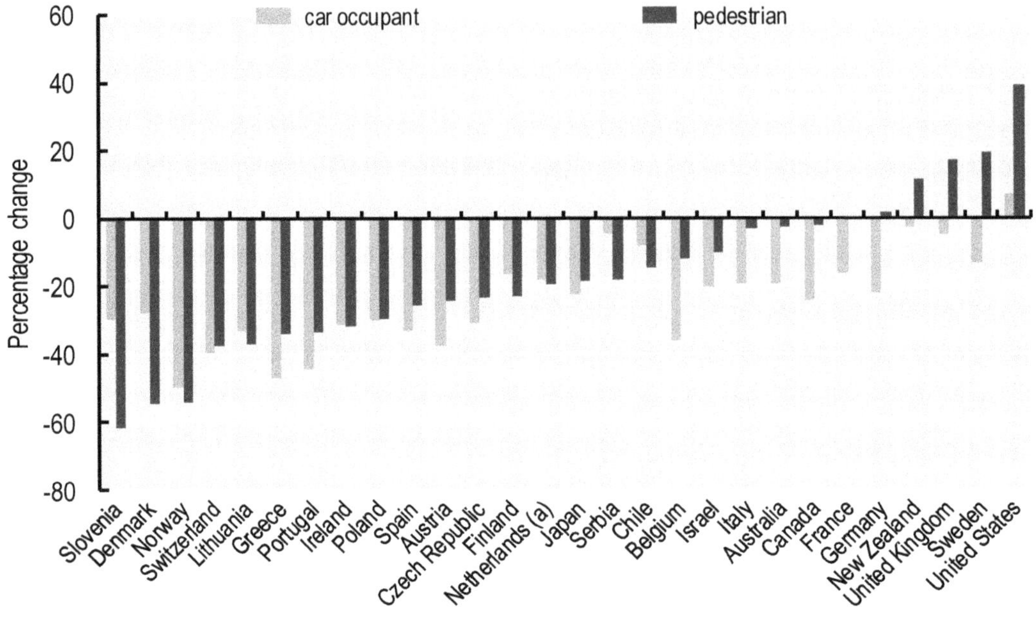

Note: (a) Real data (actual numbers instead of reported numbers by the police). Data from Iceland and Luxembourg are not shown, since observations are too low to have meaningful percentage changes.
Source: (ITF-OECD, 2018[33]).

StatLink https://doi.org/10.1787/888933993161

As highlighted in Section 5.2, improved road safety has several indirect impacts, including on climate change mitigation, that are often overlooked. These indirect benefits go beyond the obvious prevention of crashes, and the energy and material implications of repairing or scrapping vehicles. They can be less obvious when looking at the national level, but are tremendously important in cities. With shorter trip distances and larger scope for public transport services, cities have a tremendous potential for modal shift from private vehicles towards healthier, cheaper and less energy-intensive transport modes. However, road safety is often cited as the main barrier to people cycling (Santacreu, 2018[34]), (De Ceunynck et al., 2019[35]). In cities, therefore, there exists a direct link between road safety and the wider policy objectives of public health, inclusiveness and climate change mitigation.

Progress on road safety can unlock modal shift and act as a catalyst for a virtuous circle: safer streets increase confidence to walk, cycle and use public transport (which generally implies increasing trips' walking segments) (Mueller et al., 2018[36]). This improves the health of the population, which is more physically active; it can also reduce the amount of private motor-vehicle traffic, and related GHG emissions and local pollution. Thus, safer roads can support climate change mitigation strategies that focus on a modal shift towards more walking and cycling. Conversely, low levels of road safety may hamper the effectiveness of these strategies, as it prevents people from shifting towards non-motorised modes. In both cases, monitoring the risks associated with higher exposure to motorised traffic that could come from enhanced use of cycling and walking is relevant.

Figure 5.6. Virtuous circle of road danger reduction

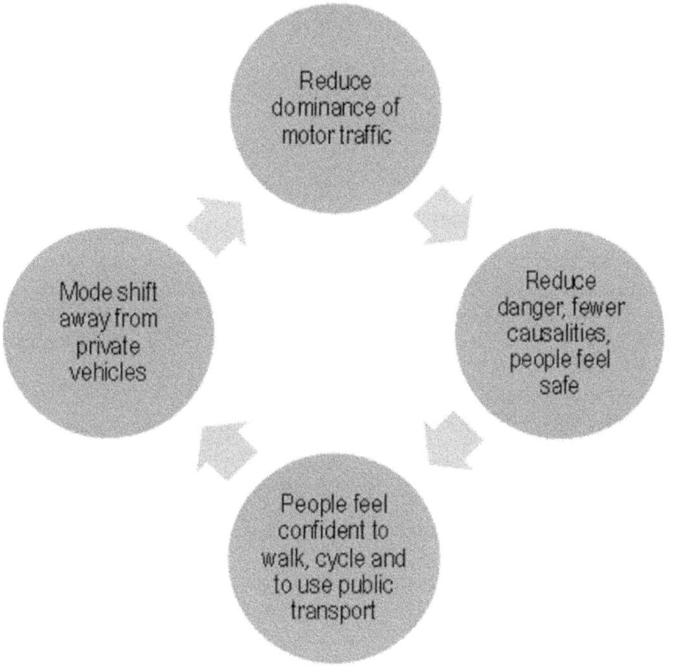

Source: (TfL, 2018[37]).

Work developed at the Catholic University in Chile complements accessibility analysis with the Environment and Urban Quality Index (EUQI), developed using pre-census data on sidewalk and street quality. Four sub-indices are calculated and serve as building blocks for the EUQI. The first sub-index is built from data on safety and security (i.e. luminary, road signs and roofed bus stops). The other three reflect walking environmental quality – environment (gardens, seats, sport fields and playgrounds); cleanliness (garbage bins and rubble); and infrastructure (sidewalk and street quality) – all of which are linked directly to improving mental and physical health (and thus with the priority below), including by encouraging walking. The EUQI index is used to complement a potential indicator (i.e. one using a decay function – see Box 5.2) that measures walkability to public transport in Santiago. This PAI calculates accessibility by foot to the ten closest transport stops (using a 400-metre threshold). Analysis using both indicators for measuring accessibility to public transport in the central business district, a higher-income (Las Condes) and a lower-income (San Miguel) neighbourhood, revealed that the lower-income neighbourhood ranked relatively high (just behind the central business district) when considering the PAI indicator only. However, the EUQI index showed that the quality of the quality of the walking environment (including because of safety reasons) to public transport in San Miguel was quite poor.

Another relevant example incorporating public security is a compound indicator developed by WhereIsMyTransport and used for analysis in Cape Town. The indicator combines spatial data on physical accessibility, affordability and public security (see Box 5.5).

Table 5.7 Summary table: Indicators for monitoring progress in ensuring safety and security and links to SDGs and OECD well-being framework

Policy priority	Proposed indicators	SDG goal and target	SDG indicators	OECD well-being domain/dimension	OECD well-being indicators
Ensuring safety and security	• # of death and serious injuries (relative to total population, travel and # of vehicles) and by severity, age, gender and type of road user • Risk of exposure to crime in transport stops.	3.6. 11.2.	• Death rate due to road traffic injuries. • Indicators can also be used to track SDG Target 11.2, which calls for safe transport systems but does not include a specific indicator.	Current well-being: material conditions. Personal Security.	Proposed indicators tracking road safety could complement current indicators (homicides and feeling safe at night)

Box 5.5 WhereisMyTransport's compound indicator: The case of Cape Town, South Africa

WhereisMyTransport is the largest source of public transport data in emerging markets, maintaining data for more than 30 cities across 4 continents. It maps both formal and informal public transport networks, making this data available to governments and mobility service providers, which can use this information to make public transport more reliable, predictable, safe and inclusive.

Applying a new approach

To obtain a better understanding of accessibility in Cape Town, WhereIsMyTransport used a multi-dimensional approach: first, it collected and processed transport data for each transport agency active in Cape Town. The transport agencies included in this case study are Metro Rail, Golden Arrow Bus Services, MyCiti BRT and the Cape Town Minibus Taxis (2018). The data were used to generate a set of general transit speed specification (GTFS)[5] extended files for each transport agency. The data were then uploaded to a platform that is designed to model multi-modal and informal transport journeys.

Three components that were considered central to understanding accessibility in emerging cities were selected for this indicator, defined as follows:

- Physical access is the ease of reaching meaningful destinations (e.g. work, school, shopping and health services) from a particular location within a particular time or cost bandwidth. WhereisMyTransport used its API to run multiple journey-planning calls with the different transport agency data, and overlaid this information with "points-of-interest" census data to show the linkages between transport and access to social amenities.
- Affordability refers to the cost of travel, which was determined using the fare data in WhereisMyTransport GTFS datasets, looking at fare cost alongside household income data to infer the percentage of income spent on public transport.
- Safety has multiple dimensions. WhereisMyTransport evaluated safety by looking at waiting times for public transport, which was captured in the GTFS data sets. Data were overlaid with openly available crime statistics for the city of Cape Town. The output is an assessment of risk of exposure to crime based on the amount of time an individual would have to wait at a given public transport stop.

Figure 5.7 shows results when mapping the compound index in Cape Town. **Map 1** illustrates accessibility in Cape Town when applying the multi-dimensional approach to the formal network. The dark blue neighbourhoods have the highest accessibility score (according to physical access, affordability and safety criteria). These neighbourhoods surround the Cape Town harbour and are part of the central business district. These are high-income neighbourhoods where residents primarily use private vehicles for travel and secondarily, the formal public transport system. This picture is missing the informal minibus taxi system, however, which is the most popular form of public transport across the city.

Map 2 illustrates accessibility in Cape Town when applying the multi-dimensional approach to both the formal and informal transport networks. By including the informal minibus taxi system in the analysis, a more accurate picture, on-the-ground picture of accessibility in the city is achieved. Low-income neighbourhoods and informal settlements are predominantly serviced by the minibus taxi network. Stemming from segregated spatial planning during the apartheid era, these neighbourhoods are located on the periphery of the city and rely on the minibus taxi network to gain access to employment and social amenities that lie in the city centre.

This case study of Cape Town highlights the importance of high-quality transport data in solving accessibility and future transport planning. It also shows that including the informally run transport system shines a light on the mobility patterns of a large proportion of Cape Town's population. Conversely, excluding the informal system renders these citizens and their transport needs "invisible" in future city planning. Finally, it shows the importance of understanding access to public transport as multi-dimensional, which will allow policy makers, planners, operators and citizens to work *together* towards mobility systems that unlock freedom of movement – and freedom of opportunity – for everyone.

Figure 5.7. Mapping the compound index

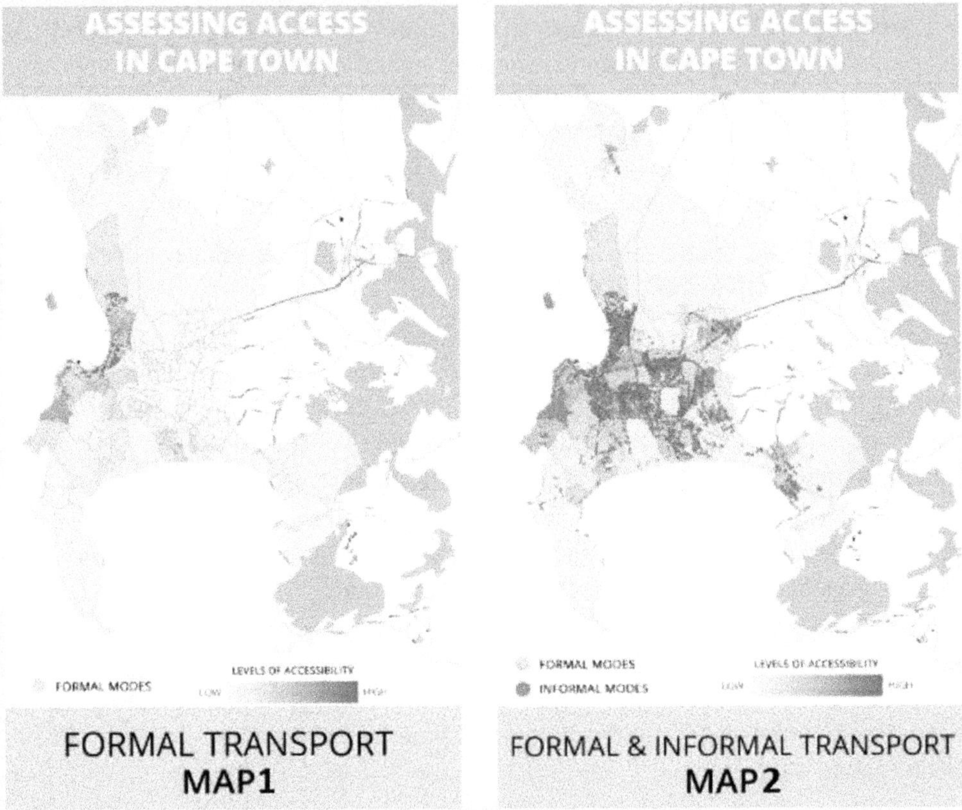

Source: Information provided by WhereIsMyTransport.

5.3.5. Reducing local pollution and noise, related health risks and habitat damage

Local pollution compromises air quality and harms health. The OECD estimated that the annual cost of pollution in terms of the value of lives and ill health amounts to around USD 3.5 trillion (US dollars) every year for OECD countries, plus the People's Republic of China and India (OECD, 2014[38]). Data and indicators showing levels, sources and health impacts of local air pollution emissions are crucial to designing effective strategies. The European Environment Agency, for instance, has a database on premature deaths attributable to PM2.5, ozone and nitrogen dioxide exposure (the principal component of nitrogen oxide [NOx]) that includes data for 41 European countries. The World Health Organization's (WHO) Global Health Observatory collects data for a majority of countries on mortality and burden of disease from ambient air pollution (expressed as annual deaths attributable to ambient air pollution). The WHO Global Urban Outdoor Air Pollution Database also gathers data on annual mean concentrations of PM2.5 and PM10 for a large number of countries and cities. Adopting general air quality standards that are consistent with international health standards set by the WHO is important to guide regulation in different sectors.

Specific data on transport-related local pollution are necessary to ensure that effective policies can be implemented in the sector. As Table 5.8 shows, it is particularly important that these data are available at the local – and even micro – level, for different pollutants and also from real-world emission testing. These data could contribute to a better understanding of the transport sector's role in achieving SDG Target 11.6 (reduce the adverse per capita environmental impact of cities). Data could also expand on this by providing information on pollutants beyond PM2.5 and PM10 (e.g. nitrogen oxide [NO_X] emissions), as well as help monitor the sector's contribution to SDG Target 3.9 (mortality rate attributed to household and ambient pollution). In the case of the OECD well-being framework, indicators could also contribute to understanding transport's contribution to environmental quality (currently measured only through national average PM2.5 concentrations). Accurate data on local air pollution emissions are an important input for ensuring that vehicle standards and policies promoting the renewal of the vehicle fleet can contribute to both GHG mitigation and pollution reduction, avoiding potential trade-offs between them. A number of studies highlight the relevance of using data that come from testing under on-road driving conditions, rather than laboratory certification testing (Box 5.6). The *Handbook on the external costs of transport* published by the European Commission provides relevant guidance for estimating air pollution costs from transport, as well as cost factors for individual European countries (for some pollutants differentiated by urban and rural areas), and a total cost estimate for the EU28 for 2016. The *Handbook* includes the following pollutants: NH_3, NMV, SO_2, NOx, PM2.5 and PM2.10. The total air pollution cost for the EU28 is estimated at EUR 71.8 billion, of which passenger transport accounts for 55%, mostly attributable to road passenger transport (54%).

As with GHG emissions, accounting for well-to tank pollution emissions (rather than tank-to-wheel emissions only) is necessary. The *Handbook on the external costs of transport* provides guidance and estimates for European countries on well-to tank emissions that include the following pollutants: NOx, non-methane volatile organic compounds (NMVOC), SO_2, PM2.5 (exhaust) and PM10 (non-exhaust).The *Handbook* estimates that pollution makes up around 38% of total well-to-tank external costs from road transport in the EU28 (with the other 62% coming from climate change costs).

Noise from transport can also harm health and is an external cost that needs to be considered. The WHO has established that environmental noise is linked to a number of negative health impacts, including increased risk of ischaemic heart disease, stress-related mental health and cognitive impairment for children (WHO, 2007[39]). The WHO also finds that road traffic accounts for most community noise in cities. The European Environment Agency (EEA) estimates that 1 out of 4 Europeans (i.e. 125 million people) suffers negative impacts from road traffic owing to noise exceeding a 55 decibels (dB) Lden[6] annual average (EEA, 2016[40]). While improvements in vehicles and roads are expected to help with this problem, growing urbanisation (which increases exposure) and increasing traffic volumes are expected to increase the overall negative impacts (van Essen et al., 2019[14]).

Box 5.6 Measuring air pollution from transport accurately

To indicate accurately health risks related to air pollution from transport, measurements of air pollution have to reflect on-road driving conditions rather than simply conditions in laboratory tests. In congestion, with stop-and-go traffic, for example, the difference between test-bed results and real-world monitoring of tailpipe emissions with on-board test equipment or roadside remote sensing can be considerable, skewing views on which technology is effective in protecting health. Real-world testing is a particular issue for diesel vehicles: only the most recent technology standards for heavy-duty vehicles (U.S. Environmental Protection Agency [EPA] 2010 and Euro VI) are able to account for real-world emissions; previous standards mandated technologies that only showed improvements in the laboratory.

Based on the impact of real-world conditions, there are two main recommendations: implement technology standards that include testing and enforcement in real-world conditions swiftly, and address adverse real-world conditions. For example, newer heavy-duty vehicle standards like U.S. EPA 2010 and Euro VI already perform well in early on-road tests. Countries developing new standards should use these as the benchmark and not adopt earlier EPA or EU standards that have been found to be deficient.

Source: Based on (ITF-OECD, 2017[41]).

The European Commission's *Handbook on External Costs of Transport* (van Essen et al., 2019[14]) includes noise among the external costs of transport. While the suggested threshold for considering noise a nuisance is 50 dB Lden, estimations in the *Handbook* take a 55 dB Lden threshold, based on the EEA Noise Maps. Estimations for noise costs and cost factors (per unit of travel) are based on estimations of exposure and increasing prices per dB, themselves based on estimates by the UK Department for Environment, Food and Rural Affairs. As discussed in the *Handbook*, these estimates are consistent with WHO recommendations. Estimations also use weighting factors for noise for different vehicle types and type of roads, i.e. urban (up to 50 km/h speeds) and other roads (80 km/h or higher speeds). The total cost of noise generated by transport in the EU28 for 2016 is estimated at EUR 63.6 billion, with 67% stemming from passenger transport and 23% from freight road transport.

Finally, transport can also generate habitat damage, which the *Handbook on External Costs* divides into habitat loss (i.e. ecosystem loss, which can be the consequence of additional land dedicated to transport and have important impacts on biodiversity); habitat fragmentation (i.e. division of ecosystem due to transport projects, e.g. motorways or railways); and habitat degradation (i.e. negative impacts on ecosystems owing to the release of air pollutants and other toxic substance, e.g. heavy metals) (van Essen et al., 2019[14]). While the document also acknowledges other possible negative impacts (e.g. visual intrusions, light emissions from vehicles), it focuses on the three impacts mentioned, providing costs for the EU28 in 2016, and cost factors for different infrastructure and member countries. Estimations are based only on habitat loss and fragmentation costs, based on the methodologies developed for a study in Switzerland by the Swiss Federal Office for Spatial Development.[7] The total cost for 2016 is estimated at EUR 39.1 billion.

Table 5.8 Summary table: Indicators for Reducing local pollution and noise, associated health risks and habitat damage and links to the SDGs and the OECD well-being framework

Policy priority	Proposed indicators	SDG goal and target	SDG indicators	OECD well-being domain/dimension	OECD well-being indicators
Reducing local pollution and noise, associated health risks and habitat damage	• Transport-related pollution emissions (PM2.5, PM10, NOx, etc.) measured in real-world driving conditions by type and both at national and local level (as well as pollution in transport construction sites). • Indicators linked to health (e.g. annual premature deaths attributable to on-road vehicle emissions). • Noise levels (dB). • Toxic substance emission and release from transport projects (e.g. heavy metals). • Land-use conversion and biodiversity impacts.	11.6. 3.9.	• Annual mean levels of fine particulate matter (e.g. PM2.5 and PM10) in cities (population weighted). • Mortality rate attributed to household and ambient air pollution.	Current well-being: quality of life. Health status. Current well-being: quality of life. Environmental quality. Future well-being: resources.	• Life expectancy • Perceived health • Annual exposure to PM2.5 air pollution • Water quality • Threatened species • Forest area

5.4. Conclusion

This chapter discussed how shifting the focus of mobility policy and investment priorities from increasing physical movement to ensuring access to goods, services, opportunities and amenities is central to delivering ambitious climate and other well-being goals. It established a number of priorities for the sector that are key to supporting the delivery of wider well-being and sustainability goals (reflected by the SDGs and the OECD well-being framework). Finally, it argued that developing and using indicators that can translate these priorities into measurable outcomes for tracking progress and setting criteria is key to effectively place the priorities discussed at the centre of decision-making and identifying potential synergies and trade-offs of policies and interventions (including climate action).

References

Aguilar Jaber, A. and D. Glocker (2015), “Shifting towards Low Carbon Mobility Systems”, http://www.internationaltransportforum.org/jtrc/DiscussionPapers/jtrcpapers.html (accessed on 30 June 2019). [4]

Blackburn, A. (2019), *Transport SDG Indicators at UNECE,(presentation at Expert Group Meeting on Transport Indicators under SDG monitoring)*. [20]

C40 (2019), *C40 Climate Action Planning Resource Centre*, https://resourcecentre.c40.org/resources/measuring-ghg-emissions (accessed on 28 June 2019). [13]

Christodoulou, A. (2019), *Measuring accessibility and congestion in European cities (presentation at the Expert Group Meeting on Transport Indicators under SDG monitoring)*. [25]

CNT (2018), *Center for Neighborhood Technology*, https://www.cnt.org/ (accessed on 3 July 2019). [27]

De Ceunynck, T. et al. (2019), *Determinants and barriers of walking, cycling and using Personal e-Transporters: a survey in nine European cities*, https://www.polisnetwork.eu/uploads/Modules/PublicDocuments/d1.1.2-a-survey-in-nine-european-cities.pdf (accessed on 3 July 2019). [35]

EEA (2016), *Transport and public health — European Environment Agency*, https://www.eea.europa.eu/signals/signals-2016/articles/transport-and-public-health (accessed on 3 July 2019). [40]

Fulton, L. et al. (2017), *Transportation Three Revolutions in Urban*, https://itdpdotorg.wpengine.com/wp-content/uploads/2017/04/UCD-ITDP-3R-Report-FINAL.pdf (accessed on 30 June 2019). [7]

Geurs, K. (2018), "Transport Planning With Accessibility Indices in the Netherlands Discussion Paper", http://www.itf-oecd.org (accessed on 30 June 2019). [16]

GLA (2018), *Mayor's Transport Strategy*, http://www.london.gov.uk (accessed on 3 July 2019). [23]

GLA (2017), "Draft Mayor's Transport Strategy challenges and opportunities.". [22]

Guerra, E. and M. Kirschen (2016), "Housing plus Transportation Affordability Indices: Uses, Opportunities, and Challenges", http://www.itf-oecd.org (accessed on 2 July 2019). [28]

IEA (2018), *Tracking Clean Energy Progress*, https://www.iea.org/tcep/ (accessed on 25 June 2019). [15]

Inayathusein, A. and S. Cooper (2018), "London's Accessibility Indicators: Strengths, Weaknesses, Challenges | ITF", https://www.itf-oecd.org/london-accessibility-indicators (accessed on 28 June 2019). [21]

IPCC (2018), *IPCC: Global Warming of 1.5 C*, https://ipcc.ch/report/sr15/ (accessed on 17 October 2018). [2]

ITF (2019), *ITF Transport Outlook 2019*, OECD Publishing, Paris, https://dx.doi.org/10.1787/transp_outlook-en-2019-en. [5]

ITF (2019), *Road Safety in European Cities Performance Indicators and Governance Solutions Case-Specific Policy Analysis*, http://www.itf-oecd.org (accessed on 29 July 2019). [32]

ITF (2018), *Policy Directions for Establishing a Metropolitan Transport Authority for Korea's Capital Region Case-Specific Policy Analysis*, http://www.itf-oecd.org (accessed on 30 June 2019). [8]

ITF (2017), *ITF Transport Outlook 2017*, OECD Publishing, Paris, https://dx.doi.org/10.1787/9789282108000-en. [3]

ITF-OECD (2019), *Benchmarking Accessibility in Cities*, https://www.itf-oecd.org/benchmarking-accessibility-cities (accessed on 3 July 2019). [26]

ITF-OECD (2019), *Improving Transport Planning and Investment Through the Use of Accessibility Indicators Case-Specific Policy Analysis*, http://www.itf-oecd.org (accessed on 28 June 2019). [12]

ITF-OECD (2018), *Road Safety Annual Report 2018*, http://www.itf-oecd.org/road-safety-annual-report-2018 (accessed on 3 July 2019). [33]

ITF-OECD (2018), *The Social Impacts of Road Pricing Summary and Conclusions*, http://www.itf-oecd.org (accessed on 3 July 2019). [29]

ITF-OECD (2017), *Income Inequality, Social Inclusion and Mobility Roundtable Report 2017 Income Inequality, Social Inclusion and Mobility*, https://www.itf-oecd.org/sites/default/files/docs/income-inequality-social-inclusion-mobility.pdf (accessed on 4 June 2019). [19]

ITF-OECD (2017), *Strategies for Mitigating Air Pollution in Mexico City | ITF*, https://www.itf-oecd.org/strategies-mitigating-air-pollution-mexico-city (accessed on 23 June 2019). [41]

Litman, T. (2008), *Evaluating Accessibility for Transport Planning Evaluating Accessibility for Transportation Planning*, http://www.vtpi.orgInfo@vtpi.org (accessed on 30 June 2019). [10]

Lucas, K. (2018), "Editorial for special issue of European transport research review: transport poverty and inequalities", *European Transport Research Review*, Vol. 10/1, p. 17, http://dx.doi.org/10.1007/s12544-018-0288-6. [18]

Luderer, G. et al. (2018), "Residual fossil CO2 emissions in 1.5-2 °c pathways", *Nature Climate Change*, Vol. 8/7, pp. 626-633, http://dx.doi.org/10.1038/s41558-018-0198-6. [6]

Mattioli, G. et al. (2017), *Developing an index of vulnerability to motor fuel price increases in England*, http://eprints.uwe.ac.uk/30778/1/Mattioli%20Philips%20Anable%20Chatterton%202017%20Developing%20an%20index%20of%20vulnerability%20to%20motor%20fuel%20price%20increases%20in%20England.pdf (accessed on 3 July 2019). [30]

Mueller, N. et al. (2018), "Health impact assessment of cycling network expansions in European cities", *Preventive Medicine*, Vol. 109, pp. 62-70, http://dx.doi.org/10.1016/J.YPMED.2017.12.011. [36]

OECD (2016), *Multi-dimensional Review of Peru: Volume 2. In-depth Analysis and Recommendations*, OECD Development Pathways, OECD Publishing, Paris, https://dx.doi.org/10.1787/9789264264670-en. [9]

OECD (2014), *The Cost of Air Pollution: Health Impacts of Road Transport*, OECD Publishing, Paris, https://dx.doi.org/10.1787/9789264210448-en. [38]

OECD/ECMT (2007), *Managing Urban Traffic Congestion*, http://www.cemt.org (accessed on 30 June 2019). [24]

OECD/IEA (2019), "CO2 Emissions from Fuel Combustion", http://dotstat.oecd.org/?lang=en#. [1]

Peralta-Quiros, T. and C. Rodríguez Hernández (2016), *Balancing Financial Sustainability and Affordability in Public Transport*, http://www.itf-oecd.org (accessed on 2 October 2018). [17]

Santacreu, A. (2018), *Cycling Safety*, http://www.itf-oecd.org (accessed on 3 July 2019). [34]

Schroten, A. et al. (2019), "Sustainable Transport Infrastructure Charging and Internalisation of Transport Externalities: Executive summary", http://dx.doi.org/10.2832/246834. [31]

Silva, C. and A. Larson (2018), "Challenges for Accessibility Planning and Research in the Context of Sustainable Mobility | ITF", https://www.itf-oecd.org/challenges-accessibility-planning-sustainable-mobility (accessed on 30 June 2019). [11]

TfL (2018), *Vision Zero action plan*, http://content.tfl.gov.uk/vision-zero-action-plan.pdf (accessed on 3 July 2019). [37]

van Essen, H. et al. (2019), "European Commission", http://dx.doi.org/10.2832/27212. [14]

WHO (2007), *Housing, Energy and Thermal Comfort Housing, Energy and Thermal Comfort A review of 10 countries within the WHO European Region The WHO Regional Office for Europe*, http://www.euro.who.int/pubrequest. (accessed on 1 July 2019). [39]

Notes

[1] A 1994 report developed by the Standing Advisory Committee for Trunk Road Assessment in the United Kingdom provided an important reference on evidence of induced demand (OECD, 2016).

[2] N_2O and CH_4 emissions are converted to CO_2eq using the Global Warming Potential.

[3] This estimate is based on delay costs; deadweight lost costs are estimated at EUR 46.2 billion.

[4] IRTAD is a permanent group dedicated to road safety in the ITF-OECD. With 80 members from 41 countries, the group has the objective of improving knowledge about road safety. It serves as a forum for countries to exchange information on methodologies for data collection and analysis.

[5] General transit speed specification is a common format for recording data on transport schedules.

[6] Weighted average between day, evening and night noise.

[7] INFRAS en Ecoplan, 2018. *External Effects of Transport 2015 in Switzerland ('Externe Effekte des Verkehrs 2015'). Update study of the calculations of environment, accident and health costs of road, rail, air and water transport 2010-2015,* Bern: Swiss Federal Office for Spatial Development.

6 Creating a sustainable food system

This chapter applies a well-being lens to the agricultural sector and, more broadly, to food systems. It first proposes a change in perspective towards policy making that places climate mitigation, the protection of the environment and human health at the same level of priority as economic objectives. Such an approach highlights the synergies and trade-offs between climate and other well-being priorities, with some examples presented in the chapter. The second part of the chapter proposes a set of indicators that can contribute to tracking progress and steering policies towards the multiple priorities discussed. It then discusses the relationship of these indicators proposed with the indicators attached to the Sustainable Development Goals and the OECD Framework for Measuring Well-being and Progress, and their potential value in providing a more comprehensive picture of synergies and trade-offs between climate and other well-being goals.

The statistical data for Israel are supplied by and under the responsibility of the relevant Israeli authorities. The use of such data by the OECD is without prejudice to the status of the Golan Heights, East Jerusalem and Israeli settlements in the West Bank under the terms of international law.

In Brief

Creating a sustainable food system

Agriculture has achieved major success in fighting hunger, feeding the world and contributing to economic development, including by providing employment to 28% of workers worldwide. Agriculture also provides agro-environmental services to society, such as flood risk mitigation, and resilience to droughts. However, this success has come at a price. Many of the undesirable impacts on the environment and on human health stem from the intensification of farming practices to meet growing global food demand (e.g. excessive use of fertilisers, pesticides and antibiotics).

The food system is a major contributor to climate change, responsible for around 30% of global GHG emissions, including methane from ruminants' digestion and paddy rice cultivation, nitrous oxide emissions arising from fertilisers and animal waste and indirect emissions from land-use change. Agriculture uses one-third of the land surface and is a major driver of deforestation. If unchecked, climate change impacts such as heatwaves, droughts and floods will threaten food security and the viability of current agricultural production patterns.

Furthermore, the current food system does not provide a healthy diet for everyone, even if it has the necessary capacity and produces sufficient total calories. Malnutrition remains a global issue and obesity rates are growing: 159 million children under the age of 5 suffer from stunted growth; 1.9 billion adults are overweight or obese. Meanwhile, one-third of the produced food is wasted or lost.

Importantly, agriculture and forestry have the potential to remove carbon dioxide from the atmosphere, which could significantly increase the feasibility of stringent mitigation goals. The most efficient options include afforestation, land restoration and the development of sustainable bioenergy. The latter can contribute to mitigation in other sectors but require rigorous life-cycle assessment to avoid damaging land-use changes and associated GHG emissions and biodiversity loss.

A shift in perspective is needed to better integrate growing challenges to the sustainability of the food system. Economic criteria (GDP, trade, farmers' income) are currently the main drivers for decisions in agriculture and associated food systems. Integrating wider social objectives (e.g. healthy diets, climate, sustainable resource management) as priorities is key. Addressing the sustainability of the food sector also requires examining the whole food value chain, including the demand side as well as the institutions and markets in which these are embedded.

Applying a well-being lens can help governments make visible the hidden costs of the current food system and identify the potential to achieve synergies (i.e. health, improved environment, carbon storage) and better manage potential trade-offs (e.g. jobs, food access and affordability) between climate and broader well-being goals. For instance, a particular focus on workers' protection and training might facilitate the sector's transition.

New indicators will be needed to measure and monitor performance and to facilitate the achievement of two-way alignment between climate and other well-being goals. For example, the development of reliable indicators on food accessibility and affordability, especially for lower-income households, would help decision-makers to address relevant trade-offs, thus improving two-way alignment. To inform policy development, performance measurement also needs to evolve towards full-cost accounting. This shift in perspective offers a framework for designing more efficient and more comprehensive policies for the food system.

Infographic 6.1. Creating a sustainable food system

Although we now produce enough food to feed the world, the food system is not sustainable and contributes to:

- 30% of GHG
- Air and water pollution
- Biodiversity loss

In addition, **malnutrition** remains a global issue, as does **food waste** along the value chain.

- 1.9 billion adults are overweight or obese
- 159 million children under 5 suffer from stunted growth
- Nearly one-third of the food produced is lost

A well-being approach allows us to look at the whole food system, delivering multiple benefits while **reducing emissions** throughout the economy as well as **removing CO2 from the atmosphere**.

- Farming
- Agro-industry
- Retail
- Consumers

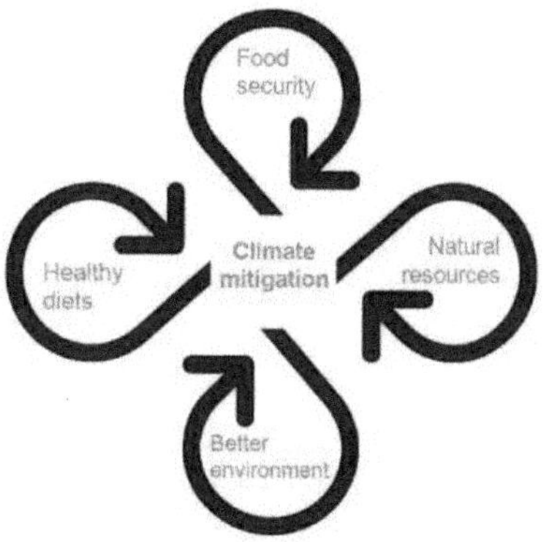

To accelerate climate action, we urgently need to:

Reframe measurement

- Adjust accounting to include well-being impacts in agriculture productivity measures
- Include life-cycle assessment of bioenergies
- Incorporate food accessibility and affordability criteria

Refocus policies

- Deploy sustainable land-use practices
- Set the proper price signal to encourage good practices
- Move from animal-based proteins to plant-based proteins

6.1. Introduction

Chapter 1 argues for applying a **well-being lens** to policy making as a central step to reflecting and assessing the synergies and trade-offs of climate policies, and thus for achieving a **two-way alignment**[1] between climate and broader well-being objectives. Adopting a well-being lens implies that:

- Societal goals are defined in terms of well-being outcomes (including limiting climate change through mitigation) and are systematically reflected in decision-making across the economy.
- The decisions taken consider multiple well-being objectives, rather than focusing on solving a single objective or a very narrow range of objectives.
- The relations between the different sectors and elements of the system in which a policy intervenes are well understood.

This chapter builds on that discussion and applies a well-being lens to the agriculture sector and the food system.

The agriculture sector of the 21st century represents one of the most important achievements of human civilisations in terms of producing large amounts of relatively affordable food that is theoretically more than sufficient to feed the world's growing population. Yet the food system[2] as a whole also faces some major challenges, both in terms of environmental sustainability and human well-being.

The negative impact of the current food system on aspects of well-being, such as health or the environment, have been underestimated as the sector has been mainly steered by income, markets and productivity goals. The current food system puts pressures on the very resources (water, soil quality) and ecosystems on which it depends, threatening its own sustainability. Many of these pressures are linked to the intensification of farming practices to meet growing global food demand (e.g. excessive use of fertilisers, pesticides and antibiotics, industrial livestock systems, unsustainable grazing), the specialisation and uniformity of landscapes, and land conversion for agriculture (Hardelin and Lankoski, 2018[1]).

Agricultural production is responsible for around 10-12% of global greenhouse gases (GHGs).[3] The combined agriculture, forestry and land-use sectors are responsible for around one-quarter of global GHG emissions (Smith et al., 2014[2]). Most of the direct emissions from agriculture are due to methane from enteric fermentation of ruminants (39% of the global GHG emissions from agriculture in 2016, in CO_2eq[4]), manure applied to pasture (16%) and rice cultivation (10%). Synthetic fertilisers, which emit nitrous oxide (N_2O) into the atmosphere, account for 13% of GHG emissions from the agricultural sector world-wide (i.e. just under 2% of global GHG emissions). In parallel, the net carbon sink caused by environmental changes due to human activity, including the increased fertilisation due to more carbon in the atmosphere, is the equivalent of 29% of total human-caused CO_2 emissions (Arneth et al., 2019[3]).

Climate mitigation is vital for the food system: a 2 degree Celsius (°C) increase in world temperature above the late 20th-century level would pose major risks for food security (Field et al., 2014[4]). With the potential for yields to be negatively affected (though heterogeneously world-wide, as some regions may actually benefit), surface water and groundwater resources will decrease, endangering the viability of irrigation systems in some parts of the world. More frequent and intense extreme-weather events (heat waves, extreme precipitation, coastal flooding) related to climate change could also threaten agriculture production.

Crucially, the importance of the agriculture sector for climate change mitigation lies not only in the potential to reduce GHG emissions, but also in its potential contribution to removing carbon dioxide from the atmosphere. According to the Intergovernmental Panel on Climate Change (IPCC) (IPCC, 2018[5]), smoother emission pathways for a 1.5°C scenario include net negative emissions by the second half of the 21st century. The most efficient options for these types of emissions lie in agriculture and forestry, notably through afforestation and the development of sustainable bioenergies, which contribute to mitigation in other sectors.

Bioenergies have the potential to mitigate climate change, under certain conditions, and are therefore included in many low-emission development strategies (see, for instance, (Popp et al., 2017[6])). However, a large range of literature shows that the production of biofuels might emit more GHGs than they store, notably owing to changes in land use (see (Fargione et al., 2008[7]) and (Searchinger and Heimlich, 2015[8])). The most recent report of the IPCC on climate change and land (Arneth et al., 2019[3]) highlights the fact that the land use for bioenergy can conflict with food production and hence jeopardise food security, with higher population growth increasing this risk. The deployment of land-based mitigation measures such as bioenergy and afforestation, is therefore limited. In the case of bioenergy, land-use competition could be alleviated by using advanced (second- and third-generation) biofuels. Ensuring the sustainability of bioenergies through a life-cycle assessment of their emissions is therefore crucial.

Agricultural production also affects well-being more broadly, notably through the pressure exerted on biodiversity, and thus on a number of ecosystem services,[5] such as pollination or natural control of plant pests.[6] Land-use change owing to the expansion of arable land is also an important contributor to carbon dioxide (CO_2) emissions (IPCC, 2018[5]) and biodiversity loss (Díaz et al., 2019[9]) (Newbold et al., 2014[10]), at a time when agricultural land already covers one-third of the terrestrial land surface (Díaz et al., 2019[9]). To what extent these pressures can be managed, while also providing adequate diets for a growing population and meeting the potentially fast-growing demand for bioenergy products, is the key challenge.

Stimulating yields in order to provide enough commodities while limiting land use can be part of the answer. According to (Arneth et al., 2019[3]), increasing food productivity could contribute significantly to the mitigation of GHG emissions in agriculture, as it would reduce the pressure for agriculture land expansion. Sustainable intensification, which consists in restoring already degraded land to increase food production and carbon sequestration, would benefit both climate and ecosystems, but its feasibility varies significantly according to the ecosystem and the area. It should be noted, however, that higher yields do not necessarily result in less agricultural expansion. (Rudel et al., 2009[11]) find that agricultural intensification has not generally led to a country stabilising or reducing its cropland area (see also (Ewers et al., 2009[12])): the predominant experience is that an increase in productivity has gone hand in hand with an increase in the agricultural area. Moreover, the higher use of inputs might compensate the climate benefits of land sparing, as showed the intensified production of rice and pigs in Vietnam in the last two decades (Arneth et al., 2019[3]).

Furthermore, the current food system does not entirely succeed in meeting the objective of providing a healthy diet for everyone, even though it has the necessary capacity and produces sufficient total calories. The World Health Organization (WHO) (WHO, 2018[13]) estimates that 452 million adults world-wide are underweight, and 159 million children under the age of five suffer from stunted growth; meanwhile, 1.9 billion adults are overweight or suffer from obesity. Considering the criticality of the food system to human development and the challenges it still faces, "zero hunger" is the second of the 17 Sustainable Development Goals (SDGs) (see Section 6.3).

The importance of the agriculture sector for climate change mitigation lies not only in the potential to reduce emissions, but also in its potential contribution to removing carbon dioxide from the atmosphere.

Policy makers have becoming increasingly aware in recent years of the new challenges facing agriculture, and efforts have been made to integrate environmental objectives in agriculture policies. The 2016 Declaration on Better Policies to Achieve a Productive, Sustainable and Resilient Global Food System, signed by the ministers and representatives of 47 countries, states several shared goals for agriculture and the food sector, including:

- access to safe, healthy and nutritious food
- enabling producers everywhere, big and small, male and female, to operate in an open and transparent global trading system, and to seize available market opportunities to improve their standards of living
- sustainable productivity and resource use
- the provision of public goods and ecosystem services
- inclusive growth and development.

However, no strong global shift in agriculture policies or their management has been observed since (see, for instance, (OECD, 2019[14]), which monitors public support for agriculture).

Putting this declaration into practice, the adoption of a well-being lens[7] for agriculture requires a broader perspective on policy making, which calls for strengthening other dimensions of the food system beyond market and income criteria. A comprehensive, multi-criteria approach emphasises broader priorities, such as providing access to a healthy diet, ensuring a healthy and safe environment, mitigating the risks of climate change and sustainably managing natural resources (land, water, soils and genetic diversity).

Such an approach can prevent inefficient policies, enabling policy makers to identify measures that enhance synergies, anticipate trade-offs and ultimately facilitate two-way alignment between climate change mitigation and other SDGs (discussed in Chapter 1). In this perspective, policy makers can take decisions in full knowledge of the associated difficulties, which they may choose to curb or compensate. For instance, a particular focus on workers' protection and training might facilitate the sector's transition.

The necessary change in perspective entails taking a food system approach that analyses change in multiple levers, including the supply (agriculture) and demand sides (final consumption). The system should respect natural cycles (water, nitrate) on the production side, as well as emphasise access to a healthy diet for all.

To create policies that lead to a sustainable food system, performance measurement needs to evolve towards full-cost accounting, i.e. a comprehensive set of indicators reflecting the impact of the food system on multiple well-being dimensions, in line with policy priorities discussed. Such indicators would help policy makers establish targets and track progress in delivering such priorities. They can also contribute to setting criteria for policy decisions, and facilitate the necessary co-ordination of actions between sectors and between countries.

Section 6.2 covers climate change mitigation policies for agriculture. It discusses how the change in perspective might help redefine the relative priorities and trade-offs between different goals. It emphasises policy measures that may have only a small – or even negative – impact on total production, but could be highly beneficial in terms of promoting healthier diets and a healthier environment. It also discusses how different policy-design, evaluation and compensatory actions can vitally enhance synergies and help minimise potential negative effects when implementing the climate policies, potentially enhancing public acceptability.

6.2. Agriculture through a well-being lens

Agricultural production can generate both positive and negative effects (Table 6.1). The provision of food is the essential function of agricultural production and is a precondition for human well-being. At the same time, agricultural production may have a negative impact on many dimensions of present and future well-being, including the sustainability of agriculture and the future availability of food. For instance, the intensive use of fertilisers or pesticides has harmful consequences on the environment, including water and soil quality, and biodiversity (OECD, 2018[15]). Agricultural production also generates direct

GHG emissions (Smith et al., 2014[16]). The extension of agricultural land causes carbon releases due to deforestation or the destruction of other types of ecosystems (like peatland or savannah).

As the environment provides ecosystem services, agriculture in turn can provide agro-environmental services to society, such as flood risk mitigation and resilience to droughts (by improving agricultural soil quality)[8], carbon sequestration (e.g. by improving soil quality, since good soil contains more organic matter, or putting additional plants like trees or hedges on agriculture land), water cycling and habitat for a diversity of species. Table 6.1 presents a number of positive and negative impacts from agriculture.

The impacts of agricultural production can also create a feedback effect on the medium- to long-term sustainability of agriculture, affecting future food availability and the sector's capacity to provide sustainable bioenergies that could be used to generate negative CO_2 emissions. Agriculture depends on biodiversity[9] for a multiplicity of supporting services, such as pest and disease control; soil fertility and animal pollination; provisioning services, such as food, fibre, medicines or freshwater; and regulating services, such as soil and air quality, climate regulation or pollination. The sector is also strongly impacted by climate change (see Box 6.1). For example, a global warming of 1.5°C will probably decrease yields locally in tropical regions and is also likely to affect food nutritional quality, which may significantly impact on food security and the viability of livestock rearing in some regions; in a 2°C warming scenario, yields in temperate regions would also be decreased (IPCC, 2018[5]).

Table 6.1. Selected impacts of agricultural production and the food system on well-being

	Positive effects	Negative effects
Climate	Carbon sequestration in agricultural soil Potential contributions of bioenergy to decarbonisation in other sectors	GHG emissions, coming mainly from livestock and fertilisers (see Box 6.1) Land-use change related to agriculture leads to a loss of carbon sink
Health	Food security Nutritious food Genetic	Occupational hazard for farmers, owing to their exposure to pesticides and strenuous work Risk of polluted food Spread of bacteria having developed resistance to antimicrobials and antibiotics used increasingly on intensive livestock farms Zoonotic diseases, exacerbated by intensive livestock production Unhealthy dietary patterns resulting in increasing rates of overweight and obesity, diets with insufficient micronutrients
Ecosystems	Ecosystem restoration in the agricultural system	Loss of ecosystem services due to soil degradation: agriculture damages soils: i) physically (soil erosion due to wind exposure, compaction due to tillage and heavy machinery); ii) chemically (acidification due to excessive application of ammonium-based fertilisers and pesticide contamination in soils); and iii) biologically (loss of soil organic matter and fauna) (FAO, 2015[17]) Habitat loss due to deforestation: agriculturally driven habitat loss is a factor in the declines of a vast majority of the threatened mammal and bird species
Water	Flood risk mitigation in the agricultural system Groundwater recharge	Water pollution (phosphorous and nitrate water pollution from chemical fertiliser use) Groundwater depletion from intensive irrigation
Air		Atmospheric pollution due to emissions of reactive nitrogen (ammonia, nitrogen oxides and PM 2.5) from agricultural land and biomass burning; pesticide pollution
Socio-economic and cultural dimension	Landscape structure Increased income for actors of the food system (wages, profits and rents, taxes) Tourism and leisure	

Box 6.1. Climate and the food system

As show in Figure 6.1, agriculture, forestry and other land use accounts for as much as 25% of global anthropogenic GHG emissions ((Vermeulen, Campbell and Ingram, 2012[18]); (Smith et al., 2014[2])). Of this total, emissions related to land-use change account for 7-14% of global anthropogenic GHG emissions (or 36% of food system-related emissions), mainly from carbon releases due to deforestation or the conversion of peatlands into agricultural land.

Direct emissions account for 10-12% of global anthropogenic GHGs (or 46% of food system-related emissions) (Lankoski, Ignaciuk and Jésus, 2018[19]). These include N_2O emissions from soils, fertilisers, and manure and urine from animals, and methane production from ruminant animals and paddy rice cultivation (Herrero et al., 2013[20]).

Figure 6.1. GHG emissions from food systems

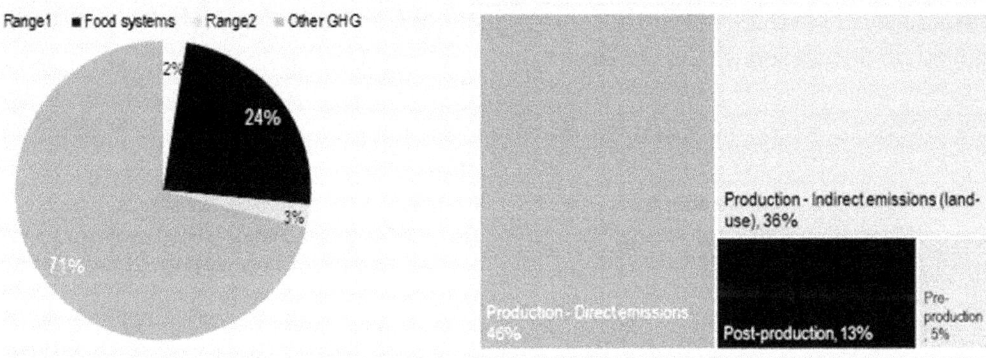

Note: Pre-production includes fertiliser manufacture, energy use in animal-feed production and pesticide production. Post-production includes primary and secondary processing, storage, packaging, transport, refrigeration, retail activities, catering and domestic food management, and waste disposal. The midpoint of the range was used whenever a range of emissions was provided in (Vermeulen, Campbell and Ingram, 2012[18]).
Source: Authors, based on (Smith et al., 2014[2]) and (Vermeulen, Campbell and Ingram, 2012[18]).

StatLink https://doi.org/10.1787/888933993180

Feeding a rapidly growing population has been achieved in part through the increased use of synthetic fertilisers. This has amplified the global nitrogen cycle (OECD, 2018[15]), with resulting environmental problems at different spatial and temporal scales. In particular, increased emissions of N_2O, a powerful and relatively long-lived GHG, have caused a small but significant climate forcing between 1750 and 2011 (about 0.17 Watt per meter square [$Wm^{-2,}$] compared to an estimated 1.68 Wm^{-2} for carbon dioxide ([O_2]) (see (IPCC, 2013[21])). Methane (CH_4) emissions have also increased rapidly owing to the growing number of ruminants, but also to oil and rice cultivation emissions. This powerful, but short-lived GHG also increases in tropospheric ozone levels, threatening human health and damaging ecosystems.

The lifetime of different GHGs determines their global warming potential (GWP) and hence the appropriate climate mitigation strategy. CH_4 is a short-lived gas that remains in the atmosphere for 12 years (Pierrehumbert, 2014[22]); its GWP over the course of a century is 28 times higher than that of CO_2 (Myhre et al., 2013[23]). N_2O, on the other hand, remains in the atmosphere for 114 years, and its GWP is 265 times superior to that of CO_2. Consequently, the reduction of N_2O emissions is a priority for long-term mitigation strategies, compared to the reduction of methane emissions, which will have quicker but more limited effect over the longer term. In other words, a one-off reduction of a very long-lived GHG like CO_2 is equivalent to a permanent reduction of the emissions rate of a short-lived GHG like methane.

Animal farming is responsible for the lion's share of direct agricultural emissions (Blandford and Hassapoyannes, 2018[24]), with ruminants accounting for more than 80% of total livestock emissions (Herrero et al., 2013[20]). In addition to direct emissions, livestock farming and the crops produced to feed livestock also contribute to deforestation. Post-production emissions arise from the food processing and retail sectors relying increasingly on abundant synthetic packaging (Alpro and Murphy-Bokern, 2010[25]), and from the "food miles" racked up to deliver the highly processed and unseasonal products to which consumers have become accustomed (Schnell, 2013[26]).

Capturing GHGs in biomass, notably through sustainable bioenergy production, is an important potential mitigation option for the future, particularly to achieve stringent mitigation targets such as 1.5°C (IPCC, 2018[5]). According to the IPCC, the easier scenarios for limiting global warming to a 1.5°C increase by 2100 include net negative emissions in the second half of the century, which means that more carbon will be removed from the atmosphere than emitted. Several options exist for removing carbon from the atmosphere. The more easily available and plausible options involve forestry and agriculture. The feasibility and potentially negative consequences of other options – including afforestation and reforestation, bioenergy with carbon capture and storage (BECCS), and changed agricultural practices (e.g. biochar, soil carbon sequestration) – are uncertain. According to (Smith et al., 2016[27]), BECCS is the plausible option with the highest storage potential, while bioenergies have the advantage of reducing emissions in other sectors by providing a lower-emitting fuel.

As the question arises of ensuring a food system capable of feeding the world population (SDG 2), as well as contributing to wider well-being and SDGs, a well-being approach encompassing several priorities integrates the numerous well-being dimensions at stake. This perspective is consistent with the definition of food security set at the World Food Summit in 1996: "Food security exists when all people, at all times, have physical and economic access to sufficient, safe and nutritious food that meets their dietary needs and food preferences for an active and healthy life".

An analysis of agriculture policies would integrate the following priorities: ensuring food security and contributing to healthy diets, limiting climate change, maintaining a healthy and safe environment, and ensuring the sustainable management of natural resources. Table 6.3 presents the links between these priorities and the SDGs, as well as with the domains and dimensions of well-being set by the OECD Framework for Measuring Well-being and Progress (henceforth the OECD well-being framework).

A comprehensive view of the food system, integrating all of its dimensions and actors, is necessary to achieve these objectives in an efficient way. Taking a broader perspective not only leads to a realignment of objectives, but also encourages an integrated vision of the whole system that goes beyond the agriculture sector and encompasses transformation, distribution and consumption. Figure 6.2 provides a comprehensive view of the food system, the different actors and the four capital stocks at stake, underlining the complexity of the relationships and the need for a global approach.[10]

Figure 6.2. Capital stocks and value flows in eco-agri-food systems

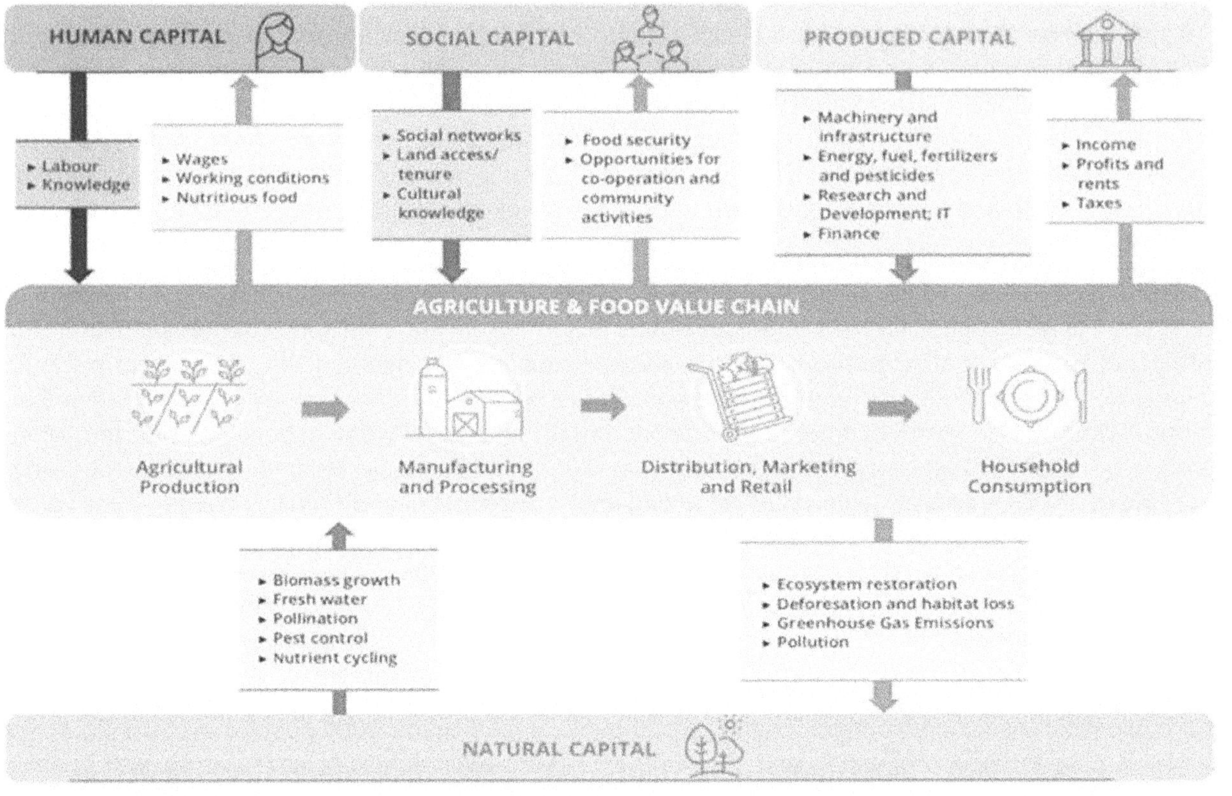

Source: (TEEB, 2018[28])

Policies and measures focusing on a single objective or only on the agriculture sector might overlook important trade-offs – e.g. between climate mitigation policies and food security – and miss opportunities for synergies. (Fujimori et al., 2019[29]) highlights that "carelessly designed climate mitigation policies" would increase the number of people at risk of hunger by 160 million by 2050 if nothing is done to prevent it.[11] Similarly, policies aiming for food-price competitiveness may appear inefficient if they result in cutting production costs at the expense of the environment or human health. Furthermore, other sectors, such as the health system or the water system, pay for the damage wrought by agriculture on food and the environment. Specifically, the food provided by the current system may have unwanted health outcomes that are costly for the population and are not accounted for (see Box 6.2).

Current production is also focused on energy-rich staples (like wheat or corn), at the expense of legumes and a broad range of minor crops with higher nutritional value (Hawkes, 2006[30]) (DeFries et al., 2015[31]). Furthermore, systems with less breeding efforts focused on productivity have resulted in increased nutritional density (Barański et al., 2014[32]) (AFSSA, 2003[33]).Two billion people world-wide have diets with insufficient micronutrients, leading to a range of health problems throughout their lifespans, such as risks of stunting, reduced immune function (and resulting risks of infection), loss of productivity, reduced mental capacity and chronic disease (Bailey, West Jr. and Black, 2015[34]); (Schaible and Kaufmann, 2007[35]); (IFPRI, 2016[36]). The Health Plus Programme copes with this issue by introducing crops that are naturally higher in nutrients in emerging and developing countries. Box 6.2 presents some studies that have examined the hidden costs of the current food system providing large quantities of food at low prices.

Box 6.2. The hidden costs of the food system

While food prices have decreased relative to income and become more affordable (Dorward, 2013[37]), the food system induces costs to human health and the environment that are not included in food prices, and whose weight is instead spread across society. Even though no single approach has allowed drawing an estimation of the total hidden costs of food system, there exists a wide literature that estimates them. The below examples of such estimations show the amounts at stake for countries and hence, the relevance of investing in policies:

The use of chemicals in agriculture involves costs borne by health systems:

- A study estimated annual endocrine disrupting chemicals-related health costs incurred in the United States through pesticide exposure alone at USD 42 billion (US dollars) (Attina et al., 2016[38]). In the European Union, organophosphate pesticides were estimated to produce the costliest outcomes in terms of exposure to endocrine disrupting chemicals, amounting to USD 121 billion per year.
- In the United States, antimicrobial-resistant infections have been linked to 8 million additional hospital days and health costs of USD 20-34 billion per year (Paulson et al., 2015[39]).

Malnutrition (which encompasses both under- and over-consumption) affects an estimated 2 billion people, putting a heavy price on society not only in terms of health expenses, but also in terms of cognitive-skill loss.

- IFPRI (2016[36]) estimates this cost at USD 3.5 trillion globally, i.e. 11% of world GDP.
- The WHO highlights that stunting in early childhood not only affects future health (mortality and morbidity), but also cognitive development (WHO, 2017[40]).
- In terms of unhealthy diets, a report by the McKinsey Global Institute concluded that, based on "disability-adjusted life years" data, obesity has an economic impact of about USD 2 trillion, or 2.8% of global GDP (McKinsey Global Institute, 2014[41]).
- The WHO estimated the direct costs of diabetes alone, often resulting from obesity, at more than USD 827 billion per year globally (WHO, 2016[42]). In the United States, the annual cost of diabetes in 2017 was estimated at USD 327 billion, including USD 237 billion in medical costs and USD 90 billion in reduced productivity (American Diabetes Association, 2018[43]).

Agricultural practices may threaten the ecosystem services from which they benefit and hence, future profitability. A major illustration is the drastic reduction in insect populations worldwide, which is mainly due to habitat loss and land-use change to intensive agriculture, as well as urban sprawl and pollution, mainly from agriculture inputs (Sánchez-Bayo and Wyckhuys, 2019[44]).

- The global economic value of pollinators to the agricultural sector has been estimated at USD 235-577 billion per year (Potts et al., 2016[45]).
- Similarly, (Sandhu et al., 2015[46]) estimate that the global value of biological pest control and nitrogen mineralisation due to ecosystem services for targeted crops (peas, beans, barley and wheat) amounts to USD 34 billion per year.

Using literature (Costanza et al., 2014[47]), the latest Group of Seven (G7) report on biodiversity estimates that the total cost of ecosystem services (climate regulation, pollination and water regulation) amounts to USD 125-140 trillion per year (OECD, 2019[48]).

A shift towards a healthier and more sustainable diet is necessary address the challenges outlined above, creating important synergies between climate and wider well-being goals. Policies encouraging less emission-intensive food baskets may have a significant mitigation potential ((Poore and Nemecek, 2018[49]); (Bajželj et al., 2014[50]); (Wollenberg et al., 2016[51])) while also benefitting health. Diets in many countries are not in line with the nutritional recommendations of the WHO: meat and sugar consumption exceeds dietary guidelines, while fruits and vegetables consumption is below the recommended intake (OECD forthcoming, 2019[52]). For instance, 70% of adults over 18 were overweight[12] in the United States in 2016, 67% in the United Kingdom, 64% in Mexico, 61% in Romania and 51% in Guatemala. In Singapore, according to (Epidemiology & Disease Control Division, Ministry of Health and Institute for Health Metrics and Evaluation., 2019[53]), dietary risks were among the leading risk factors affecting health. In Europe, the Institut du Développement Durable et des Relations Internationales (IDDRI), a French think tank, estimates that shifting towards diets in line with WHO nutritional recommendations would result in a 40% reduction of GHG emissions from agriculture and better health outcomes (Poux and Aubert, 2018[54]). The EAT-Lancet Commission on Food Planet and Health (EAT-Lancet Commission, 2018[55]) recently reported that reaching a healthy diet globally would require dividing the global consumption of red meat (beef, lamb and pork) by nearly three (more than six in North America).[13]

A dietary shift towards more plant-based proteins can contribute significantly to climate objectives, as the production of plant-based proteins generally emits smaller amounts of GHGs[14] than that of animal-based proteins – of which beef emits the most. (Popp, Lotze-Campen and Bodirsky, 2010[56]) highlight that, if the current dietary trends and population growth were to continue, non-CO_2 emissions (methane and N_2O) would triple by 2055. By contrast, scenarios that would limit climate change to 1.5°C by the end of the century all include a rapid drop of methane emissions before 2025, and most include a decrease in N_2O (IPCC, 2018[5]). This involves a slump in the numbers of ruminant livestock, as most methane emissions come from enteric fermentation. Such a change in dietary patterns would mitigate climate change through two distinct channels: first, it would reduce direct emissions from animals; second, it would ease pressure on land use, since a large proportion of crops are grown to feed livestock. In its report on climate change and land (Arneth et al., 2019[3]), the IPCC estimates that changing diets has a major GHG reduction potential (from 3 $GtCO_2eq$ per year for a Mediterranean diet to 8 $GtCO_2eq$ per year for a vegan diet).

Taking a broader perspective not only leads to a realignment of objectives, but also encourages an integrated vision of the whole system that goes beyond the agriculture sector and encompasses transformation, distribution and consumption.

Analysing the food system as a whole highlights synergies between actors and objectives. A good way to ensure that farmers implement environmental practices over the long term is to ensure that these practices are economically viable. This implies mobilising the whole value chain and reorganising markets to create new opportunities. First, all actors would need to promote the provision of healthier and more sustainable food (e.g. through the development of labels by farmers and agro-industrial companies, and highlighting these labels on packaging and in stores' shelf placement). Second, the new patterns of production would need to be accompanied by a reorganisation of key actors. In particular, practices striving for a more sustainable agriculture, notably due to higher crop rotation or legumes used as intermediate crops (see Part 2 of this report for details on sustainable agricultural practices), would need to be based on a higher level of diversity in the supply of grains and plants. This new diversity has to be managed and valued by the whole value chain, from the harvest, through transformation by the agro-industry, to the final retailers. The worldwide development of organic farming and food is a good example of how accumulated changes at every link of the food chain lead to the development of a parallel market chain. As consumer demand grows for healthier and more sustainable food, farmers and cooperatives, supported by public subsidies, respond through advertising, new labelling schemes, a greater variety of products, and so on. Part 2 of this report provides more details on organic agricultural practices.

A holistic approach to the food system aiming for a sustainable use of resources advocates a greater integration of waste management at every stage of the food chain, using different levers. According to the World Resources Institute (WRI, 2018[57]), based on Food and Agriculture Organization of the United Nations (FAO) estimates, nearly one-third of the global food production in terms of weight, and one-quarter in terms of energy content, is not consumed, wasting the resources used to produce it. Reducing waste at every level by using sustainable practices from production to final consumption is the optimal solution, as it reduces the need for food production and releases the pressure for higher yields in order to meet food security goals. It is a lever to reduce environmental pressures from the overexploitation of resources. Figure 6.3 shows the distribution of lost food and wasted food, highlighting that the bulk of waste in developed countries comes from consumption (61% in North America and Oceania, 46% in industrialised Asia and 52% in Europe), but there are also significant losses during production, handling and storage (23% in North America and Oceania, 40% in industrialised Asia and 35% in Europe). In developing countries, the main problems concern production, handling and storage. When the waste cannot be avoided, it may be re-used by reintegrating it into the natural cycles of nutrients. Synthetic fertiliser can be replaced by organic waste from municipal waste or crop residues, which has the potential to mitigate GHG emissions if managed properly. Finally, as these wastes have an organic component, they can be used to create energy, with proper infrastructures connecting the power plants to the (gas or electricity) energy grid (see examples in Chapter 4 on the residential sector). This has a strong mitigation potential, since waste may appear as a substitute not only for fossil fuels, but also for biofuels, which are responsible for deforestation and land pressure.

Figure 6.3. Food loss and waste in developing and developed countries

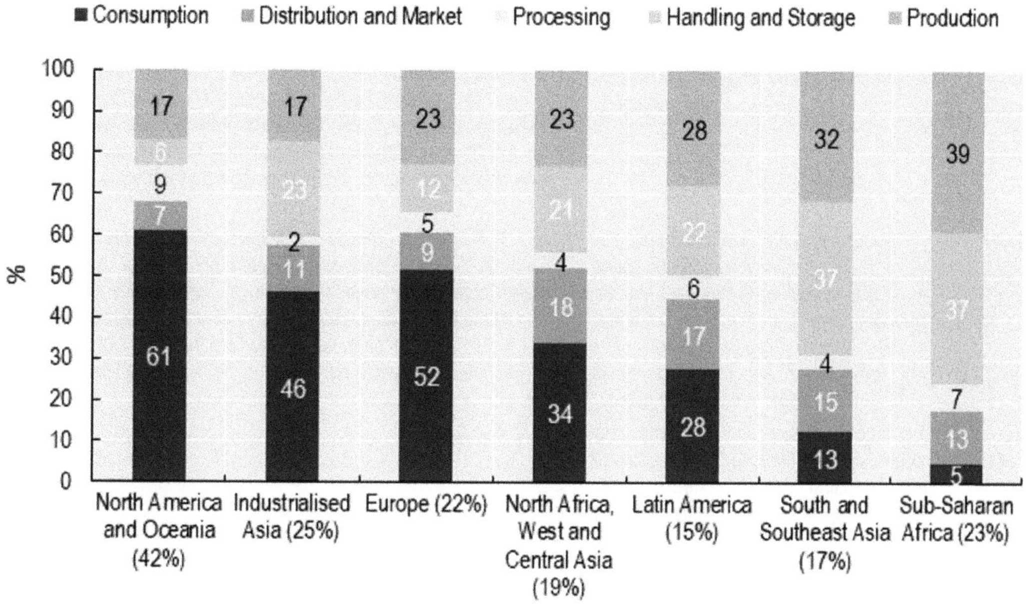

Note: % underneath x-axis is the share of total food available that is lost or wasted (in terms of weight per year).
Source: WRI analysis, based on FAO.

StatLink https://doi.org/10.1787/888933993199

Numerous questions remain on how governments structured around functional or sectoral ministries, often with different budgets and sometimes contradictory agendas, can apply such a holistic approach. Shared policy goals would lead to more co-ordination between institutions and ministries. Most of the time, agriculture policies are supported by one ministry specialised in the agriculture sector and decisions are taken accordingly, often to support farm incomes and production. Taking a well-being approach would require other ministries (e.g. environment and health ministries) and local institutions to demonstrate a greater degree of involvement in decision-making. Showing the benefits of such a holistic approach, Table 6.2 synthesises the main synergies and trade-offs in the food system highlighted by a well-being lens integrating multi-dimensional objectives and a systemic view.

Table 6.2. Potential two-way alignment benefits from applying the well-being lens to the agriculture sector

Other policy priority	Contributing to limiting climate change	
	Generating synergies	Avoiding/reducing trade-offs
Food security and the provision of a healthy diet	Intensifying production by hectare can prevent conversion of unmanaged land to agriculture and hence maintain carbon sinks. Healthier diets by reducing intake of meat and animal products can result in significant GHG emission reductions. Growing leguminous crops has the potential to contribute to a stable climate (since they can be used to fertilise soil and therefore limit the use of chemical fertilisers), resulting in more diversified diets and higher nutrition. Ecological practices can provide job opportunities while reducing GHG emissions and improving on-farm carbon sequestration.	Climate policies may increase food prices, leading to affordability and accessibility issues, especially for low-income households. In particular, there might be a conflict for land use between bioenergies and food that can make food prices higher and more dependent of energy prices. This trade-off between mitigation and food security might strongly hinder the deployment of bioenergies (Arneth et al., 2019[3]). Sustainable practices are more labour-intensive and may therefore increase food prices. Policies encouraging healthier and more climate-friendly diets can curb the detrimental effects on households' purchasing power, e.g. through reductions in the amount of animal protein in diets in favour of plant proteins (legumes, oil seeds), which are much cheaper. They would also reduce the pressure put on land, since livestock occupies lot of land, both for grazing and growing crops to feed the animals. Employment in agriculture may be affected by any reshaping of the food system. For instance, jobs in livestock could be destroyed if meat consumption decreases. According to (Jean Chateau, 2018[58]), farm workers would among the most impacted by the implementation of a carbon tax. However, climate mitigation practices in agriculture are more labour-intensive than conventional practices, and thus have the potential to offset any negative impacts in the livestock-labour market. Training could help facilitate this transition of jobs and workers.
Maintain a safe and healthy environment	Reducing fertiliser use could result in reduced nutrient run-off and water pollution, leading to healthier aquatic ecosystems. It also reduces ammonia volatilisation, which participates in the formation of particulate matters and therefore improves air quality.	Tillage is a practice that helps remove the weeds and alleviates topsoil compaction. While reducing tillage may contribute to GHG mitigation, it may also increase the need for pesticides. Conservation tillage, which consists in letting the previous year's crop residue on fields before and after planting, reduces soil erosion, helps to reduce the impact of food production on soil structure and avoid run-off. It can be considered as an alternative in many cases.
Sustainable management of natural resources	Forest conservation efforts can maintain carbon sinks and reduce GHG emissions while benefitting other ecosystem services Restoration of agriculture land and agroforestry can increase carbon storage while providing habitat for on-farm biodiversity.	

6.3. Indicators for monitoring agriculture's contribution to well-being

This section presents and discusses different indicators that can contribute to steering food systems towards sustainability. These indicators could be used together, as criteria to guide policy decisions, but also as a way to track the performance of a given food system and the effectiveness of policies in delivering the goals defined in Section 6.2: food security defined as access to a healthy diet, the limitation of climate change, a healthy and safe environment, and the sustainable management of natural resources.

The food system is an essential component of the SDGs of the 2030 Agenda for Sustainable Development and constitutes SDG 2, "zero hunger". That goal is divided into five different sub-targets:

- end hunger and ensure access by all people … to safe, nutritious and sufficient food all year-round
- end all forms of malnutrition … and address the nutritional needs of adolescent girls, pregnant and lactating women and older persons
- double the agricultural productivity and incomes of small-scale food producers
- ensure sustainable food production systems and implement resilient agricultural practices
- maintain the genetic diversity of seeds, cultivated plants and farmed and domesticated animals and their related wild species … and promote access to and fair and equitable sharing of benefits arising from the utilisation of genetic resources.

As highlighted in Chapter 1, the SDG targets and the well-being priorities defined in section 6.2 overlap substantially, since both approaches aim to be inclusive and place economic goals on the same level of priority as others. Sustainability and access to healthy diets are central to both approaches. The global indicator framework developed for the SDGs – especially SDG 2 – provides a useful set of indicators to monitor well-being. Other SDGs relating to the food system provide some indicators in line with a well-being analysis of the food system: SDG 3 (good health and well-being), SDG 6 (clean water and sanitation), SDG 8 (decent work and economic growth), SDG 14 (life below water), SDG 9 (industry, innovation and infrastructure), SDG 11 (sustainable cities and communities) and SDG 12 (responsible production and consumption). However, they often require complementary information: even though agriculture may affect these SDG indicators, they do not explicitly mention its specific impact. Table 6.3 summarises the links between these policy priorities and the SDGs, as well as with different dimensions and domains of the OECD well-being framework. Sustainability and access to healthy diets are central to both approaches. The global indicator framework developed for the SDGs, especially SDG 2, provides a useful set of indicators to monitor well-being.

The summary tables in each section links a number of useful indicators to the SDGs and the OECD well-being framework. These tables are not exhaustive, but aim to open discussions. Most of the indicators presented have been developed nationally, or at international organisations like the OECD. Although the OECD well-being framework provides information on dimensions (air quality or water quality) impacted by agriculture, it does not include any information on the specific impact of agriculture and hence cannot be used as a unique criterion. The Biodiversity Indicator Partnership (BIP) listed 64 indicators to track the progress towards the Aichi Biodiversity Targets,[15] and more particularly towards a sustainable agriculture, aquaculture and forestry (Aichi Target 7) and the limitation of pollutions detrimental to ecosystem functions and biodiversity (Aichi Target 8). The European Union developed its own set of indicators to monitor its agriculture policies. Current discussions on the next EU common agricultural policy for 2020-24 include nine objectives[16] and quantitative targets EU Member States must reach through their own national strategic plans. Thus, indicators[17] measuring the targets underlie the EU agricultural policy in order to assess its efficiency. The United States Department of Agriculture (USDA) has also developed a set of indicators to track the environmental impacts of agriculture (Hellerstein, Vilorio and Ribaudo, 2019[59]).

The summary tables also include many of the agri-environmental indicators developed by the OECD to monitor the environmental performances of its (then 34) member countries (OECD, 2013[60]). The agri-environmental indicators have the potential to compare the environmental performance of agriculture in these countries and monitor progress over time since the 1990s. They cover many dimensions of the environmental impacts of agriculture, such as land cover, nutrient balance, pesticide use, water abstraction and water quality, GHG emissions and soil quality.

Table 6.3. Policy priorities for the agriculture sector and their links to the SDGs and the OECD well-being framework

Policy priority	Sub-objectives	SDG goal and target	OECD Well-being domain	OECD Well-beingdimension
Ensure food security and healthy diets	Food production.	2. End hunger, achieve food security and improved nutrition and promote sustainable agriculture.	The well-being framework does not include any dimension on food availability.	The well-being framework does not include any dimension on food availability.
	Food affordability and accessibility.	2. End hunger, achieve food security and improved nutrition and promote sustainable agriculture.	The well-being framework does not include any dimension on food availability.	The well-being framework does not include any dimension on food availability.
	Healthy diets.	2.2. By 2030, end all forms of malnutrition.	Future well-being: resources. Current well-being: quality of life.	Human capital Health status
	Farmers' living conditions and skills.	2.3. By 2030, double the agricultural productivity and incomes of small-scale food producers.	Current well-being: material conditions.	Income and wealth Job and earnings
Limit climate change	Reduce GHG emissions in agriculture.	13. Take urgent action to combat climate change and its impact.	The well-being framework does not include any dimension on food availability.	Resources – future
	Carbon sequestration.		The well-being framework does not include any dimension on food availability.	Resources – future
	Bioenergy contribution to mitigation in other sectors.		The well-being framework does not include any dimension on food availability.	The well-being framework does not include any dimension on food availability
Maintain healthy and safe environment by minimising the pollution of air, water and soil from agriculture	Air quality.	3.9. By 2030, substantially reduce the number of deaths and illnesses from hazardous chemicals and air, water and soil pollution and contamination.	Current well-being: quality of life.	Environmental quality.
	Water quality.	3.9. By 2030, substantially reduce the number of deaths and illnesses from hazardous chemicals and air, water and soil pollution and contamination.	Current well-being: quality of life.	Environmental quality.
	Reduced degradation of soils.		Current well-being: quality of life. Future well-being: resources.	Environmental quality.
	Maintenance of biodiversity and ecosystem services.		Future well-being: resources.	Natural capital.
Sustainable management of the planet's natural resources – land, water and virgin raw materials	Circular economy.	12. Ensure sustainable consumption and production patterns.	Future well-being: resources.	Natural capital.
	Efficient use of water resources.		Future well-being: resources.	Natural capital.
	Efficient material use.	12. Ensure sustainable consumption and production patterns.	Future well-being: resources.	Natural capital.

6.3.1. Ensuring food security and healthy diets

Four types of indicators – total food production, food affordability and accessibility, dietary health impacts and farmers' living conditions – track the food system's capacity to provide food security and healthy diets. All these dimensions are necessary to reach long-term food security and Table 6.4 proposes a set of indicators to track them. Organisations tracking agricultural performance have long mainstreamed indicators on food production and single-factor agricultural productivity (e.g. yields), often driving policy decisions regarding agriculture While the SDG indicator framework includes the volume of production per labour unit of farming or pastoral enterprise size, other institutions focus on indicators of production (value added of agriculture in the OECD Green Growth Dashboard) or the factor productivity. Altogether, these indicators are complementary and provide comprehensive information on the agriculture sector's capacity to produce efficiently, in terms of productive marketed factors (land, labour, intermediate inputs and capital). However, these indicators are not sufficient to estimate the overall efficiency of agricultural production, since they overlook unpriced factors (e.g. biodiversity) and potential negative externalities (water pollution), which leads to overestimating factor productivity.[18] To answer this issue, research by the International Platform on Biodiversity and Ecosystem Services (IPBES) or TEEB to measure unpriced ecosystem services may help integrate them in sectoral accounts and the measure of factor productivity. For instance, IPBES assessed that pollination service created a value estimated at USD 235-577 billion in global agriculture in 2015 (Potts et al., 2016[45]). As such, it should be included as a factor of production in the calculation of the sector's total factor productivity, which would automatically decrease.

Indicators from the OECD well-being framework or the SDG framework provide little information on food affordability. The existing indicators in the SDG framework and other international organisations focus on the variability of food prices. Although a high volatility of food prices may strongly harm consumer well-being, information on the general level of prices is more important, particularly for low-income or otherwise vulnerable groups. The FAO has introduced the concept of food insecurity, which is used by several countries to track policies. The United States, for instance, measures food insecurity through answers to a representative household survey, capturing the concept's different dimensions (i.e. availability, accessibility, utilisation and stability). However, applying a well-being approach entails clearly assessing and disentangling different factors, particularly the economic barriers to a healthy and adequate diet. Understanding these barriers is crucial to analysing the potential effects of environmental and climate mitigation measures on households' capacity to pay for a healthy diet. An indicator comparing households' food expenses to income would be an accurate measure in this respect. Going further, the price of a healthy food basket for households (that is nutritionally adequate as defined, for instance, by (Willett et al., 2019[61])) relative to income would add precious information on the affordability of healthy food.[19] The availability of this indicator by decile of income would also provide useful information concerning the distributional impact of policies.

The SDG framework includes useful indicators on the prevalence of undernourishment and the populations that suffer from food shortages. However, proper and precise indicators on other kinds of malnutrition are hard to find. This is because a healthy diet is defined as a balance between nutrients for a given individual. As a result, aggregate data on nutrient inputs are insufficient, since they do not tackle inequality issues: the total input can be enough to feed the population, but may hide strong inequalities. Besides, many of the diseases (e.g. obesity, cardiovascular problems, diabetes) linked to unbalanced diets are determined by several factors (people's daily activity, genetic propensity), and the actual role of food is hard to determine. Nevertheless, the indicators on the prevalence of these diseases appear as imperfect but useful proxies of malnutrition issues, as they can stand as a proxy to track the adoption of healthier diets, and can be completed by more accurate estimates of the role played by food and diets. Tracking general health indicators, like life expectancy, may also provide relevant information on how agriculture may affect different well-being dimensions.

Table 6.4. Summary table: Indicators for monitoring progress in ensuring food security and healthy diets and links to SDGs and OECD well-being framework

Policy priority	Sub-objectives	Proposed indicators	SDG indicators	OECD Well-being domain/dimension	OECD Well-being indicators
Ensuring food security and healthy diets	Food production	Value added in agriculture.[2] Total factor productivity in agriculture.[4]	Volume of production per labour unit by classes of farming/pastoral enterprise size.	Framework does not have related indicators.	Framework does not have related indicators.
	Food affordability and accessibility	Commodity price variability.[4] Consumer price of food products (index).[4] Food security index (FAO). Share of food expenses or cost of a healthy food basket for households generally and for poor-income households specifically.	Indicator of food-price anomalies.	Future well-being: resources. Human capital. Health status. Current well-being: quality of life.	Framework does not have related indicators.
	Healthy diets	Extent to which food education is mainstreamed in: national education policies curricula teacher education; and student assessment	Prevalence of undernourishment. Prevalence of moderate or severe food insecurity in the population. Prevalence of stunting among children under 5 years of age. Prevalence of malnutrition among children under 5 years of age, by type (wasting and overweight). Mortality rate attributed to cardiovascular disease, cancer, diabetes or chronic respiratory disease.	Future well-being: resources. Current well-being: quality of life. Human capital. Health status.	Obesity prevalence. Life expectancy.
	Farmers' living conditions and skills	Agricultural entrepreneurial income.[4] Rural employment rate.[4] Degree of rural poverty.[4] Rural GDP per capita.[4] Workers' turnover (proportion of workers entering and leaving the profession). Proportion and number of children engaged in child labour in agriculture. Life expectancy for agricultural workers. Specific training in agricultural schools on sustainable practices.	Average income of small-scale food producers, by sex and indigenous status.	Current well-being: material conditions. Income and wealth. Job and earnings.	Household income. Employment Earnings. Job strain.

1. This indicator is included in the OECD well-being framework.
2. This indicator is included in the OECD Green Growth Dashboard.
3. This indicator was developed by OECD as an agri-environmental indicator.
4. This indicator was developed to monitor the EU common agricultural policy.
5. This indicator was developed by the USDA.
6. This indicator was listed by the BIP to track progress towards the Aichi Targets.

Climate change mitigation in the food system also requires action on the consumer side. Informing people on the health, environmental and climate-related impacts of food is therefore crucial. Public education seems like an efficient lever. Hence, this report proposes monitoring demand policies through an indicator on food education.

Farmers' living conditions determine the long-term viability of agriculture and are therefore key determinants for food security. Ensuring a sustainable food production requires maintaining and developing a skilled workforce. For this reason, the SDG framework include farmers' income as an indicator for SDG 2 ("zero hunger"). However, information on incomes should be completed by information on the many other dimensions of working conditions, including the agriculture sector's compliance sector with international labour rights, farm workers' life expectancy relative to the rest of the population and occupational risks.

Finally, implementing a sustainable agriculture calls for more technical training for farmers. Sustainable practices often require a sound knowledge of ecosystems and agronomy, as precision agriculture relies on optimising and reducing inputs and takes into account environmental factors. Indicators on farmers' training to estimate the sector's ability to respond the sustainability challenges should therefore be developed and tracked.

6.3.2. Limiting climate change

The food system can contribute to climate change by emitting GHGs; by sequestering carbon in soils and in agricultural production (plants and animals); and by contributing to the mitigation of emissions from other sectors, through the sustainable production of bioenergy (see section 6.1). While the SDG framework does not feature an indicator on GHG emissions, such information can be easily found – even at the sectoral level – as other institutions (e.g. the FAO) have developed indicators on GHG emissions in agriculture enabling for international comparisons. Table 6.5 proposes a set of indicators to monitor agriculture's contribution to climate change.

A well-being approach calls for developing an indicator on carbon footprints. Although carbon footprints are difficult to estimate because they require information on the whole food chain, they have the potential to provide useful information if determined by a sound methodology. One limitation of considering national carbon emissions is that this indicator focuses on the production side at the national level and hence do not account for the climate impact of imported food.

Information on carbon sequestration and land-use change caused by agriculture is hard to collect, since many factors are at play. The carbon sequestration capacity of agricultural soil depends on farming practices (e.g. agroforestry sequesters carbon) and initial soil quality, neither of which is reflected in existing indicators. Such an indicator is crucial for climate-policy makers as sequestration capacity should be estimated regularly, ideally at the parcel level.

The climate effect of the food system also arises from how the sector affects land use. Estimating the precise impact of agriculture on deforestation is not straightforward. The impact differs strongly among the different regions of the world, as urban sprawl also disturbs the distribution of land and can indirectly pressure forest areas by displacing agricultural land. As proof of this heterogeneity, almost all of the deforestation (-7 million hectares) between 2000 and 2010 occurred in tropical areas; by contrast, forested land increased in North America, Europe and Northeast Asia, while agricultural land decreased (FAO, 2016[62]). Consequently, an adequate analysis of the role of agriculture in the loss of natural land can be provided by using two complementary indicators, developed in the OECD Green Growth Dashboard: i) the share of land conversion from natural or semi-natural land to cropland; and ii) the share of land conversion from cropland to artificial lands. The analysis and comparison of the trends identified by both indicators could help identify the drivers of land conversion.

The production of bioenergies is crucial for climate stability. It needs to be monitored in a life-cycle assessment of both bionergies' direct mitigation impact, and their likely conflict with food production or natural lands over land use. A first set of indicators could track the production of first-generation and advanced bioenergies through their contribution to the energy sector, i.e. the units of energy produced (as a total or as a share of the total energy produced). Another set of indicators could monitor land use for bioenergy as a total, as a share of total land use and as a share of agricultural land.[20] The share of agricultural land would be particularly useful to assess land-use conflict with food, as the production of bioenergy does not necessarily correlate with its land use. Some bioenergies are made through intermediate crops, crop residuals (for second-generation biofuels) or the methanisation of manure, and therefore do not conflict directly with food production.

Table 6.5. Summary table: Indicators for monitoring progress in limiting climate change and links to SDGs and OECD well-being framework

Policy priority	Sub-objectives	Proposed indicators	SDG indicators	OECD Well-being domain/ dimension	OECD Well-being indicators
Limiting climate change	Reduce GHG emissions in agriculture	Nitrogen use efficiency Energy use in agriculture[3] CO_2 emission per unit of value added in agriculture: methane emissions, N2Oemissions GHG emissions in agriculture:3 4 methane emissions, N_2O emissions Food consumption carbon footprint	Framework does not have related indicators.	Future well-being: resources. Natural capital	GHGs from domestic production CO_2 emissions from domestic consumption
	Carbon sequestration	Natural and semi-natural vegetated land, % total[2] Cropland, % total[2] Conversion from natural and semi-natural land to cropland, % since 1992 Ratio of agricultural land consumption rate to population growth rate Carbon sequestration per hectare of agriculture land	Framework does not have related indicators.	Future well-being: resources. Natural capital	Forest area.
	Bioenergy contribution to mitigation in other sectors	Bioenergy production (in GWh or as a total of produced energy and as a share of the total arable land) Biofuel production by type (bioethanol and biodiesel) and generation (first and second) and as a share of the total arable land in GWh	Framework does not have related indicators.	Future well-being: resources. Natural capital.	Framework does not have related indicators.

1. This indicator is included in the OECD well-being framework.
2. This indicator is included in the OECD Green Growth Dashboard.
3. This indicator was developed by OECD as an agri-environmental indicator.
4. This indicator was developed to monitor the EU common agricultural policy.
5. This indicator was developed by the USDA.
6. This indicator was listed by the BIP to track progress towards the Aichi Targets.

6.3.3. Maintaining a healthy and safe environment (air, water, soil and biodiversity)

A healthy and safe environment is provided by good air, water and soil, as well as high levels of biodiversity. All these dimensions are intrinsically related, since each is determined by the others (for instance, biodiversity cannot flourish without good air, water and soil quality, and reciprocally). Table 6.6 proposes a set of indicators to monitor them.

Collecting indicators on agriculture's impacts on air and water quality is no easy task. First, determining the precise role of agriculture is complicated by the fact that many other factors, like industrial, household or transport pollutants, may affect air and water quality. Second, measuring air or water quality has many different dimensions, given the many potential pollutants (nitrate, phosphorous, sulphur, pesticides, etc). A comprehensive indicator should therefore include all these dimensions. For instance, the ecological quality of water basins defined in the European Commission's water directive[21] encompasses physiochemical and ecological criteria that were to be reached by 2015. The OECD provides indicators on the pollution of waters in agricultural areas, but does not cover agricultural pollutants in other areas. Developing a similar indicator on air quality would be useful, although it may impose high collection costs, given the precision of the information needed.

The SDG framework provides good information on soil quality by including an indicator on the share degraded land, but it is still under development and does not specify the type of degraded land (e.g. forest or agricultural land). Besides, many factors may cause the degradation, including the changing climate. The specific impact on agriculture can be estimated by using other existing indicators, such as the share of agricultural land with erosion risk or the share of organic matter in arable land. Neither the SDG nor the OECD well-being frameworks feature an indicator on the role played by certain agricultural practices on land erosion, owing to the difficulty to estimate this effect. As a proxy, the SDG framework proposes a soil carbon indicator, which is still under development. The USDA follows the evolution of the share of conservation tillage, which aims to reduce the negative impact of tillage on soil quality (see Table 6.2).

Tracking the biodiversity impacts of agriculture requires developing indicators on the state of biodiversity and the pressure exerted on it. Few existing indicators allow precise monitoring of impacts, although these impacts are generally well-known and documented. Biodiversity has many dimensions and several other environmental aspects can be tracked, like genetic diversity (within the same species), species diversity and habitat diversity (OECD, 2013[60]). The SDG framework indicators tackle genetic and species diversity, focusing on the diversity of plant and animal production in agriculture. The BIP suggests monitoring Aichi Target 7 (a sustainable agriculture, aquaculture and forestry) through the Living Planet Index for farmland (following population trends for vertebrates species) and the farmland birds index, which is also provided in the OECD agri-environmental indicators. The farmland birds index measures fluctuations in the populations of certain species of birds that depend on agricultural land for nesting or breeding. Farmland birds are considered good indicators of ecosystem health, as their population changes can reflect changes in the populations of other types of biodiversity (e.g. insects) that are more difficult to measure. This index is broadly used, and enables both time-based and international comparisons. However, it can only be considered as a proxy of the impact of agriculture on overall biodiversity or the biodiversity of agricultural areas. Among its shortcomings is that it does not cover the impact of agriculture on biodiversity in other areas. Moreover, the collection of this indicator relies on volunteer groups and is therefore subject to their availability (OECD, 2019[63]).

Table 6.6. Summary table: Indicators for monitoring progress in maintaining a healthy and safe environment and links to SDGs and OECD well-being framework

Policy priority	Sub-objectives	Proposed indicators	SDG indicators	OECD Well-being domain/ dimension	OECD Well-being indicators
Maintaining a healthy and safe environment	Air quality	• Mean population exposure to PM2.5.[2] • Welfare costs of premature mortalities from exposure to ambient PM2.5, GDP equivalent.[2] • Ammonia, NOx and SOx emissions.[4] • Methane emissions.	Mortality rate attributed to household and ambient air pollution.	Current well-being: quality of life. Environmental quality	Air quality
	Water quality	• Nitrogen and phosphorous balance per hectare.[2] • Share of agriculture in total emissions of nitrate/phosphate in surface water/groundwater/coastal water.[3] • Share of monitoring sites in agricultural areas where one or more pesticide are present in surface water/groundwater.[3] • Share of monitoring sites in agricultural areas that exceed recommended drinking water limits for nitrate/phosphorous/pesticides in surface water/groundwater.[3] • Trends in nitrogen deposition.[6] Trends in loss of reactive nitrogen to the environment.[6]	Mortality rate attributed to unsafe water, unsafe sanitation and lack of hygiene. Index of coastal eutrophication and floating plastic debris density.	Current well-being: quality of life. Environmental quality	Water quality
	Reduced degradation of soils	• Agricultural land classified as having tolerable water/wind erosion risk.[3] • Soil organic matter in arable land. • Soil erosion by water.[4] • Share of conservation tillage.[5]	Proportion of land that is degraded over total land area.	Future well-being: resources. Natural capital	
	Maintenance of biodiversity and ecosystem services	• Pesticide use. • Living Planet Index in farmlands, which measures vertebrate species.[6] • Wild Bird Index in farmlands, which measures wild bird species.[6] • Farmland Birds index3.[4] • Water quality index for biodiversity.[6]	Number of plant and animal genetic resources for food and agriculture secured in either medium- or long-term conservation facilities. Proportion of local breeds classified as being at risk, not at risk or at unknown level of risk of extinction.	Future well-being: resources. Natural capital	Threatened species

1. This indicator is included in the OECD well-being framework.
2. This indicator is included in the OECD Green Growth Dashboard.
3. This indicator was developed by OECD as an agri-environmental indicator.
4. This indicator was developed to monitor the EU common agricultural policy.
5. This indicator was developed by the USDA.
6. This indicator was listed by the BIP to track progress towards the Aichi Targets.

6.3.4. A sustainable management of the planet's natural resources

Sustainably managing resources requires using them efficiently and potentially moving towards a circular economy. The SDG indicators are insufficient to tackle both issues and should therefore be completed. Table 6.7 proposes a set of indicators.

The SDG framework has limited information on the degree of efficiency in the use of water or material resources in agriculture. The share of abstraction for agriculture from renewable sources seems crucial indicator on the sustainability of water use, but does not provide information on water-use efficiency, which is also a lever to reduce the impact of agriculture on water resources. More efficient irrigation practices limit irrigation water losses in watersheds. They also induce the growth of species that are less dependent on irrigation.

In this section, we propose indicators to measure water and material use efficiency as the quantity of resource consumed per added value in agriculture (consumption here corresponds to the share of water that does not go back into its environment once used). These indicators would inform policy makers on how policies and practices can improve resource efficiency, and – if international comparisons are provided – on the possibility of implementing more efficient practices elsewhere. However, a growing number of empirical studies show that resource-efficiency measures might have unwanted effects on the total availability of freshwater (Scheierling and Tréguer, 2018[64]), which should be carefully anticipated and monitored.

Monitoring how non-organic material is used in the overall food system should also be considered, since a large share of waste in the food system is attributable not to food, but to packaging. These wastes may create severe environmental damages and therefore should be reduced. Hence, the present paper proposes devising indicators that measure the material footprint of consumed food, defined as the weight of material needed for final food consumption.

The SDG framework provides information on the share of food loss and food waste, but fails to tackle the issue of circularity. Complementary indicators should provide information on how food waste is managed, i.e. the share of waste that is re-used in the agricultural sector (as fertiliser) or outside the sector (e.g. in the energy sector). Similarly, indicators on the uses of materials and water, and their efficiency, can be completed by indicators on how unused and wasted resources are treated.

Table 6.7. Summary table: Indicators for monitoring progress in a sustainable management of the planet's natural resources and links to SDGs and OECD well-being framework

Policy priority	Sub-objectives	Proposed indicators	SDG indicators	OECD Well-being domain/dimension	OECD Well-being indicators
A sustainable management of the planet's natural resources	Circular economy	Share of recycled and managed food waste.	Food loss index and food waste index. National recycling rate, tonnes of material recycled.	Future well-being: resources. Natural capital.	Framework does not have related indicators.
	Efficient use of water resources	• Water stress, total freshwater abstraction as % total available renewable resources.[2] • Water consumption per added value in agriculture. • Share of agricultural production using irrigation. • Renewable freshwater resources.[1] • Water abstraction in agriculture.[4]	Change in water-use efficiency over time. Level of water stress: freshwater withdrawal as a proportion of available freshwater resources.	Future well-being: resources. Natural capital.	Freshwater abstraction.
	Efficient material use	• Material footprint, material footprint per capita, and material footprint per GDP in agriculture/in the food system by type of material (biomass, fossil fuels, metals, mineral). • Tonnes of material recycled in agriculture	Material footprint, material footprint per capita, and material footprint per GDP.	Future well-being: resources. Natural capital.	Framework does not have related indicators.

1. This indicator is included in the OECD well-being framework.
2. This indicator is included in the OECD Green Growth Dashboard.
3. This indicator was developed by OECD as an agri-environmental indicator.
4. This indicator was developed to monitor the EU common agricultural policy.
5. This indicator was developed by the USDA.
6. This indicator was listed by the BIP to track progress towards the Aichi Targets.

6.3.5. Comprehensive indicators

As the well-being approach aims to analyse policies with a comprehensive view, trans-sectoral indicators on the food sector can be a useful complement to the indicators detailed above. The SDG framework includes an indicator on the share of sustainable agricultural production, as well as several indicators on practices adopted by policy makers and firms to achieve more sustainability. However, there exists no proper, consensual definition of what constitutes sustainable agriculture, since the concept encompasses many different notions (environmental impact, viability, etc.) and is likely to vary depending on the prevailing resources and conditions (including climatic conditions). The FAO, in collaboration with the Global Strategy to improve agricultural and rural statistics, has been developing an indicator since 2015. The indicator is multidimensional and encompasses 11 sub-indicators and themes, covering productivity, profitability, risk, soil, water, fertiliser, pesticide, biodiversity, wages, food insecurity and land property rights. For example, GHG emissions can be reduced through policies promoting healthier diets. The need for social policies accompanying price increases due to the application of a GHG tax also becomes more evident when analysing social and economic impacts at the level of the food system. A broad and balanced set of policy measures, covering the entire food system, offers the greatest potential for climate change mitigation relative to current approaches, while at the same time improving the sector's sustainability, ensuring food security and benefitting other well-being goals.

Sustaining well-being depends on keeping a balance between food provision and other ecosystem services (e.g. climate regulation and water quality), including those that will allow the production of food in the future. The measurement system used to inform policy decisions and track progress needs to reflect the impact of the policy actions on the different dimensions of well-being in both the present and the future. Only then can sustainability considerations be embedded in policy making.

A key issue for the agricultural sector – and food systems more generally – is ensuring that land use contributes to durable carbon sequestration, and that the mitigation demand for bioenergy emanating from other sectors of the economy does not undermine food security or drive unsustainable land-use conversion and associated CO_2 emissions. The most stringent mitigation scenarios foresee a major role for bioenergy, which may raise challenges for food security and affordability, as well as for other areas of well-being. The trade-offs between mitigation and other well-being goals may be reduced if countries are able to take early mitigation action that decreases the need for the large-scale deployment of CO_2 removal technologies (such as BECCS), and can constrain the growth in energy demand and achieve behavioural shifts resulting in different dietary choices (IPCC, 2018[5]).

By being aware of which situations produce a trade-off, what these trade-offs are and where they arise, policy makers can strike a balance between the provision of present and future services, as well as between visible (e.g. food provision) and invisible (e.g. nutrient cycle) services. Although specific goals will need to be prioritised, trade-offs can be minimised and synergies fostered, resulting in more effective, politically acceptable and coherent policies (i.e. two-way alignment).

6.4. Conclusion

The agriculture sector we have inherited in the 21st century represents one of the most important achievements of human civilisation, as it produces large amounts of food, which are more than sufficient to feed the world population. Paradoxically, it also results in some of the greatest challenges to the environment, health and overall well-being.

The way food is currently produced has significant environmental and climatic impacts. Furthermore, the degradation of biodiversity – and thus ecosystem services – caused by agricultural production threatens its own viability. In order to transition to a sustainable agriculture sector, this chapter argues that agriculture and climate change mitigation policies need to:

- Take a food system approach that analyses change levers on both the supply (agriculture) and demand sides;
- Look beyond food production and GHG emissions to analyse the sector' sustainability in terms of ecosystem services and, more broadly, well-being.

Food systems are at the nexus of health and well-being, poverty alleviation, climate change and nature protection. Hence, they offer a unique opportunity to reduce GHG emissions and store carbon, while minimising trade-offs and creating synergies with other well-being goals. For example, GHG emissions can be reduced through policies promoting healthier diets. The need for social policies accompanying price increases due to the application of a GHG tax also becomes more evident when analysing social and economic impacts at the level of the food system. A broad and balanced set of policy measures, covering the entire food system, offers the greatest potential for climate change mitigation relative to current approaches, while at the same time improving the sector's sustainability, ensuring food security and benefitting other well-being goals.

Sustaining well-being depends on keeping a balance between food provisions and other ecosystem services (e.g. climate regulation and water quality), including those that will allow the production of food in the future. The measurement system used to inform policy decisions and track progress needs to reflect the impact of policies on all the different dimensions of well-being in both the present and the future. Only then can sustainability considerations be embedded in policy making.

A key issue for the agricultural sector – and food systems more generally – is ensuring that land use contributes to durable carbon sequestration, and that the mitigation demand for bioenergy emanating from other sectors of the economy does not undermine food security or drive unsustainable land-use conversion and associated CO_2 emissions. The most stringent mitigation scenarios foresee a major role for bioenergy, which may raise challenges for food security and affordability, as well as for other areas of well-being. The trade-offs between mitigation and other well-being goals may be reduced if countries are able to take early mitigation action that decreases the need for the large-scale deployment of CO_2 removal technologies (such as BECCS), and can constrain the growth in energy demand and achieve behavioural shifts resulting in different dietary choices (IPCC, 2018[65]).

By being aware of which situations produce a trade-off, what these trade-offs are and where they arise, policy makers can strike a balance between the provision of present and future services, as well as between visible (e.g. food provision) and invisible (e.g. nutrient cycle) services. Although specific goals will need to be prioritised, trade-offs can be minimised and synergies fostered, resulting in more effective, politically acceptable and coherent policies (i.e. two-way alignment).

References

AFSSA (2003), *Evaluation nutritionnelle et sanitaire des aliments issus de l'agriculture biologique*, http://www.afssa.fr (accessed on 27 August 2019). [33]

Alpro, |. and D. Murphy-Bokern (2010), *Sustainable Eating-Part Understanding the Carbon Footprint of our Food*, http://www.wrap.org.uk (accessed on 25 June 2019). [25]

American Diabetes Association (2018), "Economic Costs of Diabetes in the U.S. in 2017.", *Diabetes care*, Vol. 41/5, pp. 917-928, http://dx.doi.org/10.2337/dci18-0007. [43]

Arneth, A. et al. (2019), *IPCC Special Report on Climate Change, Desertification, Land Degradation, Sustainable Land Management, Food Security, and Greenhouse gas fluxes in Terrestrial Ecosystems Summary for Policymakers*, IPCC, https://www.ipcc.ch/site/assets/uploads/2019/08/4.-SPM_Approved_Microsite_FINAL.pdf. [3]

Attina, T. et al. (2016), "Exposure to endocrine-disrupting chemicals in the USA: a population-based disease burden and cost analysis.", *The lancet. Diabetes & endocrinology*, Vol. 4/12, pp. 996-1003, http://dx.doi.org/10.1016/S2213-8587(16)30275-3. [38]

Bailey, R., K. West Jr. and R. Black (2015), "The Epidemiology of Global Micronutrient Deficiencies", *Annals of Nutrition and Metabolism*, Vol. 66/2, pp. 22-33, http://dx.doi.org/10.1159/000371618. [34]

Bajželj, B. et al. (2014), "Importance of food-demand management for climate mitigation", http://dx.doi.org/10.1038/NCLIMATE2353. [50]

Barański, M. et al. (2014), *Higher antioxidant and lower cadmium concentrations and lower incidence of pesticide residues in organically grown crops: A systematic literature review and meta-analyses*, http://dx.doi.org/10.1017/S0007114514001366. [32]

Blandford, D. and K. Hassapoyannes (2018), "The role of agriculture in global GHG mitigation", *OECD Food, Agriculture and Fisheries Papers*, No. 112, OECD Publishing, Paris, https://dx.doi.org/10.1787/da017ae2-en. [24]

Costanza, R. et al. (2014), "Changes in the global value of ecosystem services", *Global Environmental Change*, Vol. 26, pp. 152-158, https://doi.org/10.1016/j.gloenvcha.2014.04.002. [47]

DeFries, R. et al. (2015), *Metrics for land-scarce agriculture*, http://dx.doi.org/10.1126/science.aaa5766. [31]

Díaz, S. et al. (2019), *IPBES, Summary for policymakers of the global assessment report on biodiversity and ecosystem services of the Intergovernmental Science-Policy Platform on Biodiversity and Ecosystem Services*, https://www.ipbes.net/sites/default/files/downloads/spm_unedited_advance_for_posting_htn.pdf. [9]

Dorward, A. (2013), "Agricultural labour productivity, food prices and sustainable development impacts and indicators", *Food Policy*, Vol. 39, pp. 40-50, http://dx.doi.org/10.1016/J.FOODPOL.2012.12.003. [37]

EAT-Lancet Commission (2018), *Summary Report of the EAT-Lancet Commission: Healthy Diets From Sustainable Food Systems*, https://eatforum.org/content/uploads/2019/01/EAT-Lancet_Commission_Summary_Report.pdf (accessed on 30 January 2019). [55]

Epidemiology & Disease Control Division, S. Ministry of Health and Institute for Health Metrics and Evaluation. (2019), *The Burden of Disease in Singapore, 1990–2017: An overview of the Global Burden of Disease Study 2017 results | Institute for Health Metrics and Evaluation*, Seattle W.A, IHME, http://www.healthdata.org/policy-report/burden-disease-singapore-1990-2017 (accessed on 28 June 2019). [53]

Ewers, R. et al. (2009), "Do increases in agricultural yield spare land for nature?", *Global Change Biology*, Vol. 15/7, pp. 1716-1726, http://dx.doi.org/10.1111/j.1365-2486.2009.01849.x. [12]

FAO (2016), *Forests and Agriculture: Land-use Challenges and Opportunities*, FAO, http://www.fao.org/3/a-i5588e.pdf (accessed on 4 June 2019). [62]

FAO (2015), *Status of the World's Soil Resources*, Food and Agriculture Organisation - Intergovernmental Technical Panel on Soils (ITPS), http://www.fao.org/3/i5199e/I5199E.pdf (accessed on 1 April 2019). [17]

Fargione, J. et al. (2008), "Land clearing and the biofuel carbon debt.", *Science (New York, N.Y.)*, Vol. 319/5867, pp. 1235-8, http://dx.doi.org/10.1126/science.1152747. [7]

Field, C. et al. (2014), *IPCC, 2014: Summary for policymakers. In: Climate Change 2014: Impacts,Adaptation, and Vulnerability. Part A: Global and Sectoral Aspects. Contribution of Working Group II to the Fifth Assessment Report of the Intergovernmental Panel on Climate Change*, https://www.ipcc.ch/site/assets/uploads/2018/02/ar5_wgII_spm_en.pdf (accessed on 28 June 2019). [4]

Fujimori, S. et al. (2019), "A multi-model assessment of food security implications of climate change mitigation", *Nature Sustainability*, Vol. 2, pp. 386-396, http://dx.doi.org/10.1038/s41893-019-0286-2. [29]

Gove, M. (2018), *Secretary of State Michael Gove Speech: Farming for the next generation*, https://www.gov.uk/government/speeches/farming-for-the-next-generation (accessed on 12 March 2019). [66]

Gustavsson, J. et al. (2011), *Global Food Losses and Food Waste*, http://www.fao.org/3/a-i2697e.pdf (accessed on 27 June 2019). [68]

Hardelin, J. and J. Lankoski (2018), "Land use and ecosystem services", *OECD Food, Agriculture and Fisheries Papers*, No. 114, OECD Publishing, Paris, https://dx.doi.org/10.1787/c7ec938e-en. [1]

Hawkes, C. (2006), *Uneven dietary development: Linking the policies and processes of globalization with the nutrition transition, obesity and diet-related chronic diseases*, http://dx.doi.org/10.1186/1744-8603-2-4. [30]

Hellerstein, D., D. Vilorio and M. Ribaudo (2019), *Agricultural Resources and Environmental Indicators, 2019*, USDA, http://www.ers.usda.gov (accessed on 21 May 2019). [59]

Herrero, M. et al. (2013), "Biomass use, production, feed efficiencies, and greenhouse gas emissions from global livestock systems", *Proceedings of the National Academy of Sciences*, Vol. 110/52, pp. 20888-20893, http://dx.doi.org/10.1073/pnas.1308149110. [20]

IFPRI (2016), *Global Nutrition Report 2016 From Promise to Impact Ending Malnutrition by 2030*, http://dx.doi.org/10.2499/9780896295841. [36]

IPCC (2018), *IPCC: Global Warming of 1.5 C*, https://ipcc.ch/report/sr15/ (accessed on 17 October 2018). [65]

IPCC (2018), *IPCC: Global Warming of 1.5°C*, https://ipcc.ch/report/sr15/ (accessed on 17 October 2018). [5]

IPCC (2013), *Climate Change 2013: The Physical Science Basis. Contribution of Working Group I to the Fifth Assessment Report of the Intergovernmental Panel on Climate Change*, https://www.ipcc.ch/report/ar5/wg1/ (accessed on 20 March 2019). [21]

Jean Chateau, R. (2018), "Impact of Green Growth Policies on Labour Markets and Wage Income distribution", *OECD Environment Working Paper*, Vol. 137. [58]

Lankoski, J., A. Ignaciuk and F. Jésus (2018), "Synergies and trade-offs between adaptation, mitigation and agricultural productivity: A synthesis report", *OECD Food, Agriculture and Fisheries Papers*, No. 110, OECD Publishing, Paris, https://dx.doi.org/10.1787/07dcb05c-en. [19]

McKinsey Global Institute (2014), *Overcoming obesity: an initial economic analysis*, http://www.mckinsey.com/mgi. (accessed on 18 February 2019). [41]

Myhre, G. et al. (2013), "Anthropogenic and Natural Radiative Forcing", in *Climate Change 2013: The Physical Science Basis. Contribution of Working Group I to the Fifth Assessment Report of the Intergovernmental Panel on Climate Change*, Cambridge University Press, http://www.climatechange2013.org/images/report/WG1AR5_Chapter08_FINAL.pdf (accessed on 25 June 2019). [23]

Newbold, T. et al. (2014), "A global model of the response of tropical and sub-tropical forest biodiversity to anthropogenic pressures", *Proceedings Royal Society*, Vol. 281/1792, http://dx.doi.org/10.1098/rspb.2014.1371. [10]

OECD (2019), *Agricultural Policy Monitoring and Evaluation 2019*, OECD Publishing, Paris, https://dx.doi.org/10.1787/39bfe6f3-en. [14]

OECD (2019), *Biodiversity: Finance and the Economic and Business Case for Action*, OECD, http://www.oecd.org/environment/resources/biodiversity/G7-report-Biodiversity-Finance-and-the-Economic-and-Business-Case-for-Action.pdf (accessed on 4 June 2019). [63]

OECD (2019), "Report prepared for the G7 Environment Ministers' Meeting, 5-6 May 2019", in *Biodiversity: Finance and the Economic and Business Case for Action*. [48]

OECD (2018), *Human Acceleration of the Nitrogen Cycle: Managing Risks and Uncertainty*, OECD Publishing, Paris, https://dx.doi.org/10.1787/9789264307438-en. [15]

OECD (2013), *OECD Compendium of Agri-environmental Indicators*, OECD Publishing, Paris, https://dx.doi.org/10.1787/9789264186217-en. [60]

OECD forthcoming (2019), "Towards policies encouraging healthier food choices". [52]

Paulson, J. et al. (2015), "Nontherapeutic Use of Antimicrobial Agents in Animal Agriculture: Implications for Pediatrics", *PEDIATRICS*, Vol. 136/6, pp. e1670-e1677, http://dx.doi.org/10.1542/peds.2015-3630. [39]

Pierrehumbert, R. (2014), "Short-Lived Climate Pollution", *Annual Review of Earth and Planetary Sciences*, Vol. 42/1, pp. 341-379, http://dx.doi.org/10.1146/annurev-earth-060313-054843. [22]

Poore, J. and T. Nemecek (2018), "Reducing food's environmental impacts through producers and consumers.", *Science (New York, N.Y.)*, Vol. 360/6392, pp. 987-992, http://dx.doi.org/10.1126/science.aaq0216. [49]

Popp, A. et al. (2017), "Land-use futures in the shared socio-economic pathways", *Global Environmental Change*, Vol. 42, pp. 331-345, http://dx.doi.org/10.1016/J.GLOENVCHA.2016.10.002. [6]

Popp, A., H. Lotze-Campen and B. Bodirsky (2010), "Food consumption, diet shifts and associated non-CO2 greenhouse gases from agricultural production", *Global Environmental Change*, Vol. 20/3, pp. 451-462, http://dx.doi.org/10.1016/J.GLOENVCHA.2010.02.001. [56]

Potts, S. et al. (2016), *Summary for policymakers of the assessment report of the Intergovernmental Science-Policy Platform on Biodiversity and Ecosystem Services on pollinators, pollination and food production*, https://www.ipbes.net/system/tdf/downloads/pdf/ipbes_4_19_annex_ii_spm_pollination_en.pdf?file=1&type=node&id=28363 (accessed on 18 February 2019). [45]

Poux, X. and P. Aubert (2018), *Une Europe agroécologique en 2050 : une agriculture multifonctionnelle pour une alimentation saine*, IDDRI, http://www.iddri.orgUneEuropeagroécologiqueen2050:uneagriculturemultifonctionnellepourunealimentationsaine (accessed on 30 January 2019). [54]

Rudel, T. et al. (2009), *Agricultural intensification and changes in cultivated areas, 1970-2005*, http://www.pnas.org/cgi/content/full/ (accessed on 4 March 2019). [11]

Sánchez-Bayo, F. and K. Wyckhuys (2019), *Worldwide decline of the entomofauna: A review of its drivers*, http://dx.doi.org/10.1016/j.biocon.2019.01.020. [44]

Sandhu, H. et al. (2015), "Significance and value of non-traded ecosystem services on farmland", *PeerJ*, http://dx.doi.org/10.7717/peerj.762. [46]

Schaible, U. and S. Kaufmann (2007), "Malnutrition and infection: complex mechanisms and global impacts.", *PLoS medicine*, Vol. 4/5, p. e115, http://dx.doi.org/10.1371/journal.pmed.0040115. [35]

Scheierling, S. and D. Tréguer (2018), *Beyond Crop per Drop - Assessing Agricultural Water Productivity and Efficiency in a Maturing Water Economy*, World Bank Group, http://documents.worldbank.org/curated/en/352321530075399351/pdf/127625-PUB-Date-6-28-2018-PUBLIC-Beyond-Crop-per-Drop.pdf (accessed on 27 June 2019). [64]

Schnell, S. (2013), "Food miles, local eating, and community supported agriculture: putting local food in its place", *Agriculture and Human Values*, Vol. 30/4, pp. 615-628, http://dx.doi.org/10.1007/s10460-013-9436-8. [26]

Searchinger, T. and R. Heimlich (2015), "Avoiding Bioenergy Competition for Food Crops and Land", *World Resources Institute*, https://www.wri.org/publication/avoiding-bioenergy-competition-food-crops-and-land (accessed on 25 June 2019). [8]

Smith, P. et al. (2014), *Agriculture, Forestry and Other Land Use (AFOLU)*, IPCC, https://www.ipcc.ch/site/assets/uploads/2018/02/ipcc_wg3_ar5_chapter11.pdf (accessed on 30 January 2019). [2]

Smith, P. et al. (2014), *AR5 Chapter11: Agriculture, Forestry and Other Land Use (AFOLU)*, IPCC, https://www.ipcc.ch/site/assets/uploads/2018/02/ipcc_wg3_ar5_chapter11.pdf (accessed on 4 June 2019). [16]

Smith, P. et al. (2016), "Biophysical and economic limits to negative CO2 emissions", *Nature Climate Change*, Vol. 6/1, pp. 42-50, http://dx.doi.org/10.1038/nclimate2870. [27]

TEEB (2018), *TEEB for Agriculture & Food: Scientifc and Economic Foundations*, http://teebweb.org/agrifood/wp-content/uploads/2018/11/Foundations_Report_Final_October.pdf (accessed on 2 August 2019). [28]

UNEP (1994), *Convention on Biological Diversity*, UNEP, Geneva. [67]

Vermeulen, S., B. Campbell and J. Ingram (2012), "Climate Change and Food Systems", http://dx.doi.org/10.1146/annurev-environ-020411-130608. [18]

WHO (2018), *Malnutrition*, https://www.who.int/news-room/fact-sheets/detail/malnutrition (accessed on 24 July 2019). [13]

WHO (2018), *Obesity and overweight*, World Health Organisation, https://www.who.int/news-room/fact-sheets/detail/obesity-and-overweight (accessed on 24 July 2019). [69]

WHO (2017), *Stunted Growth and Development. Context, Causes and Consequences*, WHO, https://www.who.int/nutrition/childhood_stunting_framework_leaflet_en.pdf?ua=1 (accessed on 4 June 2019). [40]

WHO (2016), *Global report on diabetes*, http://www.who.int/about/licensing/copyright_form/index.html (accessed on 18 February 2019). [42]

Willett, W. et al. (2019), "Food in the Anthropocene: the EAT-Lancet Commission on healthy diets from sustainable food systems", *The Lancet Commissions*, http://dx.doi.org/10.1016/S0140-6736(18)31788-4. [61]

Wollenberg, E. et al. (2016), "Reducing emissions from agriculture to meet the 2 °C target", *Global Change Biology*, Vol. 22/12, pp. 3859-3864, http://dx.doi.org/10.1111/gcb.13340. [51]

WRI (2018), *Creating a sustainable food future*, World Resources Institute, https://www.wri.org/our-work/project/world-resources-report/publications. (accessed on 20 February 2019). [57]

Notes

[1] Creating two-way alignment between climate action and the broader goals of human well-being and sustainable development means that: i) action in non-climate policy areas should support, rather than undermine, the pursuit of climate change mitigation goals; and ii) climate change mitigation will be more attractive when it also meets other important societal goals (e.g. clean air and improvements in health) that are likely to materialise over a shorter timescale.

[2] "Food systems" are defined here as all the stages needed to feed the population, from producing, to transforming, distributing, consuming and disposing of food (Gustavsson et al., 2011[68])

[3] This figure excludes CO_2 emissions from agriculture. Fossil-fuel use for machinery is captured in the energy sector.

[4] Source: FAOstat.

[5] Ecosystem services are the gains humans get from properly functioning ecosystems. They include supporting services (habitat), provisioning services (food, freshwater), regulating services (climate regulation, pest control) and cultural services (tourism, recreation, folklore).

[6] See, for example the UK Secretary of State for the Department of the Environment, Food and Rural Affairs' speech of 4 January 2018: "The pressures placed on our global environment by this growth … will be formidable – whether it's greenhouse gas emissions in our atmosphere contributing to global warming, desertification and soil erosion reducing the space for cultivation, deforestation leading to the disappearance of valuable carbon sinks and precious habitats, air pollution from traditional industry and intensive agriculture adding to health costs, waste poisoning our oceans or iconic landscapes under threat from the need for further development. Without action we face the progressive loss of the natural capital on which all growth – natural, human and economic – ultimately depends" (Gove, 2018[66]).

[7] See Chapter 1 for more information on adopting a well-being lens.

[8] The water storage capacity of soils increases in soils with higher organic matter.

[9] Biodiversity is defined here as "the variability among living organisms from all sources including, *inter alia*, terrestrial, marine and other aquatic ecosystems and the ecological complexes of which they are part; this includes diversity within species, between species and of ecosystems" (UNEP, 1994[67]).

[10] This figure is from TEEB, a framework modelled by the United Nations Environment Programme which provides a full-cost accounting and allows better understanding of the origins of potential trade-offs in the food system.

[11] The study also notes that the direct impact of climate change on yields was not assessed and the benefits of climate mitigation in terms of avoided yield loss could be substantial.

[12] Overweight is defined by the World Health Organization as a body mass index superior to 25 (WHO, 2018[69]).

[13] This is an average number for the world population and does not apply to the whole population everywhere, as many populations face undernutrition issues.

[14] There can be exceptions, e.g. in the case of plants grown in heated greenhouses or transported by airfreight, which can emit more GHG per unit of protein than some animal products.

[15] The 20 Aichi Targets were set at the 2010 Convention on Biodiversity as part of the 2011-2020 Strategic Plan for Biodiversity.

[16] Ensure fair income, increase competitiveness, rebalance power in food chain, climate change action, environmental care, preserve landscapes and biodiversity, support generational renewal, vibrant rural areas, protect food and health quality.

[17] https://eur-lex.europa.eu/legal-content/EN/TXT/?uri=COM%3A2018%3A392%3AFIN.

[18] To respond to these issues, the OECD launched the Network on Agricultural Total Factor Productivity and the Environment in 2017, gathering experts in order to build a co-ordinated framework for an "environmentally adjusted total factor productivity" indicator that allows international comparisons.

[19] Research on such an indicator is part of the ongoing Changing Access to Nutritious Diets in Africa and South Asia project conducted by the Friedman School of Nutrition at Tufts University.

[20] Agricultural land includes arable land (temporary crops, temporary meadows, land under market, kitchen gardens and temporary fallows), permanent crops and permanent pastures.

[21] Directive 2000/60/EC of the European Parliament and of the Council of 23 October 2000 establishing a framework for Community action in the field of water policy.

www.ingramcontent.com/pod-product-compliance
Ingram Content Group UK Ltd.
Pitfield, Milton Keynes, MK11 3LW, UK
UKHW051501290926
15471UKWH00008B/1340

9 789264 801